Date Due

JAN 5 4			
FEB 22			
MAR 16			
JAN 3			
JAN 28			
ℬ	PRINTED	IN U. S. A.	

MARTHA WASHINGTON

Books by

ALICE CURTIS DESMOND

FAR HORIZONS

SOUTH AMERICAN ADVENTURES

LUCKY LLAMA

FEATHERS

JORGE'S JOURNEY

SOLDIER OF THE SUN

FOR CROSS AND KING

MARTHA DANDRIDGE CUSTIS
Portrait by John Wollaston

ALICE CURTIS DESMOND

Martha Washington

OUR FIRST LADY

Dodd, Mead & Company
New York   1942

TO
MY MOTHER AND HUSBAND
AND
THE MEMORY OF
MY FATHER

CONTENTS

ILLUSTRATIONS

MARTHA WASHINGTON

AN APRIL MORNING IN TIDEWATER VIRGINIA IN THE SPRING
of 1746. The white walls of Colonel John Dandridge's New
Kent County plantation house, Chestnut Grove, stood in the
light of dawn on the south bank of the Pamunkey River.
Before the house, the lawn, shaded by the spread of giant
chestnut trees, sloped to the edge of the stream, one of the
crooked blue fingers of Chesapeake Bay that point up into
the Virginia shore.

Suddenly, out of the cool silence rose a prolonged mellow
sound. It was the work-horn, calling the Negro slaves to the
Dandridge tobacco fields that stretched out behind the house
to the pine forests. Five-thirty, and barely daylight; yet none
too early to start the tasks which must be under way before
the sun rose.

Inside the house, in a room on the second floor, curtained
with chintz of wild-rose and fern, a slim figure stirred in the
four-poster bed. Fifteen-year-old Martha Dandridge, eldest
daughter of the house, opened her brown eyes and yawned.

"Patsy! Are you awake?"

The brisk voice of Mistress Frances Dandridge, the Colonel's handsome dark-haired wife, and mother of Martha, her
three brothers, and her two sisters, came from the hall below.

Patsy, as the family called Martha when her father did
not shorten this into the boyish Pat, slipped down from her

1

high pine bed with its white valance edged with ball and cord. Untying the strings of her night cap, she hastily reached for her square-toed, high-heeled slippers of soft satin, which she cross-strapped over white cotton stockings.

Before the mirror topped with a golden eagle, she stood— rather a solemn little figure—in her high-necked bed-gown of unbleached muslin with frills of homemade lace at throat and wrists. Its voluminous folds concealed her body, slim now in its youth, and short, like all the women in the Dandridge family. Her straight, brown hair was parted in the center over large hazel eyes; unusual eyes, alive with intelligent curiosity.

From a chair, Martha took her morning garments and quickly put them on. A hooped petticoat, and over it a brown homespun dress, with a basque that fitted tightly over her stiff pack-thread stays. Around her throat she folded a white kerchief.

"Patsy!" came the second call.

Her hair in two pigtails, topped by a dainty mob cap, Martha hurried from the room and down the stairs.

"Gently, Patsy, please . . . young ladies do not run."

Frances Dandridge, clad in a starched white morning sacque over a black stuff skirt, put out her hand to stay the swift advance of the small, brown figure with hoops swinging and pigtails flying.

"Yes, Mama."

Martha was instantly sedate, head bowed, just a shadow of a pout on her lips. It was hard learning to be grown up. Doubly hard when, until recently, she had been allowed to do as she pleased.

But now she was fifteen. Almost a woman grown, her mother had said in one of her recent serious talks with her eldest daughter. And in future Patsy was to take as a pattern for living, the motto hanging on her bedroom wall:

"Never sit down before your elders unless told to do so;
Bite not your bread, but break it.
Never speak in the presence of your elders except to reply
to a question;
Take salt with a clean knife.
Hold not your knife upright, but sloping; and lay it down
at the right hand of your plate;
Make no sound with your tongue, mouth or lips while eat-
ing or drinking."

Frances Jones Dandridge was a woman of high standards, whose severity toward her six children was her way of show- ing her love for them. Ambitious, especially for Patsy, whose high spirits had been something of a trial, Mistress Dandridge resolved that this year should see a curbing of her eldest child.

From a long line of scholars and clergymen, Frances' own character had been formed, making her at thirty-six, the efficient, if rather strict mistress of Chestnut Grove. Her father, Orlando Jones, had been Burgess from New Kent. Her mother was Martha Macon, daughter of Gideon Macon, secretary to the Governor, Sir William Berkeley. It was to this grandmother young Martha owed her good old English name. But Frances resembled more her own grandfather, the Reverend Roland Jones, a graduate of Oxford, and the first rector of Bruton Parish in Williamsburg.

It was Frances Dandridge, who, on hearing that a tutor from England had arrived in New Kent, had insisted that the Colonel invite him to Chestnut Grove to give lessons to her boys, John and William and Bartholomew. Girls did not need book learning. But since the tutor was coming, Patsy and Anna Maria, nicknamed Nancy, might as well learn to read and write and cipher.

That Patsy was none too pleased by the arrival of Thomas Leonard, the tutor, was shown by the reluctance with which she approached the daily lessons. His teaching was quite different from her previous instruction with her father. Those lessons usually ended, when hardly begun, with the Colonel remembering that he must speak to an overseer in his tobacco fields and father and daughter dashing off on a horseback ride together.

Each morning since the tutor's coming, six months earlier, the Dandridge children, neatly dressed, with hair combed and hands clean, had met in the schoolroom for lessons before the breakfast hour. The boys continued their studies most of the day. For Nancy and Martha there was afternoon instruction in household duties from their mother, with little time left for play. And Patsy, who had no fondness for books, was ready to rebel.

"You're late for lessons, dear," her mother reminded her. "Your cap is rumpled, your braids not smooth. You'll please make yourself neat and join Thomas Leonard and the other children in the schoolroom."

Murmuring a polite assent, Martha turned to a mirror to straighten her cap.

In a small back room, fitted up for school purposes with tables and benches, she found tall, beetle-browed Thomas Leonard and his class. His past was well known in the colony —an indentured servant, a political prisoner from England, working out his freedom and paying for his passage by teaching the children of the Virginia planters. A week more at Chestnut Grove, and then Thomas, with his deep frown and

CHESTNUT GROVE, BIRTHPLACE OF MARTHA DANDRIDGE, IN 1746

CHESTNUT GROVE, BIRTHPLACE OF MARTHA DANDRIDGE, IN 1942

Photograph by the author

les for genders and exceptions. But the moment a sentence
was dropped, the tutor was alert.

"Come now, Mistress Patsy, you mustn't skip," he scolded.

Martha's voice droned on; the time passed slowly. William's head nodded, and John forgot to prod him. Dimpled
Nancy bent her blonde head over the horn-book, a wooden-handled board covered with a transparent sheet of yellowish
horn and bound with brass, from which she was learning the
nine digits and the alphabet.

Spelling followed the reading lesson, a half hour Martha
detested. She could not remember to spell a word the same
way twice. Especially did she persist in spelling "do" as
"doe," "no" as "noe," and "go" as "goe." If "hir" did not
spell "her," she wondered, pray what did it spell? And "bin"
was surely more reasonable than "been," "tha" than "they."

Next came a half hour of "cyphers" from *Cocker's Arithmetick*. While this lesson gave Patsy little joy, it was less
painful than spelling. Working away in her stiff young hand-writing at "Reductions Ascending" and "Reductions De-scending," which a child of today would call addition and
subtraction, she could not keep her eyes from the window
that faced on the Pamunkey, a pretty stream hastening to
lose itself in the York.

Now she longed to be down at the plantation wharf,
watching the river life! She might hear news of the arrival
of *The Scottish Thistle*, a packet from Liverpool, loaded
with goods ordered by Colonel Dandridge from his London
agent. Would the ship arrive today, she wondered?

The breakfast bell interrupted Martha's thoughts. Hastily
shutting her book, she stood with the children, awaiting the
tutor's permission to leave the room. After sitting for two
hours, it was hard for Martha to resist the temptation to

cultured voice, would be on his way to an
and the Dandridge children would go happil
lessons under their easy-going father.

This morning, nine-year-old Bartholomew, t
ous of the boys, and named for his father's frie
mew Selden, a lawyer of Hampton, was reciting
from the *New England Primer* the prayer beginn
I lay me down to sleep . . ." Bartholomew liked
liked the sound of his voice in the simple prayer.

His twelve-year-old brother, William, named
father's brother, did not join in Bartholomew's en
as he sat beside him on the hard bench. It must be a
that William, sleepy-eyed, was nodding over his *Gr*
of the English Tongue, a large book in fine type, but
the grammar rules conveniently in rhyme as an ai
memory. William was awakened by a nudge from the el
Dandridge boy, John, fourteen now and his father's nar
sake, who under Thomas Leonard's tutelage had discover
a new interest in Greek.

Nancy, a chubby little girl of seven, dressed in blue-
checked calico, sat on a stool near the tutor, her thoughts
fixed hungrily on her belated breakfast. Lessons, even the
fascinating business of writing out the alphabet on her slate
in tipsy capitals, were hard to do with the odor of smoking-
hot batter bread drifting up from the cookhouse.

Taking her seat on the bench beside Bartholomew, Martha
opened her *Lilly's Grammar*. The first task of the day was
reading. While she read aloud in a firm, quick voice, the tutor
sat before his class at a tilt-top table, mending a goose-quill
pen with his knife and dissolving ink-powder into writing
fluid. So absorbed did he seem that Martha dared to omit a
few lines of the dull text, lists of nouns and their declensions,

stretch her young legs and race down the hall. But remembering her mother's rebuke, she dropped a curtsy to Thomas Leonard and walked sedately away.

The spicy smell of hot gingerbread drew the hungry scholars towards the dining room. Holding pretty Nancy by the hand, Martha led the way into the white-paneled room. Again Martha and Nancy curtsied, this time to their parents, seated at opposite ends of the long oak table. John, as the oldest son, made a formal bow, followed quickly by the less courtly bobbing of boisterous William and poetic little Bartholomew. Then they were free to take their places on the oak benches between their father and mother.

Colonel Dandridge had been up since daylight and at his desk, arranging the farm work for the day. Mistress Dandridge had been checking supplies in her cookhouse long before the work-horn sounded over the tobacco fields. Both had slept well and long, for the myrtleberry candles in use in the household were not bright enough to tempt late hours for reading or sewing.

Martha, seated happily by the side of her bluff, good-looking father, tied a bib around Nancy's neck. Then she turned to her own pewter porringer with its fish-tail handle, full of cereal and cream.

Breakfast in the Dandridge family was a bounteous meal. On the oak table rested pewter platters of broiled ham and eggs, breast of wild turkey, stacks of crisp fried hominy cakes, spoon bread, hot gingerbread and beaten biscuit. From the heavy teapot, one of the family's cherished pieces of silver, bearing as it did the lion's head crest of the Dandridges of Great Malvern, Worcestershire, Mistress Frances poured the scalding drink into handleless cups of Canton ware. In a high chair beside her, baby Frances crowed and waved her spoon to attract her mother's attention.

"Well, children, how did the lessons go today?" asked John Dandridge, a ruddy-cheeked squire in knee breeches and a homespun coat. His smile for his eldest daughter was especially warm. "And you, Pat, are you developing into the brains of the family?"

Remembering her spelling, Martha blushed.

"Patsy is showing her skill in domestic accomplishments," said his wife. "Things of greater importance to a woman than book learning. Try this grape jelly, Colonel Dandridge. Your daughter made it."

Martha blushed again, this time with pride.

Under the tutelage of her mother, the girl was rapidly learning the art of cooking. While once she had spent most of her time out of doors, each day proudly accompanying her father as he made his inspection ride over the plantation, now she was being taught the use of every copper pan hung around the big hearth in the kitchen, every brass kettle swung from the stout crane.

There were the big iron pot for boiling the indispensable Virginia ham; the lidded ovens standing on four feet that coals might burn beneath them; the skillet, with its ascending aroma from frying chickens; the hoe, slanting before the fire to receive the thin delicious hoe-cakes of Indian meal. At first, Martha had not liked the kitchen tasks. But gradually she came to enjoy the daily experiments with breads and preserves, cakes and puddings.

Now, as she lifted a spoon of quivering grape jelly, amethyst purple, onto a square of batter bread, she felt a surge of happiness, happiness made doubly sweet because her adored father had just swallowed with relish an enormous bite of the same fare.

"Very good jelly, Patsy," he said with gusto. "And while you're about it, Mrs. Dandridge, how about a little bit more?"

His daughter beamed. To Martha, the robust, hearty-voiced Colonel was the most important person in the world.

To New Kent County, Virginia, John Dandridge was also a man of importance. In addition to being an extensive tobacco grower, he was county clerk, colonel of his military district, and a vestryman of Saint Peter's, the local parish.

Leaving a brother Francis and a sister, Mary Langbourne, in London, the Dandridge brothers, John and William, had come from their native Worcestershire to Virginia. After living for a while at Hampton, they moved north to the Pamunkey River, the south branch of the York. John had built Chestnut Grove in 1722, eight years before his marriage. William, three years before that, had built Esling Green, on the north shore of the Pamunkey, in King William County. John became a tobacco planter, and William, a member of the King's Council and the more restless of the brothers, took up a naval career. As Captain Dandridge, he had commanded His Majesty's ships, the *Wolfe*, the *South Sea*, and the *Ludlow Castle*, until his death three years ago.

Martha had loved her gallant Uncle William. With the other Dandridge children, she had spent many happy days at Esling Green, his large Georgian brick house on the opposite shore of the river. Its halls were built in the form of a cross. At each end was a wide staircase with such an easy rise that once Martha, in a hoydenish mood, had ridden her horse, Fatima, up one flight and down the other. Uncle William had applauded the feat of horsemanship. But his wife, Aunt Unity, the heiress of Colonel Nathaniel West, and a great-great niece of the third Lord Delaware, had lifted her hands in horror. What did Frances Dandridge mean by permitting her eldest daughter to run wild, a greater tomboy than any one of her three sons?

What Mistress Dandridge thought of her daughter's behavior was revealed in tight-lipped disapproval. But for once the Colonel took a hand in the rearing of his child.

"Let Patsy alone!" he roared. "She's not harmed William's staircase. And, by heavens, *how she can ride!*"

Today, when John Dandridge finished his breakfast, he turned to his daughter and said, "Would you like to go to the planter's store with me this morning, Pat?"

Martha's heart leaped. But before she could voice her eager acceptance, her mother interrupted.

"Not today, Colonel Dandridge. Patsy has her sewing stint with me after breakfast. Later she must practice on the spinet; after dinner, Thomas Leonard will instruct her in dancing. With the Governor's Ball at Williamsburg only two weeks away, there's no time to be lost. Patsy scarcely knows a minuet from a rigadoon."

Martha's small, regular features contracted. The high temper, against which she was to struggle all her life, rose within her.

"I don't want to go to the ball," she burst out. "I want to stay home with the other children, and my horse and my garden . . .'

There was a shocked silence.

Even Colonel Dandridge's genial voice grew stern. "Patsy, you're fifteen years old. It is time for you to be presented at Court."

Martha dared not meet her mother's gaze. She knew that it had long been Frances Dandridge's desire to introduce her daughter to Williamsburg society. As the capital of the colony of Virginia, the little town, situated midway between the York and James Rivers, was the center of colonial life and the gayest on the continent. Its Court, revolving about the governor, was a miniature of the London Court of George II, ruler of America. Thought of the vice-regal ball gave the frightened girl an idea. Williamsburg ladies and gentlemen dressed in the latest fashions from England, brought to them by slow sailing ships, and only six months old.

"I can't go to the ball," Martha said flatly. "I haven't anything to wear."

To her surprise, her mother smiled. "Don't worry about a gown, Patsy. You will go to the Governor's Ball, as planned. And you'll look very sweet in whatever you wear."

Martha, who had expected a stern rebuke for her impertinent outburst, was dumb with surprise. Why had her mother excused her behavior? Why had her father, on leaving the table, exchanged mysterious glances with his wife?

Puzzled, Martha fetched her "housewife," a silk-lined morocco roll for holding sewing materials. Following her mother into the family sitting-room, she seated herself on a stool at the feet of Mistress Dandridge, erect in a wing chair at the side of the ample fireplace.

Her back stiffly supported by pack-thread stays, feet demurely set square on the floor and scarcely showing beneath her hooped skirt, Martha began work on a lawn kerchief. As the girl's needle moved in and out of the sheer fabric, her thoughts were far away. She was riding Fatima beside her father, mounted on his big hunter, Jupiter. She was wearing her old riding habit, stained with mud. The hours passed pleasantly, with no interruptions by Thomas Leonard—no reading, no ciphers, no detestable spelling.

Daydreaming, her determined little face set, Martha finished the kerchief. Next there were samples of hemming and cross-stitching to be done; tent-stitching, over-seaming and looping for her mother's approval. Cooking had been hard for Martha to learn. Sewing came easily. As a child of five she had been able to knit mittens and stockings. At thirteen, she had made a pair of long white hose with open work design for her father. She could mend her clothes, work samplers, edge handkerchiefs with needle-point.

Frances Dandridge leaned over to compliment her daughter on her neat, even stitches. "And I'll be glad, dear, when your temper is as even as your stitches," she added. "Some day you may have to manage a plantation of your own, and then you'll thank me for all I've taught you."

Three o'clock found Martha seated at the red cedar spinet, her hands running lightly over the short keyboard as she applied herself to the trills of *Down to Devon* and *The Bristol Belle*. She had an ear for music, and a sure, rhythmic touch. No one in the house, not even Mistress Dandridge, herself a fine musician, could excel Patsy at the spinet. The rollicking tunes set the feet of the slaves to dancing. They brought Colonel Dandridge from his study, pipe in hand, to stand at the door and listen.

But, alas, they also brought Thomas Leonard, whose coming reminded the young musician that the time for her dancing lesson had arrived.

Her knowledge of intricate steps and ballroom etiquette, an important part in the education of a young Virginia lady, had its beginning that afternoon as the tutor drew bashful Martha to her feet. Deftly he led her, cheeks flushed and head held high, through the movements of the minuet.

Within the hour, the girl had learned to curtsy, to take a gentleman's hand, and to sweep her skirts in the figures of the dance. One thing she discovered was a necessary part of the technique of the minuet—the pointed foot must be so straight that not a wrinkle appeared in the quilted petticoat. And, of course, that meant that the quilt must be of a strength and richness sufficient to stand alone. All of which set Patsy, who had never owned a petticoat of silken quilt, to worrying once more over what she would wear to the Governor's Ball.

Mistress Dandridge, holding baby Frances on her lap as she chaperoned her daughter from a corner of the room, saw Martha's troubled expression. What was the matter? Surely Patsy did not doubt her dancing ability! She had a youthful, coltish grace, her mother noted with approval.

The dancing lesson was stopped short by a shout from outside, followed by noise and confusion and the voices of slaves on the plantation wharf, far down the lawn.

"Colonel Dandridge, the ship from England is here! Hurrah for the *Scottish Thistle!*"

Dancing was forgotten in the excitement of the arrival of the boat. Children, parents and tutor rushed from the house and went hurrying down to the dock.

From the great arm of the Atlantic called the Chesapeake Bay, up the broad, winding stream fringed by woodlands and giant sycamores, the sailing ship had glided. Before the excited gaze of Colonel Dandridge and his family, it dropped anchor in midstream, completing its three-thousand-mile journey from England.

The Colonel was the first to greet the red-faced, hearty-voiced captain when he was rowed ashore, full of stories of his adventurous voyage across the Atlantic. The slaves of the plantation helped the sailors unload the goods John Dandridge had ordered, and load tobacco as payment for articles to be sent over the following year.

Meanwhile, the Dandridge family trooped back to the house to give the captain the meal of his life, and to listen to news from England.

Martha, her brothers and sister Nancy, could hardly wait to see the gifts that the treasure ship had brought. There was for Mistress Dandridge a bed with four tall posts, and a pine highboy to match. For the Colonel, a plum-colored suit and tri-cornered hat; for John and William and Bartholomew, small suits and hats made exactly like their father's. There was a gun for John, Junior, now old enough to hunt with the Colonel; books for Bartholomew, who could not get enough of them; a similar collection for William, who sulked and begged for a gun such as John had been given; a doll for Nancy; and for Martha, a new bridle and saddle for Fatima.

But the excitement was not over.

That evening, as Martha undressed for bed, her mother came into her room, followed by two slaves who deposited on the floor a small pigskin trunk studded with brass nails. When this was opened, Patsy's brown eyes blinked at the splendor of its contents. There were bolts of soft velvet and glossy satin in cream and jade and violet, sent by Martha's Aunt Mary, Mrs. Robert Langbourne, from her London home in Fetter Lane. There were yards of heavy flowered silk in the lovely pattern of the English Rose. Ruffles of sheer lace and muslin tuckers. Gloves and satin slippers. Fans of lace and bejeweled gauze. Lawn kerchiefs and petticoats laced with ribbons.

Martha stood before this froth of feminine finery, eyes aglow. Would her mother wear these fine clothes when they went to Williamsburg? But Frances Dandridge was not decking herself with velvet and laces. She was lifting the bolt of heavy silk in the English Rose pattern and draping the shimmering folds across her daughter's shoulders.

"See, Patsy," she said, warm excitement in her voice, "this is your Court dress. Colonel Dandridge had your Aunt Mary buy it for you in London."

A ball gown from London!

Martha, whose most festive frock was a chintz cotton, could hardly believe her ears. And when she spied a quilted petticoat in the trunk, she was speechless with joy. Quickly she wrapped it around her. Under the weight of the silk quilt, rich enough to stand alone in the minuet, the girl trembled. No wonder her parents had not been concerned about a proper ball gown for their eldest daughter!

As she folded the rich material, Frances Dandridge could not resist pointing her usual moral. She reminded the glowing Patsy that her father's decision to present her with this fine outfit was a reward for a good girl who had worked hard at subjects she disliked—spelling and ciphers.

Martha's heart leaped with love and gratitude. *"Dear Mama, thank you—"* She threw her arms around her mother and hugged her.

A week passed, and then another. From dawn until dusk, the sewing room of the Chestnut Grove plantation hummed with activity as Mistress Dandridge, assisted by Martha and a corps of sewing women, cut and snipped and basted and fitted the materials from London into dresses, sacques, cloaks and mantles.

For many long hours, Martha stood patiently while the rose flowered silk was molded to her young form. The bodice, cut demurely low, was a tight sheath from which her neck gleamed modestly. The tight sleeves were elbow length, trimmed with flowing lace. Over a side hoop, the largest

Martha had ever owned, the stiff blue quilt was draped, the open skirt of the flowered silk revealing its silken beauty decorated with rows of cream lace.

Finally, the day of the departure for Williamsburg arrived. The ball gown, the lace fan, the gloves from London, the high-heeled satin slippers were all packed in the pigskin trunk and fastened onto the back of the family coach.

That vehicle stood before the door of the plantation house. The Colonel and his lady were seated in it, among their bandboxes—the Colonel, elegant in his suit of plum-colored broadcloth that had come from England, his lady very fashionable indeed in her imported bonnet of green silk and mantle of padded velvet.

"Tell Mistress Patsy the carriage awaits her," her mother ordered a slave for the third time.

Just then, through the pillared entrance, emerged a short slim figure, slowed from a reckless run into a walk—Martha Dandridge, ready for the ride to Williamsburg.

But here was no dignified young lady in her traveling costume of brown woolen stuff and prim tan bonnet. Here was Patsy, her father's Pat, hatless and in her old riding habit.

Her conventional mother was horror-struck. Whoever heard of a well-born young woman wanting to ride on horseback to the Governor's Ball?

"Return to your room, Martha, and attire yourself in suitable garb for the journey," she said sternly. "And make haste!"

But as the girl turned dejectedly back into the house, her father, who had always felt a sympathetic bond with the eager, energetic girl, came to her rescue.

"Come, come, Frances," he said. "Let Pat ride her horse

to Williamsburg. Let her enjoy herself as a child—it may be
for the last time!"

The master of the house had spoken. Frances Dandridge
bowed her head in submission, and the Colonel gave the
coachman the order to start. Cracking his whip over the
horses, he sent the coach lumbering down the sandy lane that
led from the plantation house to the road. Beside it, the spirited Fatima trotted, with happy Martha on her back.

At the turn of the road, the girl looked back at the square
white house of Chestnut Grove, with its brick chimneys at
either end. The picture she carried away was that of the
magnificent chestnut trees that gave the house its name. Beneath them stood a modest country home, with, what seemed
to Martha, outstretched arms. Her father's voice echoed in
her ears: *"It may be for the last time . . ."*

In Colonial Virginia, there was a formal debut when a
girl reached her teens, at which time she was considered mar-
riageable. At twenty she was a disappointed spinster. Something told Martha that, at fifteen, she was leaving her girlhood behind her.

Her heart throbbed quickly. What would be her fate at
Williamsburg? Would the flowered gown, the quilted petticoat, look well on her? Would she dance the minuet with
grace? Whatever happened, this much she knew—she would
return from her journey a full-fledged young lady.

So Martha Dandridge rode Fatima on the road to Williamsburg, sitting her side-saddle loosely, holding her reins
with the ease of long habit—a spontaneous, natural girl, who
had grown up on a comfortable Virginia plantation, taking
an elder sister's place in responsibility towards her sisters and
brothers, learning to love animals and flowers, and to be
useful in the home; striving to curb a hot temper and to

build up character and judgment, just as many other girls, daughters of the landed gentry, have done.

But no other Virginia girl who ever lived had this one's rich experiences. No other one trod such paths of war, of statehood, of glory, bringing comfort and strength to others, until her name became so closely associated with the history of America that it was known to every school child. Virginia is full of traditions, treasured nowadays, of this girl who grew up in New Kent, who grew famous, and then grew old, always loving her native state—the girl who lived to be Martha Washington, our first First Lady.

Chapter Two   *The Golden Horseshoe*

IT WAS ONLY TWENTY-FIVE MILES FROM CHESTNUT GROVE to Williamsburg, capital of the colony of Virginia, yet it was the next day before the Dandridges reached their destination. Across bridgeless streams the horses splashed, almost submerging the hard-working steeds and leaving Patsy soaked to the elbows of her riding habit. Time and again the heavy coach sank hub-deep in wallows of sand, which changed to sloughs of mud in wet places. But always the straining horses managed to pull free. And on the afternoon of the second day, the mud-spattered vehicle, bearing the weary Colonel and his wife, rolled down the Duke of Gloucester Street, the main thoroughfare of Williamsburg.

The capital was only a small colonial town of some two hundred houses, yet to the girl from New Kent it seemed a very large city. Big-eyed with excitement, she looked at the stately brick houses with steep hipped roofs, and the less pretentious white cottages set close to the street, each with its garden of box-bordered flower beds. Interspersed between them were taverns and shops with signs in flowing script.

Coaches and chaises, filled with gentlemen in tri-cornered hats and hoop-skirted ladies, swung along the Duke of Gloucester Street, which "six poles wide," extended in a straight line from the College of William and Mary to the Capitol, nearly a mile away. Over muddy country roads, through

19

sandy stretches, the landed gentry were coming into Williamsburg from their plantations on the James, the York, and the opposite shore of the Chesapeake, to occupy their town houses during *Publick Times*, as the session of the Virginia Assembly was called.

As representative of the Crown, Governor William Gooch was the social arbiter and recognition at the Palace, the near equivalent of acceptance at Court in England. So every red-faced Burgess, every bewigged tobacco planter, had brought his wife and daughters to attend the Governor's Ball which marked the opening of the legislature.

They traveled in style, many of them in English coaches drawn by four horses, and flanked by mounted outriders and servants. Few families, Martha was quick to see, had come to Williamsburg unattended, as had the Dandridges.

Reining in her horse to avoid a cloud of dust from a shiny new coach escorted by four servants, she caught a glimpse inside of the haughty faces of two young girls and an older woman.

Ruefully, Martha compared her mud-spattered riding habit with the bonnets and silk dresses of the young misses. Of all those who had come to Williamsburg to attend the ball, she was probably the dirtiest and the most disheveled. With increasing misgivings, she spoke to Fatima and tore down the street after the family coach.

Colonel Dandridge did not own a town house. When he came to Williamsburg, he was well satisfied to stop at one of the comfortable taverns, where lodged the less wealthy squires and their families.

Now before a swinging board bearing a picture of Sir Walter Raleigh—the bearded and ruffed patron of Virginia, who introduced into England the "taking" of tobacco—the

Dandridges came to the end of their journey. Here was the Raleigh Tavern, the most famous inn in Virginia. And there on the doorstep was its keeper, Henry Wetherburn.

Willing hands took Martha's horse from her. Bandboxes and trunks were lifted down from the coach and carried inside. And the Colonel and his women-folk entered the white, L-shaped building under a slanting roof.

Martha found herself in a low-raftered room crowded with people, for as well as being a social center of the town, second only to the Palace, the Raleigh was the market place of Williamsburg. Here tobacco planters mingled with statesmen and lawyers. Merchants settled accounts. Sea captains discussed their cargoes at the oak tables in the taproom.

The tavern hummed with voices. The air was thick with pipe smoke. The girl from New Kent, who had never seen so many people, felt her excitement give way to shyness. She longed to reach the quiet of her room.

But the jovial Henry Wetherburn insisted that first Colonel Dandridge and his lady should quench their thirst with a cup of his arrack punch. Then the Colonel must show his wife and daughter the Apollo Room, in the rear ell of the tavern, where all the important dinners and balls were held.

When she finally reached her little room under the eaves, next to that of her parents, Martha washed her face and hands, and then unpacked the pigskin trunk. The flowered silk ball gown, the satin slippers of delicate pink, the lace fan, each was lifted out lovingly and laid on the bed. No girl had ever had a prettier outfit.

Yet while dressing for tea in a frock of blue calico, her hands began to tremble. She stared at herself in the mirror, a red-cheeked, rather short girl with huge brown eyes and heavy straight hair. Remembering the pale, haughty faces of

the young ladies who had passed her on the Duke of Gloucester Street, Martha surveyed her own round, rosy cheeks
and sighed. With the Governor's Ball only a few hours away,
desperately she wished herself back in New Kent.

Her shyness increased as she followed her parents downstairs. Usually capable of devouring a large tea, Miss Dandridge now had no appetite at all. Pressed by her anxious
mother, she managed to swallow a biscuit, a little cold ham,
and a few sips of tea. Then she seated herself quietly beside
her father, who, having partaken of a lusty meal, was settled
down by the fireside with a copy of *The Virginia Gazette*.

The first newspaper printed in Virginia bore little resemblance to ours of today. On the front page were advertise-
ments, poems in labored verse, and pompous essays. Colonel
Dandridge was hunting among notices of runaway slaves, ar-
rivals of cargoes and records of horse races, for some bit of
European news, however stale. He found it—on page three
—"freshest Advices," over two months old, brought by the
"good ship, Virginia, safe in York river 10 weeks after
leaving Bristol, England."

"Listen to this, Patsy!" said the Colonel, turning in disgust
to the local news:

"Tonight being the opening of the Virginia Assembly,
the Representative of our Most Gracious Sovereign, his Excellency the Governor, will give a Ball and an elegant Entertainment at the Palace, to a numerous and splendid Company
of Ladies and Gentlemen; and the City will be handsomely
illuminated."

Martha felt cold fingers of fear clutch her heart. Just
thinking about the ball that night was enough to bring tears
to her eyes.

But a minute later, dismay turned to happiness.

"Cousin Nat!" Martha cried joyfully and jumped up to greet a tanned young man in a leather jacket and mud-spattered boots, who came through the crowd to join them.

It was Nathaniel, eldest child of Martha's Uncle William and Aunt Unity, in Williamsburg from Elsing Green. A handsome lad of seventeen, he was a favorite with all the Dandridges, especially Patsy.

Of course, she told him at once why the Dandridges from Chestnut Grove were in Williamsburg.

"Are you going to the Governor's Ball, Nat?" she asked eagerly.

Here was someone who would dance with her!

Unfortunately for Martha, Nathaniel was not in Williamsburg for the ball, but to attend to the exporting of his tobacco crop. Since his father's death, the boy had taken charge of the Elsing Green plantation, duties which left little time for social life. This was small loss to Nathaniel, who no longer cared for balls and meeting new girls. He was in love with thirteen-year-old Dorothea Spotswood, the daughter of ex-Governor Alexander Spotswood.

Seeing the disappointment in Martha's face on hearing that he was returning home that evening, Nat said quickly, "This is your first trip to Williamsburg, isn't it, Patsy? Have you seen Bruton Parish where your great-grandfather was rector? The Capitol where your grandfather was Burgess?"

Martha shook her head.

Nathaniel jumped to his feet. "Get your mantle then, and come with me for a walk. There's plenty in Williamsburg to show to my favorite cousin!"

"Be back shortly, Patsy," urged her mother. "You must allow an hour for dressing for the ball."

Martha fetched a red cape with a hood. Then by the side of tall Nathaniel she left the tavern and walked down the Duke of Gloucester Street, past shops of wigmakers, tailors, jewelers, saddlers, and other inns. An apothecary shop, called the "Unicorn's Horn," caught her eye; she was fascinated by the forge where the smith worked his bellows and sent the wild sparks flying, as he hammered out a sedan chair for Governor Gooch.

Nathaniel pointed out the Court House; the Powder Horn, a small octagonal building with a peaked roof, in which the arms and ammunition of the colony were stored; and the Public Gaol, with its row of prisoners in jail for debt seated before it in pillory and stocks.

Martha saw the three brick buildings of the College of William and Mary, the second college to be founded in America, following Harvard. Standing beside the entrance gate, its posts topped with statues of the royal patrons, King William and Queen Mary, the cousins gazed admiringly at the main building, a graceful brick structure, with hip roof mounted by a cupola, designed by Sir Christopher Wren.

Nathaniel told Martha how the college had a seat in the House of Burgesses and was supported by the tax of a penny a pound on all Virginia tobacco exported; that it paid (and still pays) two copies of Latin verse a year as rent to the governor; and that it had received from the College of Heraldry the only coat-of-arms ever granted an American college.

Returning to the tavern, Nathaniel and Martha passed an ivy-covered brick church standing under spreading trees beside a quiet graveyard.

Bruton Parish.

Martha had her first view of the Court Church of Williamsburg. Governor Spotswood himself had drawn the plans for the building. Under its roof, all the royal governors worshiped. Remembering that her own great-grandfather, the Reverend Roland Jones, had been the first minister of Bruton Parish, its rector for fourteen years, Martha held her head high.

Instead of "Court Church," Bruton Parish might be called the "Tobacco Church," Nathaniel told her. When the Reverend Roland Jones was rector, the law against staying away from services was enforced in tobacco fines. And his salary, a hundred pounds a year, had been paid through the medium of sixteen thousand pounds of tobacco.

Looking at Bruton Parish, Martha felt as important as she had when Cousin Nat showed her the Capitol of the colony. That handsome brick building was built as two parallel houses, connected by a covered arcade, crowned by a white cupola. In the building on the east, the House of Burgesses held its meetings. Martha's grandfather, Orlando Jones, had come there as Burgess from New Kent in 1718.

Seeing these historic Williamsburg places, where her ancestors had been prominent, made Martha feel happy and confident. She had all but forgotten about the dreadful Governor's Ball, when she beheld an imposing brick mansion at the head of a broad level of grass, its slate hip roof and white cupola agleam in the sunset.

Martha knew . . . it was the Governor's Palace. And within a few short hours, she must go there to a ball. Again the cold fingers of fear clutched at her heart.

Seeing the distress in her eyes, kindly Nathaniel guessed the reason. "Afraid to go to the ball?" he asked.

Martha nodded. "I wish I were home."

"Nonsense! You'll have a splendid time. You'll be one of

the most popular girls there."

But Nathaniel was thinking otherwise. Martha was pretty, but a debutante from New Kent needed more than fresh, girlish good looks to be noticed among the high-born young ladies at a Governor's Ball. He thought fast. Drawing out his purse, he held up before Martha a shining object.

"Here, Patsy, is your lucky piece. Wear it to the ball, and you'll meet your fate."

Martha gave a cry of delight. In her hand was a small golden horseshoe, studded with jewels 'for nailheads. "What is it, Cousin Nat?" she asked.

Thirty years ago, Nathaniel told her, the soldier-governor, Colonel Alexander Spotswood, had led a band of cavaliers, called the Knights of the Golden Horseshoe, on an exploration trip over the Blue Ridge Mountains of western Virginia. On their return, Governor Spotswood presented to each of them, as a lucky piece, a golden horseshoe bearing the motto: *Sic juvat transcendere montes*. (Thus is made easy the surpassing of mountains.)

Although Nathaniel was too young to have been a Knight of the Golden Horseshoe, Dorothea, the Governor's daughter, had given him one of the lucky pieces as a keepsake. His sweetheart's gift was Nathaniel's most prized possession. Yet, because he felt sorry for his favorite cousin, he was lending her his Golden Horseshoe to wear to the ball.

Would the talisman bring her luck, Martha wondered, as she dressed that evening in her ball gown of flowered silk? On a black velvet ribbon around her neck, she hung the Golden Horseshoe.

Her mother swept into the room with the rustle of ivory satin and caught sight of her daughter's strange ornament.

"What is that, Patsy?" she asked sharply.

Martha's eager explanation brought a frown to her mother's brow. Jewelry was not worn much in Colonial days, particularly by a miss of fifteen. Frances Dandridge asked, and rightly, what would the fashionable people at the Palace think? What would Governor Gooch and Lady Rebecca say?

What anyone said or thought was unimportant to young Martha, urgently in need of something to make easy the "surpassing" of her personal "mountain." She could be as determined as her parent, this frightened girl, and her small features were rigid, as she repeated, "Cousin Nat says it'll help—"

Colonel Dandridge's voice thundered in the hall outside, telling mother and daughter to hurry. Dropping the argument, Mistress Dandridge motioned to Patsy to gather up her flounces and come along.

The Dandridge coach was caked with mud, the horses exhausted by the journey from New Kent. So in a shabby hired vehicle, Martha and her parents rode the short distance to the Palace.

As the coach drew near the lordly Georgian brick mansion, which was the colony's symbol of royal authority, Martha's hand stole to the comforting presence of the Golden Horseshoe around her neck.

All too soon for the trembling debutante, the coachman was reining in his horses before the iron-grilled gate of the high brick wall that guarded the Governor's home. The footman jumped down from the tiny platform on the back of the coach, ran around to open the door, and out stepped Colonel and Mistress Dandridge and their daughter.

Carefully managing their hoops, Martha and her mother, followed by the Colonel, entered the Palace gates between posts topped by the British Lion and Unicorn. They crossed a courtyard and passed through a transomed doorway.

Once in the large, paneled entrance hall, Martha's curious eyes caught glimpses of richly furnished rooms opening into others of equal pomp—all the splendor with which the royal governors surrounded themselves in an effort to make their "barbarous exile" more endurable. Then she was walking demurely beside her parents into the gold and blue ballroom from which came the sound of harp and violin.

The debutante from New Kent advanced timidly, holding fast to the arm of her father, who was resplendent in a coat of rose velvet, with fawn knee breeches and silver buckled shoes. On the right of him, Frances Dandridge moved gracefully, her head held high. Martha longed for a reassuring smile. But her mother was looking straight ahead to the blue silken walls where hung the coronation portraits of George II and Queen Caroline in their ermine robes.

Bright colors everywhere. Candlelight from the heavy chandeliers shone on the men's powdered hair, gathered in black silk bags tied with bows of black ribbon; on their velvet coats, buckled shoes and jeweled swords. Candlelight shone on the ladies' gowns of stiff brocade or satin; on their tight bodices, and wide panniered hips. Their hair . . . Martha's heart stood still.

Every debutante but herself had powdered hair.

She stared with amazement at the high white pompadours, drawn up over pads of wool and garlanded with flowers, ribbons and jewels; at the other girls' painted and powdered cheeks.

Their gowns, too, cut lower at the neck, and with wider hoops, were different from her flowered silk. The truth smote her. Her dress, which had seemed so elegant in the sewing room at Chestnut Grove, was nothing less than countrified.

True, the silk had come from London, as had the fabrics draped on the slender figures of the other girls. But no plantation seamstress or proud mother had cut and fitted the gowns that graced these Virginia belles. They had been designed and sewed by professional costumers, or even had been made in London, the measurements of the debutantes accompanying the original orders for silks and satins.

Painfully conscious of her appearance, Martha took her place behind her parents in the line of people going up to pay their respects to the Governor and his Lady.

"Colonel and Mistress John Dandridge."

Standing before the Governor, Colonel Dandridge bowed low; Frances curtsied to the floor, her ivory skirts billowing around her.

"Mistress Martha Dandridge."

Now it was her turn to curtsey before His Serene Highness, William Gooch, living symbol in America of His Majesty George II, and his Lady. Looking shyly through her lashes, Martha saw a portly man in a white wig and beruffled red velvet coat. And beside him, Lady Rebecca, popular for her gifts to Bruton Parish and the College of William and Mary, queenly tonight in blue satin, looped over a pink quilt petticoat.

All this Mistress Dandridge saw as she curtsied, her eyes downcast. Then she stepped back, a fifteen-year-old debutante, blushing and ill at ease in a homemade ball gown and unpowdered hair.

A minuet was about to start. From the orchestra came the squeak of violins, the twang of harps. A group of girls were seated along the blue silk wall, chattering and giggling, and making eyes behind their fans. At her mother's suggestion,

Martha joined these young ladies, waiting to be led out to dance.

A group of white-wigged gallants in brocaded coats and silken breeches, who had been exchanging boastful stories around the punch bowl, were streaming into the ballroom, looking for partners. Across the floor they came to the young girls seated along the wall. Each young man bowed before the lady of his choice, and led her out to join the couples gathered for the minuet. As one girl after another was claimed, Martha's cheeks flushed. Was she to be left out— the only debutante to be neglected?

"Mistress Dandridge, if that be your name?"

A red-coated young officer of the staff of His Majesty's Governor stopped before her. And Martha gasped her relief.

David Mountjoy, son of a wealthy planter, who had been sent to Oxford to complete his education, was none too pleased with the partner that had fallen to his lot. But his feet ached to tread a measure. And this young girl was the only debutante left. So he led her out onto the floor—a little brown-haired maiden, who wore an odd-looking golden horseshoe around her neck. As he took her hand for the first step, his eyes could not conceal his disdain.

But Martha did not recognize young Mountjoy's scorn as such. Once among the dancers, who caused Governor Gooch to write to his brother: "The Gent^m and Ladies here are perfectly well bred, not an ill Dancer·in my Govmt," Martha became fleet of foot and happily absorbed in the minuet. Remembering what Thomas Leonard had taught her, she faced her partner. With one hand she held out her blue quilt skirt, with the other she touched David Mountjoy's hand.

The debutante from New Kent bore herself well. She remembered when to peep at her partner with a dash of coquetry and flutter her fan; when to take the short steps, the petiteness, from which the minuet gets its name; when to do the *coupee*, a high step and a balance, which is done over and over again; when to curtsey with outspread fan while her partner bowed, his hand on his heart.

A smile crept over Martha's flushed young face. The Governor's Ball was fun after all! She was being a credit to Thomas Leonard, and to her mother's advice on how a young girl should behave at her first ball.

But on David Mountjoy's face was no answering smile. The haughty young aristocrat was very bored indeed. Worse, he was mortified at being seen dancing with an apple-cheeked young miss who romped through the stately minuet as though it were a country dance. His one desire was to get rid of this girl, and seek out ·an elegant powdered-haired damsel, just returned from England, whose silken garments and stately manners told of her family's wealth and prominence.

When a brother officer dared to laugh behind his gold-laced sleeve at the spectacle of the snobbish Mountjoy leading the little country girl through the minuet, the dandy flushed. Too embarrassed to finish, he whispered to Martha, "The floor is crowded. Shall we get something to eat?"

Surprised by her partner's abrupt invitation, Patsy left the ballroom by his side. Remembering her meager tea, however, her healthy appetite reasserted itself. Supper sounded inviting!

In the next room, a long candle-lit table was heaped with such dainties as Martha had never seen. A great silver tureen of soup was at one end; a saddle of mutton at the other end. Between were silver platters of capon, oyster patties, crabs, venison, partridges, canvasback duck, turkey, and diamond-back terrapin. There were six kinds of desserts. Ices in three-storied shapes, trifle, syllabub, pies, wine cake, and a rich concoction of pastry and almond cream. From the cookhouse across the courtyard, a procession of liveried flunkies came bearing covered dishes to heap yet more food on the overloaded table.

Martha's escort had fetched her a plate of venison and creamed crabmeat, when he saw the lady of his heart across the room, tossing her ringlets and dimpling at a fellow officer who had brought her an ice.

Mountjoy seized Martha's plate from her. "Let me show you the gardens," he said hastily. "We can eat later."

Before the startled girl could speak, a firm hand on her elbow steered her toward the door.

Down the neat brick walk strolled the debutante from New Kent and her unwilling cavalier. Behind them the Palace rose majestically in the moonlight, seen now between twelve red cedars trimmed in pillared shapes like yews. From one terrace to another they went, between beds of roses and tulips and peonies, doubly fragrant now in the moonlight; beds laid out in intricate geometrical patterns, and edged with trim box in the Dutch manner.

Once away from the Palace, young Mountjoy grew more cheerful. Relieved that here he no longer would have to endure the laughter of his friends, he resolved to make the best of a bad choice. Courtesy forbade that he leave this girl at once. And in the flattering moonlight, Martha looked slender and supple as a flower. No harm to amuse himself, until they returned to the ballroom and he managed to get rid of her.

Seated on a marble bench overlooking the fish pond, David Mountjoy boasted a bit about his duties on the Governor's staff, the race horses he owned, the actresses he knew.

Martha drank in every word. She had never known anyone wealthy enough to own race horses. And, of course, she had never been to the theater. More bewitched by the conversation of this sophisticated young man than by the moonlit garden, she gazed at him and wondered. . . . Could he be her fate? Nathaniel had said if she wore the Golden Horseshoe she might meet him tonight.

But David Mountjoy was not Martha Dandridge's fate. He was merely a spoiled, purse-proud young man, and none too gallant, as she was soon to find.

For as they turned to go back to the ballroom, he caught the little country girl in his arms and kissed her.

For one horrified moment Martha stood still, enormous-eyed, shocked, and hot with maidenly anger. Then her hand shot up and, palm open, she gave her escort a resounding slap on the cheek.

The polished Colonial blade was too surprised to speak. Instead, he laughed. And that mocking laughter only served to increase Martha's anger. All she could do, except burst into tears, was to run stumbling up the path toward the bright lights of the ballroom ahead.

What would her father say? Her prim mother? Cousin Nathaniel, who had predicted— Blindly her hand moved to the Golden Horseshoe, but in vain did she clutch at her throat.

The Golden Horseshoe. on its velvet ribbon was gone! In the struggle with the young officer, the treasure had fallen to the ground.

Martha plunged back down the terrace, running as fast as her high-heeled slippers would let her. One rose bed after another bloomed only to confuse her. Where was that marble seat overlooking the fish pond? Here? No, this pool was lined with beds of tulips. There? No . . . that path led into a delphinium walk. She had lost her way.

Terror-stricken, the girl ran in the opposite direction. The Palace seemed far away. Now there was only a faint sound of music and voices. Would she ever find the spot where she had stood beside David Mountjoy?

Then someone called, "Wait, please!"

Down the moonlit path, Martha saw a man coming toward her. She saw his white wig, the gleam of his red coat. Mountjoy again? Picking up her billowing skirts, she prepared to run, stumbled, and would have fallen had not the stranger helped her.

"Have you lost this?" He held up before her startled eyes the Golden Horseshoe.

It was not Martha's late escort. Here was a man in his thirties, wearing not the red coat of His Majesty's officers, but one of gleaming brocade. He was not so tall as Mountjoy and his figure was fuller, his voice friendlier. Here was no haughty court gallant, but a man whom one could trust, as simple of manner as her Cousin Nat.

Murmuring her thanks, Martha took from the stranger the Golden Horseshoe and gave him a grateful, if teary smile. As she walked by his side back to the Palace, she felt her trembling leave her.

In the ballroom another dance was about to start.

Martha's rescuer turned to her. "May I have the honor?" he asked simply, and he made the girl feel that it was indeed an honor. Hurt by her unhappy experience with Mountjoy, she hesitated, her eyes searching the face of the man before her. He was not handsome, his nose was too long, his lips too full. But his eyes were the kindest she had ever seen.

Her answer was to curtsy. The man bowed again and offered her his arm. As Martha touched it with her finger tips, a strange peace came over her. She was not afraid now.

A rustle of astonishment swept over the row of matrons seated against the ballroom walls. All eyes were turned to where Daniel Parke Custis, heir of the wealthy Colonel John Custis, the King's Councillor, and the social catch of the season, had led out onto the floor a strange girl with plain brown hair and a flowered frock, obviously country-made.

"Who can she be?" came whispers from behind satin fans and lace-trimmed cuffs.

No one knew. Finally the wife of a planter from the south shore of the Pamunkey ventured to say, "I *think* she's the daughter of John Dandridge, the county clerk up in New Kent."

Chapter Three   Belle of Old Williamsburg

THE APRIL SUNSHINE SIFTED THROUGH THE CEDAR TREES THAT lined the bowling green of the Governor's Palace, favorite meeting place of Williamsburg blades and belles of 1749.

Martha Dandridge, graceful and slim in a morning gown of striped muslin, stood by the mark. Expertly she weighed the boxwood bowl in her hand. Then she sent it rolling across the lawn in a curve toward the white jack.

The round bowl hit the jack squarely.

"Bravo, Mistress Patsy!" chorused a group of students from William and Mary, handsome in white wigs, satin breeches and silken hose. "You bowl well . . ." was the more restrained cry of a bevy of misses in silks and powdered curls.

Acknowledging her friends' applause with a smile, Martha took her place with her team on a bench beside the green. She did bowl well, her brother John had taught her the game, but she was modest about her skill. When a more timid girl curved the bowl into the ditch, Martha did not join in the laughter of the crowd. Instead, she resolved to give the young player a pointer or two.

As the other bowlers tried their luck, Martha looked over the group of people gathered on the Governor's bowling green. One face was missing. And it was the face Martha most longed to see—that of Daniel Parke Custis.

What could be keeping Daniel? He had promised to return from his father's home, Arlington, to join her this morning for a game of bowls. But the hours were passing. Soon Colonel Dandridge would arrive to escort Martha and her mother back to Chestnut Grove, now that the King's Birthnight Ball was over. She could not leave Williamsburg without seeing Daniel. Where *was* he?

Then the memory of his calm face reassured her. Daniel had never failed her. Not once, since he had rescued her at her first Governor's Ball. He would not fail her now.

At eighteen, Martha Dandridge had none of the painful shyness from which she had suffered as a debutante. In the last three years, she had visited Williamsburg many times. Now at the Palace balls red-coated officers of the Governor's staff, as well as students at William and Mary, who "kept race-horses at ye college and bet at ye billiard and other gaming tables," fought for the privilege of handing her through the minuet. They sent her valentines, with tender sentiments tucked under a bird's wing. They wrote sonnets to her, badly spelled and sprinkled with capitals. "Florella," they called her, Martha being too homespun for so fairy-like a being. They sent her locks of their hair, tied in true lover's knots; tamed mocking birds for her, and sang sentimental serenades beneath her window.

Martha was enchanted. If this meant being a young lady, it was a very wonderful experience. But no matter how many admirers she had, always she had turned to the quiet, serious man of thirty-eight who had come to her rescue three years ago. Her thoughts turned to him now at Arlington across the Chesapeake, where Daniel Parke Custis was visiting his father.

It was no sudden thing, Martha's love for sedate, dependable Daniel, twenty years her senior. He was not the kind to sweep a girl off her feet. And while his own intentions had been serious from the start, for two years Martha had regarded him only as a good friend. Friendship had turned to love, but slowly. Aside from her father, she had never known a man so considerate of her wishes, so unfailingly kind. In Daniel she found not only her most understanding friend, but eventually the one to whom she gave her blithe young heart.

"Dear Daniel!" she sighed, as she saw him coming across the lawn, a short, stout man in a three-cornered hat, silken coat and satin breeches.

"Patsy!" Custis whispered, bending over her extended hand. "You're beautiful this morning."

The language of romance.

For Martha Dandridge was pretty rather than beautiful. Her hazel eyes were too prominent; and her face had a healthy roundness that gave it cheer, rather than classic beauty.

But today, with a singularly happy light in her eyes, she was radiant. Daniel had asked her to marry her. The country miss from the banks of the Pamunkey would become the mistress of his Williamsburg house, Six Chimneys; and, on the death of his father, of the vast Custis estate, Arlington, on the eastern shore of Virginia, now Maryland. It was to Arlington that Daniel had gone, to ask Colonel Custis's consent to their marriage.

Turning to Daniel to acknowledge his greeting, Martha whispered shyly, "Father arrives from New Kent before the dinner hour. You can speak to him then. Has *your* father—" She paused.

What was wrong? Her suitor's rather full face was sad.

"Martha, I'm sorry . . . but it's no use," he said miserably.

"Father won't give his consent. If we marry, he'll disinherit me."

Martha's cheeks went scarlet. For a moment her temper flared. Then it died in pity for this man in his thirties, still so much under his father's domination.

This was not the first time old John Custis had threatened his son with disinheritance. He had never forgiven him for not marrying his cousin, Evelyn Byrd of Westover, considered the most sumptuous estate on the James River. Evelyn, a dewy-eyed beauty, four years older than Daniel, was the daughter of William Byrd, Receiver-General of His Majesty's Revenues and President of the Council—the most important man in Virginia. Her mother had been the daughter of Daniel Parke, Governor of the Leeward Isles, and Daniel's aunt.

The wedding of Evelyn and her cousin, uniting the Byrds and Custises, Virginia's two most prominent families, would have delighted Daniel's father. But not the young people. Daniel had refused a marriage to the greatest heiress in the colony because he did not love her. As for Evelyn, she was in love with another man.

Taken to England by her father to be presented at Court, Evelyn had fallen in love with a young Catholic nobleman, Charles Mordaunt, the grandson of the Earl of Peterborough, whom her Protestant father refused to allow her to marry. William Byrd brought his daughter back to Virginia to pine away from grief. It was then that John Custis, knowing the efficacy of love on the rebound, had conceived the idea of his son marrying the pale, unhappy Evelyn. When Daniel refused, the stormy scenes that followed shook the lordly mansion at Arlington.

Evelyn Byrd, still mourning her Englishman, remained a spinster. And John Custis had not lost hope until the broken-hearted girl died on November 13, 1737, at the age of twenty-nine, and was buried at Westover by the James River, where she used to sit and watch for her lover's ship.

His father had never forgiven Daniel for his disobedience. During the twelve years following Evelyn's death, a coolness had existed between the old man, who lived alone at Arlington across the Chesapeake, and his heir who occupied his own home in Williamsburg, called Six Chimneys.

Now Daniel and Colonel Custis were quarreling again, this time over little Martha Dandridge. The elder man's anger at his son's previous disobedience was mild compared to his fury when Daniel told him of his desire to marry a girl from New Kent—"A nobody," shouted his father, "of whom no one has ever heard!"

The irascible old Colonel could hardly believe his ears. Had his son, after long years of bachelorhood, taken leave of his senses?

"Martha Dandridge . . . indeed!" John Custis took a pinch of snuff and flew into one of his famous tempers. When it had spent itself, he delivered his ultimatum; and it seemed like an echo of the past:

"Marry that girl and I'll disinherit you. I'll leave my whole fortune to Jack, my little Negro slave."

"What shall we do, Martha?" Nearing forty, Daniel was embarrassed to admit his father's power over him, yet it was his nature to be frank.

"I don't know," she answered sadly. The deep kind voice of Daniel was pleading for help for the first time, and she had no solution for their problem.

Should they elope? Elopements were a serious matter in Virginia in 1749. Where would a young couple run away to, except the wilderness? Martha knew the fate of Fanny

Custis, Daniel's unfortunate sister, who had dared to defy her father and marry Captain Dausie, the man she loved.

One night Captain Dausie stole to the cedar-screened summerhouse at Arlington, and Fanny, disguised as her own maid, had tripped out in the gray dawn to join him in a wild horseback ride to the Blue Ridge Mountains of western Virginia.

But an eloping couple could not live forever in the wilderness. Finally the Dausies had been forced to return to Williamsburg. There Fanny had lived ever since in poverty and disillusionment, "cut off with a shilling" by her bitter, influential old father.

So standing on the bowling lawn, in the bright April sunshine, Martha and Daniel went over their problem again and again, as lovers do—hopeless lovers, most of all. How could they force the Colonel to give his consent to their marriage?

"Let's not give up hope," she whispered. "There may be a way . . ." And she tried to smile as they joined their friends and finished the game of bowls.

Back in her room at the Raleigh Tavern, where she was staying with her mother, Martha flung herself on the bed and burst into tears.

Evelyn Byrd was dead. But there were other such fortunate girls in Virginia. Not as beautiful or as wealthy as Evelyn, perhaps, but girls that Daniel's father would think more suitable for him to marry than Martha Dandridge. What power had the daughter of the county clerk from New Kent against this ambitious old man, who had chosen Governor Alexander Spotswood and the Honorable William Byrd as godfathers for his son?

At dinner time, Frances Dandridge rapped on the door of her daughter's room. John Dandridge had arrived. He was asking for his favorite child.

The sound of muffled sobs greeted her. Pushing open the door, she saw a slender figure flung high on the bed, weeping forlornly.

"Tell Mama about it," was the mother's concerned request. And, her arm around the red-eyed girl, she listened to the story of Colonel Custis's cruel decision.

"Why does Daniel's father dislike me so?" wailed Martha, burying her head in the pillow.

"He doesn't dislike *you*," explained her mother. "It is Daniel and Fanny whom he hates. He wants to show his power over them."

"How do you know this, Mama?"

Frances Dandridge's face grew grave. "It's not a pretty story, Patsy. But you'd best know the kind of family you wish to marry into. Your Daniel has bad blood in his veins."

Daniel's mother had been Frances Parke, also the victim of a stormy disposition, inherited from her father, the arrogant Governor of the Leeward Islands. John Custis, a stubborn young blade, had insisted on marrying the pert, self-willed girl, although his friends warned him that he never could get on with her.

John Custis and Frances Parke were married at the bride's home at Queen's Creek, on the York River. Their honeymoon was scarcely ended before they were quarreling. As predicted, the two spoiled young people found it impossible to get along together. Living under the same roof, they finally spoke to each other only through a slave, Pompey.

One day Colonel John asked his wife, through the slave, to take a drive with him. He helped her to a seat in the carriage—and then drove straight ahead into the bay!

When the water was above the floor board, Frances asked,

"Where are you going, Colonel Custis?"

"To hell, Madam."

"Drive on," she replied. "Any place is better than Arlington."

Her husband turned the carriage around and drove home.

"Madam, I believe you would as leave meet the Devil himself, if I should drive to hell," he said bitterly.

"Quite true, sir," she answered. "I know you so well I would not be afraid to go anywhere you would go."

This war of words only ended with Frances's death. She died of smallpox, leaving a son, Daniel, and a daughter, Fanny.

"People say that John Custis hated his wife because she had the quicker tongue, and always managed to have the last word," Mistress Dandridge told her daughter. "He married Frances to tame her, and did not succeed. Fanny escaped him. But he is getting full revenge by keeping Daniel subdued."

Poor Daniel! Martha sighed. "Then nothing can be done—" She lifted tear-filled eyes. "Oh, Mama, I love him so!"

Frances Dandridge was an intelligent woman. Resourceful, too, when her children's happiness was at stake. Looking at her weeping daughter, she resolved that, if Martha wanted Daniel, neither Colonel Custis's stubbornness nor his son's lovable weakness should break her heart.

"Have hope, Patsy." She patted her daughter's shoulder. "You may yet be Mrs. Daniel Parke Custis. Leave it to me."

That afternoon Colonel Dandridge and his wife held a consultation in their room. Then Frances donned her bonnet and mantle, and hurried down the Duke of Gloucester Street to a white clapboard cottage, nestling in a garden of hollyhocks and larkspur, behind a white picket fence.

This house the Nathaniel Dandridges had taken for the legislative session. Two years before Martha's Cousin Nat of Elsing Green had married the fourteen-year-old Dorothea Spotswood, and this year, they had emerged from the happy isolation of their Elsing Green plantation, with their baby, for a few weeks of gaiety.

Over the tea cups, Martha's mother had a long talk with Dorothea. Later she sped back to the inn with surprising news for her daughter.

Martha was not to return with her parents to Chestnut Grove. She was to spend two weeks with her cousins.

That fortnight found Williamsburg at its gayest. A new and wonderful life opened for the girl from New Kent. Chaperoned by the popular sixteen-year-old matron, Dorothea Spotswood Dandridge, Martha was seen everywhere. Not just at an occasional ball, but at all the fairs, races and entertainments with which Williamsburg celebrated the *Publick Times* of the legislative session.

Mornings Dorothea and Martha had their hair crimped into curls and powdered. Then, in charming poke bonnets, they went out in a sedan chair to pay ten o'clock calls. Tripping up the brick walks, they folded their hoops into one stately mansion after another along the Duke of Gloucester Street. And to all the great ladies in town from their estates on the York and James, Dorothea said proudly, "This is my *cousin*, Martha Dandridge."

Anyone introduced by the fashionable Dorothea Spotswood—and related to her besides!—was quickly accepted in Williamsburg society. There was no more distinguished family in Virginia than the Spotswoods. The haughty ex-Governor, Dorothea's father, could show a ball which had passed through his coat at Blenheim. He had finished the Governor's Palace of which Virginians were so proud, designed Bruton Parish, and built the Powder Horn.

After the morning calls, Dorothea and Martha went shopping at cabinet makers, silversmiths and blacksmiths. At The Sign of the Golden Ball, they selected a punch and toddy ladle from the stock of piggins, candle cups and silver buckles. At the goldsmith's they bought a mother-of-pearl snuff box for Daniel, and a gold toothpick case for Colonel Dandridge.

Evenings Daniel came to call, carrying his flute in two sections in the tails of his coat. With Martha at the spinet, the lovesick couple rendered together the simple tunes of the day, while over in the corner Nathaniel pressed his Dorothea's hand.

One day they went, all four of them, to the Fair at which the common people had their fun at *Publick Times*. They watched the puppet shows, the foot races, the chasing of greased pigs. And to everyone they met, Dorothea introduced the girl from New Kent, "This is my *cousin*, Martha Dandridge."

Sundays they worshiped at Bruton Parish, where the sunlight dappled the brick walls with the shadows of the trees in the church-yard, and fell on the tombstones parading their coat-of-arms of dead parishioners. Martha, sitting proudly in the Spotswood high box pew, was thrilled to be in the church whose baptismal font had been used at Jamestown for the baptism of Pocahontas. Her eyes sought the grave in the chancel of her great-grandfather, Roland Jones, rector here for fourteen years; the grave of her grandfather, Orlando Jones, Burgess from New Kent. If Daniel could only tell his father—

Then her eyes strayed to a tablet on the wall, dedicated to

Daniel Parke, Secretary of the colony of Virginia, and His Majesty's Councillor, who "dyed ye 6th of March Anno 1679." That was Daniel's grandfather, the father of Frances Parke, and a far more famous man than any of Martha's ancestors!

Colonel Daniel Parke had been aide-de-camp to the Duke of Marlborough in the campaign in Flanders; he had carried the Duke's dispatch to Queen Anne, announcing the victory of Blenheim. For that the Queen had given him a miniature of herself set in diamonds. Later, he had been appointed Governor-General of the Leeward Islands, where a mob, excited to frenzy by his cruelty and arrogance, surrounded the Government House and killed him.

Martha seemed to hear her mother's voice: *"Your Daniel has bad blood in his veins."* She shuddered. People said her Daniel—good, kind, patient Daniel—looked like his grandfather. They had the same high-domed brow, long nose and rather full mouth. But there the resemblance ceased. There was not a more considerate, upright man in all Virginia than Daniel Parke Custis.

Dorothea and Nathaniel, warm-hearted and romantic, could not do enough for their guest. In Martha's honor, they gave a reception during the second week of her stay.

Helping her cousins receive the guests in their drawing-room, furnished with chairs and inlaid tables of mahogany— a new wood come into fashion two years earlier—was the smiling Mistress Dandridge, in voluminous pink panniers and powdered pompadour. Later, poised and radiant, she poured tea from Dorothea's silver service with the Spotswood crest. Everyone met and liked the visitor from New Kent. Everyone wanted to see more of her.

Once or twice during her visit, a "headache," to which

the lively Dorothea had never before been subject, required that she remain in her bedroom. This left Martha to act as hostess and be the center of attraction.

Before long, the name of Martha Dandridge was on everyone's lips. People spoke of her fresh face, good sense, and amiable disposition. The *Virginia Gazette* even printed a poem singing her praises.

Finally, gruff old John Custis, over in Arlington, heard about the girl. Mutual friends, knowing of Daniel's hopeless love for her, wrote to his father, speaking in high terms of Mistress Dandridge.

The Colonel's curiosity was piqued. Perhaps there was something to this girl, after all. He decided to go to Williamsburg and see for himself the person whom he had rejected as a daughter-in-law.

Early one morning Martha Dandridge strolled in Dorothea's garden to gather a bouquet of Sweet William and pink cloves. She was close by a crepe myrtle shrub, when over the box hedge she saw an eccentric-looking old gentleman in a gay waistcoat, his red wig askew, watching her.

"You've a nice garden," he said, bluntly.

Wearing a cotton morning frock, and with her hair still unpowdered, Martha smiled at the stranger. "It isn't my garden, sir. It belongs to my cousins."

The man chuckled. Daniel's sweetheart was not too good-looking, he was glad to see. He had had enough of spoiled beauties with Frances Parke. "This is nice box," he remarked, touching the hedge.

"You should see the box at Chestnut Grove, sir!" cried Martha impulsively. And before she knew it, she was telling the stranger about her garden on the Pamunkey.

Martha's hazel eyes glowed, the roses in her cheeks deep-

ened as she talked. The old man appeared interested. He asked
her questions about her family. There were her brothers, John
and William who had gone into the Royal Navy, she told
him; Bartholomew, student of the family, always with his
nose in a book. Pretty Nancy, now ten years old, could sew
as well as her eldest sister. Baby Frances—how Martha missed
the little cherub and longed to see her again!

"What do you consider the most important character assets
in a young person?" the Colonel asked abruptly.

"*A just mind and a right heart*," Martha replied promptly.

"A prudent remark, child." The old man took a pinch of
snuff from a silver snuff-box as he spoke. Sneezing violently,
he snapped the lid.

The breeze blew a whiff of snuff in Martha's direction.
She sneezed, too, and they both laughed.

"Oh, sir, I *do* wish you could see my garden at Chestnut
Grove," Martha repeated warmly. She liked this old man.
There was something familiar about him—what was it? What-
ever it was, he had succeeded in rousing her interest.

He looked at her curiously for a long time. She flushed
deeply. "My dear, I think I shall. . . ." he said. And without
another word went off down the street.

Back at Arlington, John Custis sat down to think over his
meeting with Martha. Her sweet, rosy face haunted him, her
simplicity, her charm. Obviously she had good stuff in her.

Finally he sent for a friend, J. Powers, to come to Arlington. He handed him this written memorandum:

"*I give my free consent to the union of my Son Daniel
with Martha Dandridge.*"

Somewhat surprised, Squire Powers, who had frequently
acted as mediator between the fiery father and his quiet son,

sat down and wrote Daniel the good news.

When the letter reached Daniel's house, Six Chimneys, in Williamsburg, the young man was not at home. Martha had returned to Chestnut Grove, and to be near her, love-torn Daniel had leased a plantation, the White House, in New Kent on the Pamunkey.

It was a happy day for Daniel Custis when J. Powers's letter reached him in his comfortable river mansion:

"This comes at Last to bring you the News that I believe will be most Agreeable to you of any you have ever heard —that you may not be long in Suspense, I shall tell you at once. I am Empowered by your father to let you know that he Heartily and Willingly Consents to your marriage with Miss Dandridge—that he has so good a Character of her, that he had rather you should have her than any Lady in Virginia —nay, if possible, he is more Enamored with her Character as you are with her person, and this is owing chiefly to a Prudent Speech of her own. Hurry down immediately for Fear he should change the strong inclination he has to your marrying Directly . . ."

Within an hour after the receipt of Squire Powers's message, Daniel was on his horse, galloping to Chestnut Grove with the written pledge of his father's consent. At last, he was free to ask Colonel Dandridge a most important question.

Doubly armed with the Colonel's approval, Daniel hurried to Martha's side. He found her in her wheel-shaped rose garden—the spot where she most loved to be—busy with her flowers. At the sight of her lover's happy face, she dropped a bouquet of moss roses, scattering the pink blossoms over the path.

"Daniel!" she cried. "What is it?"

He did not have to tell her. His answer was to take her in his arms.

A week later, on a June day, in a little brick church in a grove of trees, Daniel Parke Custis and Martha Dandridge were married by the Reverend David Mossum. The wedding took place, not in Bruton Parish, the Court Church of Williamsburg, but at St. Peter's in New Kent, where John Dandridge was vestryman.

Proudly the Colonel gave his eldest child in marriage. Dressed in a simple gown of white gauze, and wearing the bridegroom's gift, a necklace of pearls, Martha looked no taller than her sister Nancy as she stood by the bridegroom's side.

In a pew near by were Martha's family—her mother, out for the first time since the birth of a new baby to be named Elizabeth; Nancy, wearing her first long party dress of pink muslin; solemn Bartholomew in a blue velvet. John and William were away at sea and Frances was considered too young for weddings.

And across the aisle were the smiling Nathaniel Dandridges —Nat and Dorothea who had helped to bring about the romance.

Daniel Custis, the patient, the kind, placed on his wife's hand the gold band that told her of his love. Beneath her gown of filmy gauze, Martha's heart beat wildly. *Her husband*. The ceremony came to a close and she turned for his kiss.

Then she had the surprise of her life. It was not her new husband who gave Martha her first embrace. Daniel's crusty old father rushed forward and kissed the bride heartily on both cheeks.

"Daughter!" he said in a proud voice, which left no doubt in the minds of the guests as to his feelings. Then he stepped back, his red wig slipping as usual, to make way for the dark-eyed groom, who had taken his young wife under his arm and was kissing her gently.

The guests rode from the church to the White House, no longer leased, but now owned in full by the Daniel Parke Custises, the gift of the groom's father. Leading the cavalcade of carriages were the bride and groom, in Daniel's cream-colored coach, drawn by four white horses and flanked by six Negro outriders in white uniforms.

For three days the White House rang with the sound of music and dancing. Friends and relatives of the Dandridges, all the gentry of New Kent, came to the big white house on the Pamunkey to eat and drink and congratulate the newly-weds. And no one entered into the gaiety more completely than did Colonel John Custis. He could not get. enough of his charming daughter-in-law's society. In between parties, he wanted to walk with her in the gardens. At dinners, he was always seated beside her. "My son has made a happy choice," he said over and over again. And if people smiled at his change of heart, he was too elated to know it.

Martha had cleared the first hurdle of her life. Give others their due—her intelligent mother, the help of the Nathaniel Dandridges—but in the end, it was Martha herself who won out. The sweet, tactful maid from New Kent had tamed the fiery old Colonel when beautiful, high-born Frances Parke had failed.

Martha was to become very fond of her eccentric father-in-law. And later that year, when she stood with Daniel in the family graveyard at Arlington, looking at his grave, there would be tears of genuine sorrow in her eyes.

On the headstone was an epitaph, ordered by the Colonel himself, that ended with a unique inscription: "aged 71 years, Yet Liv'd but Seven Years which was the space of time He kept a *Batchelers* house at Arlington on the Eastern Shore of Virginia." The seven years referred to were the years John Custis had been a widower.

"Dear old thing!" Martha smiled through her tears. "He *did* have the last word."

It was october in 1756, and mistress daniel parke custis, in a scarlet riding habit, rode beside her husband across the fields of their plantation. The breeze ruffled the white plume in her tri-corne hat. It blew her brown hair, worn unpowdered at Daniel's request, across her pink cheeks.

It was good to be alive on a crisp autumn day, to be twenty-five, blessed with health and wealth and the love of a devoted husband. As the riders drew rein on a hill to let their horses rest, Martha gazed with rapture over the Virginia country-side. Against a forest of pines spread Daniel's fields of tobacco, yellow in the sun; and in their midst was the Custis's comfortable white frame house, surrounded by the workhouses of the plantation, the cabins of contented slaves. And winding its way to the sea was the river of Martha's childhood, the broad Pamunkey.

"Let's race!" she cried to her husband. "Breakfast is waiting!"

Across the fields they galloped their horses, then dropped to a trot on nearing the house. Stone gateposts carved with the head of a griffin, the Custis crest, marked the beginning of an avenue of linden trees.

The riders passed Daniel's office, a small white outbuilding where he conferred with his overseer, Macon, or the captains of the trading ships who came to his wharf for tobacco.

Near by were the other buildings of the plantation—the wash-house, smokehouse, milkhouse, bakehouse, shoemaker's shop, storehouses, and the large brick stables. The lanes between them were enlivened with swarms of dogs, chickens, ducks, pigs, and little Negroes.

At the door of their home the Custises dismounted and handed their reins to a waiting stableboy. Like most Pamun-key plantations, the front of the square white house faced the main highway in Virginia, the river. Here a row of giant tulip poplars stood like tall green soldiers ever on guard.

"Papa! Mama!"

A rather frail, dark-haired little girl rushed down the steps to greet her parents, followed by the white-turbaned black Mammy, Molly, with John Parke Custis, the Fifth, in her arms.

It was to Daniel that three-year-old Frances ran first. "Papa!" The child's eyes were adoring as she flung her arms about him. There was a more sedate kiss for her mother, who had taken her son from his nurse's arms.

"Breakfast is served, Missus Martha. . . ." came Oney's soft voice from the white-columned veranda. Holding her year-old baby against her scarlet jacket, Martha guided little Frances into the house and toward the breakfast room.

"Mama will be with you shortly," she promised. "Oney, start them with their porridge and milk." And Mrs. Custis hurried upstairs to change into a morning gown of blue muslin.

Seated at the handsome mahogany dining table Daniel had bought in Williamsburg, Martha lifted the silver teapot, bear-ing the Custis crest, and poured her husband a cup of scalding tea. She poured one for herself as well, and, sipping it, smiled at him over a bowl of purple asters. Frances was busy with her porridge bowl. Baby Jacky's snub-nose was hidden in his silver cup.

Every room of the White House breathed peace and happiness. With gleaming floor and dignified mahogany furnishings, the broad hospitable hall opened through the house to a sunny garden. Fires blazed beneath marble mantels in the living room and the sleeping rooms as well. Tall gilt mirrors reflected the sunshine and firelight and the glow of happy faces.

But these evidences of the grace and beauty of good living had not appeared by magic; they were the result of hard work each day on the part of the master and mistress.

Breakfast completed, Daniel kissed his wife good-bye and left for his office. Martha, her mind on the making of fall clothes for the slaves, hurried to the spinning house. She found the women carding wool and preparing it for spinning.

"Good morning," she greeted her workers pleasantly, as each rose and curtsied.

The wool came in bunches. It had to be untangled by drawing it through wool cards—flat pieces of wood thickly set with wire teeth like a coarse brush. Martha watched a carder take up a bunch of wool and draw it across a card which rested on her knees. As the snarls, knots, burrs and grass entangled in the wool were removed, she followed each movement with a practiced eye. When the wool lay straight and smooth, the worker twisted it into a long curl, and dropped it among others in a box beside her.

Efficient Mistress Custis stopped here and there to guide her women. But she had not always been an expert. With some embarrassment, she remembered her first days in the spinning house. How was she, a young bride, to know that before wool was dyed it must be washed? How was she to know how wool was dyed?

Feigning a knowledge that was not hers, she had timidly offered suggestions. The women had gone on without her guidance, tying the white locks into net bags and then throwing them into kettles of liquids to boil until they were the right shade. But how they had smiled, discreetly, of course, behind their young mistress's back!

Martha learned, but the learning was painful. For instance, why had not someone told her that after wool was dyed it must be greased? For every ten pounds, three pounds of melted swine's grease must be worked in to soften the wool and moisten it. Her first batch of wool had been too stiff to card.

Martha had not even known how dyes were made, and rather than let her women see her ignorance, she had run weeping to her room. There "dear Mama," as Martha always called Frances Dandridge, visiting the White House that day, had come to comfort her.

Many of the dyes came from flowers and plants growing right on the plantation, Mistress Dandridge told her daughter. Brown and yellow from the bark of red oak or hickory trees. Goldenrod blossoms, mixed with indigo and alum, made green. Red, by boiling the juice of the pokeberry. And the purple dye, which gave such a lovely color to the white wool, came from the petals of the purple iris.

It was very simple, once you knew how. Martha listened carefully. Her women should never laugh at her again.

"Oh, Mama, thank you for all you've taught me!" She flung her arms around her mother and kissed her.

Tears came to Frances Dandridge's eyes. Her eldest daughter had often thought her over-strict. At last she understood the purpose behind the rather relentless process.

But that was long ago. And now, with her eyes trained to detect any fault, Martha hurried to that part of the building where women stood at spinning wheels, preparing wool for the looms on which it would be woven into cloth.

Starting the big wheel in motion, a woman caught in her left hand the end of the yarn. As the wheel began to turn, she stepped back quickly, one, two, three steps. By walking away with the yarn in her hand, the spinner drew it out, allowing it to twist as she walked. When she had twisted as much as her three steps allowed, she glided forward with the yarn held high, letting it wind on the spindle, which was being turned by the moving wheel.

With the day's spinning well under way, Martha hastened along a brick walk to the whitewashed cookhouse—to Mistress Custis, who enjoyed good food and took pride in serving bountiful meals, the most important building on the plantation.

Keys in hand, she entered the large tile-floored room of the smoky building. From iron cranes on the hearth hung a row of hooks from which swung steaming soup kettles. Quarters of beef, suckling pigs, rows of turkeys and chickens roasted on spits over the fire. The portly brown cook, in red bandana, was baking bread in an iron bake kettle mounted on short, stout legs.

Martha Custis sniffed the delicious odor. What feathery biscuits would be served to her guests! What crisp corn pones cooked in the hot ashes! She saw the griddle, which sat on four feet just over the red coals, ready for the batter cakes.

After tasting a piece of fresh bread, to the grinning delight of the cook, the mistress hurried back to the "big house." A carriage was stopping at the front door. Could "dear Mama" have arrived so early? Anna Maria, and the others from Chestnut Grove? Or was it friends from one of the neighboring plantations?

It was the Nathaniel Dandridges and their children, arriving from Elsing Green. Martha smiled happily as she welcomed Dorothea and Nathaniel. Remembering their effective hospitality of years gone by, she could not do enough for her cousins.

The next carriage to appear contained the Dandridges from Chestnut Grove, the widowed Frances in a black crepe mantle; Nancy, seventeen now, and pretty in a poke bonnet; brother William, home on furlough, in his naval uniform; the solemn nineteen-year-old Bartholomew; Frances, a miss of twelve; Elizabeth, seven, and a six-months-old baby, Mary.

With Chestnut Grove only five miles away, scarcely a week passed without a visit from some member of Martha's family. Their two babies, Mary and Jacky, had drawn mother and daughter closer together. Sorrow was another bond between them. Martha had lost her first born, Daniel, a chubby three-year-old, two years before. And death had come twice to Chestnut Grove. The month after Martha's marriage her brother John had died. And two months ago, her beloved father, Colonel Dandridge, had passed away.

At three o'clock dinner, Martha sat at the head of her table, heaped with food in generous Virginia fashion and lighted by four candles. She was dressed in blue taffeta, a lace mob cap on her brown curls, while Daniel played the gracious host in a ruffled shirt, tie-back wig, and velvet coat. Laughter tinkled, stories were exchanged, family gossip related.

After seven years of marriage, it was still hard for Martha Custis to think of herself as mistress of the house, and of "dear Mama" as just a guest, seated down the table at Daniel's right. Rather shyly she listened to talk of cockfighting, race horses, dueling, and farming going on about her, while a succession of young Negro servants marched in, carrying pewter dishes polished until they gleamed. These were the kitchen "helpers," chiefly the cook's own children, their black faces shining, robed in white aprons to hide various trouser deficiencies.

The meal these young kitchen helpers served was a bountiful feast, even for Virginia. Terrapin and venison, Chesapeake Bay oysters, crab and wild turkey, were followed by a procession of sweets. Daniel beamed proudly at his wife. And their guests rose from the table with many a compliment for their young hostess.

But it was to her mother that Martha looked for a hint of approval. Only when she saw that Frances Dandridge was smiling did she know that her party had been a success.

After dinner the Dandridges and Custises gathered in the parlor to play the game called "Pawns for Redemption." But soon Nancy wanted to dance, and Daniel called for the plantation fiddler, as important a person at the White House as the barber, shoemaker, or carpenter. And old and young joined in dancing country dances. "Hunting the Squirrel" led to "The Cushion Dance," which last, of course, was but an excuse for the lads to kiss their partners.

They were hospitable, light-hearted people, these tobacco planters of New Kent, and their plantations the scene of a continual round of parties. Several times a week, Daniel and Martha traveled to one isolated house or another for three o'clock dinner, cards, dancing, or an evening of songs around the spinet, followed by refreshments of hot mulled wine and fruit cake.

When the roads of New Kent were too rough for carriages, they rode on horseback, followed by a black servant.
Balls, "fish fryes," christenings, cockfights, horse races and
weddings—quiet Daniel Parke Custis, twenty years older than
Martha, might have liked the peace of his fireside in the evening. But he liked even more to see his vivacious young wife
having a good time. And a royal good time she had!

The pleasures of plantation society on the Pamunkey so
appealed to the tastes of the Custises that, each spring and
fall, they left the White House with regret. But being a
fashionable young couple, *Publick Times,* when the Virginia
Assembly was in session, found them moving to their Williamsburg home for a more worldly existence.

Martha now traveled in state to Williamsburg in the
Custis coach, driven by two postillions wearing the red and
white family livery, and followed by a cavalcade of mounted
servants leading extra horses. In the capital she no longer
stayed at a public inn. She lived in elegance at her husband's
handsome town house, Six Chimneys.

This mansion, built in 1714, had a charm and dignity that
set it apart from the other residences of the town. Rising out
of great clumps of dark, glistening boxwood, the gables of
the house were dominated—as its name implied—by six sturdy
chimneys. Its size can be judged by the number of these
chimneys. But only the detached cookhouse remains today
of what was once the show place of Williamsburg.

Also still standing is an ancient yew tree, said to have been
planted at the front door by Martha herself. We think of
the young mistress of this fine house pausing beside the yew,
as yet a young shrub, and remembering that night, so long
ago, when as a shy unknown of fifteen she had made her

debut at the Governor's Ball.

Now, as Mrs. Daniel Parke Custis, every door in Williamsburg was open to her. There were visits in the stately Georgian mansions that lined the Duke of Gloucester Street, pleasant intimacies with their rich and powerful owners. And a ball at the Palace was not complete without the Daniel Parke Custises—Daniel being a close friend of the new governor, Robert Dinwiddie.

On the morning of a ball—and that was almost every morning during the season—a hairdresser came to Six Chimneys to powder, "crisp" (curl), burn and generally damage Martha's lovely brown hair. At the plantation, she wore it unpowdered, under a dainty mob cap, because Daniel preferred it that way. But in Williamsburg, Mrs. Custis affected the showy pyramids that London decreed were the fashion.

Her "head done," Martha would sit all afternoon afraid of the least bit of wind, her head propped up against pillows, because the hairdresser could not attend to everyone the afternoon of the ball.

How her neck ached! But that night, as she and Daniel entered the new ballroom built onto the rear of the Palace, her heart beat with triumph under her tight bodice. Tiny Martha Custis might look a trifle top-heavy, so immense was the creation on her head, a mass of ringlets on which was perched a pair of pink lace wings, six blue silk tassels to match her gown, and a wreath of artificial roses, but well she knew she was one of the best-dressed women in the room. Her headdress was the highest, her hoop the widest. The lace handkerchief tucked in her bracelet, the diamond-studded rosettes gleaming on her tiny slippers, would be copied all over Virginia.

And so the days in Williamsburg glided pleasantly by for

the wife of prominent Daniel Parke Custis. Martha must order her costumes to wear to the balls held in candlelit rooms to the music of harpsichord, flute and bassoon. She must plan routs to be given in her own drawing room with its Adam mirrors and Chinese Chippendale furniture. There were such important matters as brocades and laces to be selected, and what sort of bonnet to wear with her new sealskin tippet, sent from London at her husband's request to adorn her purple velvet mantle.

Ever generous to his young wife, it seemed, as Daniel grew older, that no gift was quite fine enough for her.

Early in the spring he had written Robert Cary, his agent in London:

"I desire a handsome watch for my wife, a pattern like the one you bought for Mrs. Burwell Bassett, with her name around the dial. There are just twelve letters in her name— Martha Custis—a letter for each hour marked on the dial plate."

While Martha had admired the timepiece owned by Anne Bassett, wife of Colonel Burwell Bassett of Eltham, she had never hoped to own so rare an ornament. In Colonial times, a watch was a highly prized possession, owned by few men and even fewer women. Martha's watch arrived in November, just in time for her to wear it to the races. And when she saw it, she threw her arms around her husband's neck and kissed him.

It was an exquisite gift, still treasured at Washington's Headquarters, Newburgh, New York. Made by Bawie of London, the watch had a gold case with a circle of white enamel, inlaid with gold, around the edges of the face and back. Over each numeral on the dial was a letter of her name,

MARTHA CUSTIS, beginning with the figure 1.

"What a childlike creature she is!" Daniel thought, looking at his wife's happy face. Martha returned his glance, smiling rapturously. Dear Daniel!

That was the season when Daniel and Martha had their portraits painted by the fashionable artist, John Wollaston; companion paintings of three-quarter length. Most of November, 1756, they lingered in Williamsburg, posing for the artist. Daniel stood with one hand on a table, the other on his hip, showing his canary satin vest, in much the same way that his grandfather, Daniel Parke, had posed for Sir Godfrey Kneller. Martha stood so straight that, although she was short and growing a trifle plump, she appeared tall and slim. Their eyes were as almond-shaped as those of a Chinese, not because Martha or Daniel had eyes of that shape, but because John Wollaston painted small, slanted eyes in every portrait, earning for himself the nickname "Almond-eyed Wollaston."

Martha was painted as Daniel liked her—her brown hair unpowdered, combed back from her brow and garlanded with strings of pearls. Her dress was his favorite, a rich silk with a low square neck, and in the front a butterfly bow of ribbon. The lace at her elbow fell in cascades to show her rounded arm as she reached to pluck a rose.

Martha was young and full of life. Small wonder that the forty-five-year old Daniel loved her, and delighted to shower her with gifts. Too long he had lived in the shadow of his stubborn old father. Martha had awakened him, taught him to laugh, to use his mind, to really enjoy life.

On nights when there were no games of cards, routs or balls, Martha and Daniel would go to the new theater, built just back of the Capitol.

The theatrical season was at its peak, on a night in November, 1756, with the Virginia Assembly in session and Williamsburg crowded with visitors. The barn-like wooden building was packed to the doors. Every seat in the pit, reserved for the common people, as well as in the boxes for the gentry, was taken. The play was Shakespeare's *Othello*, followed by a farce.

For hours servants with the white on red of the Custis livery had been solemnly holding box seats. A few minutes before the curtain rose at six o'clock, Martha and Daniel appeared with their friends, Richard and Anne Nicholas.

Martha had seldom been prettier than she was that evening in a pink satin gown, with wreaths of artificial roses festooned on the full skirt and in her powdered hair. Holding an ermine tippet around her bare shoulders, against the cold of the unheated building, she stood looking out over the crowded pit before she took her seat.

Standing just below was a man—a young giant of about twenty-four, in the blue uniform of a Virginia soldier. He was an unusually noticeable figure, more than six feet tall, broad-shouldered, yet of a slender and athletic build.

"Who is that?" Mrs. Daniel Parke Custis asked Richard Carter Nicholas, indicating the officer with her fan.

"That's George Washington," answered Nicholas. "Colonel of the Virginia troops—hero of Braddock's march. Isn't he a fine-looking man?"

So that was George Washington, the young colonel of the Virginia forces! The French and Indian War had been going on for some time, and Martha had heard Daniel and the other men speak of Colonel Washington with admiration. Even sheltered ladies such as Mistress Custis knew of the bloody battle at the Monongahela River on July ninth, over a year ago. The English had been surprised by the Indians, and their allies, the French; Edward Braddock, general of the British regulars, sent to drive the French from Fort Duquesne, had been killed; and only the Colonial leader, George Washington, had emerged from the defeat with glory. With a coolness and bravery that spread his fame to Europe, the young colonel had reorganized the defeated British and led them to fight a dogged rear guard action that brought them eventually from the ambush.

But all this had occurred off in the western wilderness. At home, and of greater interest to Martha, Governor Dinwiddie had commissioned his friend, Daniel Parke Custis, a colonel of the militia of New Kent, so now she could proudly refer to her husband as "the Colonel." Beyond that, the French and Indian War had not touched so much as the surface of her life.

But this night Martha looked down again, and with increasing interest, at George Washington, Virginia's military hero. She noticed his strong, regular features, the dignified way he carried his head on his superb neck. How handsome he is! How distinguished! she thought. But the stage-hands were snuffing out the smoking candles in the footlights. As the theater went dark and the tragedy of *Othello* began, Martha lost sight of the man.

Absorbed in the woes of the Moor, Othello, she forgot all about the soldier in the pit. But during the intermission, when the half-frozen audience gathered around the stove in the foyer, she saw him again—a big young man, with a captivating shyness of expression, making his way through the crowd.

"There's Colonel Washington!" Martha exclaimed softly, as though greeting an old friend.

"May I present him to you, Patsy?" asked Richard Nicholas. "I know him well."

But Martha Custis and George Washington were not destined to meet that night. Just as she was about to bow her approval of the introduction, the next act of *Othello* was announced, and Daniel escorted her back to their box. When Richard Nicholas looked again, George Washington had gone.

On Martha's return to the White House that winter, she took with her a happy secret. The doctor in Williamsburg had told her that about the time the roses bloomed Frances and Jacky would have a new brother or sister.

So the quiet plantation life began anew, with a baby layette to make, as well as hours of sewing on Daniel's ruffled shirts. The weeks sped quickly. Martha spent long hours in her wing chair beside the window, little Frances at her knee, busy with her own sewing stint.

Glancing often at her precious gold and enamel watch, Mrs. Custis thought how it was ticking away the days she must wait for her baby—happy days. Little did she know that it was ticking away her last month of unclouded happiness. Ahead lay heartbreak.

On the evening of April first, Daniel took his daughter Frances on his knee for her usual story hour. She was begging for another tale of the haunted Stone House on York River. "Tell me more, Papa, please . . ."

Martha, playing with Jacky across the room, wanted to protest. Frances was not well. She had caught a cold; her cough was troublesome. She should be in bed, thought her practical mother, not listening to stories of ghosts that might give the frail, over-imaginative child a nightmare and break her sleep.

But Daniel had begun.

"When Alexander Spotswood was governor, the pirate Blackbeard used to waylay ships along the Virginia coast, robbing and murdering their crew," he told his little daughter. "Finally the pirate's grim head was brought home on the bowsprit of a Virginia ship, and a drinking-cup made of the skull that held his wicked brains. Of course, having been murdered, Blackbeard could not rest in his grave, Frances. So on moonlight nights his phantom sloop still spreads its ghostly sails on the York River; putting into Ware Creek, the bloody horror of a headless body wends its way to the Stone House to hide its stolen treasure . . ."

"His *headless* body, Papa . . ." Frances cried, her eyes big and shining, spots of color on her pale cheeks.

That was too much for Martha. "Come, Frances," she ordered briskly, "bedtime . . ."

Protests from daughter and father. "Why, Patsy—" There was hurt in Daniel's voice, "—the story isn't over!" But the young mother was firm. Taking her daughter's hand, she hurried Frances off to her trundle bed.

In the middle of the night, Martha was awakened by Frances, a small white figure, standing beside her.

"Let me in with you, Mama," Frances begged. "I'm afraid."

At the anguish in the child's voice, Martha threw back the quilt and took Frances into her arms. The little girl was trembling violently. She must speak to Daniel, forbid more ghost stories—but no—Martha felt Frances's hot cheek. The child was not trembling with fear, but shivering and burning with fever.

Alarmed, Martha sprang from her bed. She spoke quickly to Daniel, who bent over the child, touched her hot face, and was himself greatly concerned. They sent for a doctor. There were no telephones in those days, and a Negro on horseback had to ride many miles to fetch him. Martha tried every remedy she knew, but as the hours slipped by, Frances grew worse.

When the doctor finally reached the White House plantation, he found a desperately sick child, whose parents pleaded distractedly with him to save her. Sadly, he shook his head. There was little he could do but await the end.

By nightfall, the innocent soul of Frances Parke Custis had slipped away from the frail little body lying in her mother's four-poster bed.

Frances Dandridge, hastily summoned, tried to comfort her bereaved daughter. "You must think of yourself," she whispered, "and the new baby."

But Martha was not to be comforted. Her grief finally made her so ill that the doctor feared there would be no baby when the roses bloomed.

On the seventh of May, when Anna Maria Dandridge was married, Martha was still too weak to attend the wedding at Chestnut Grove. Feeling scarcely stronger than his wife, Daniel agreed to go, taking to Martha's favorite sister the handsomest gifts to be bought in Williamsburg.

Nancy Dandridge was making a match equal in wealth and prestige to Martha's own. At eighteen, she had chosen from a flock of beaux the twenty-three-year-old widower, Colonel Burwell Bassett, whose first wife, now dead, had been Anne Chamberlayne, the owner of the famous watch. His family was distinguished. In 1665, the original colonist, Captain William Bassett, had directed the erection of the fort at Jamestown.

The Bassett home, Eltham Hall, was only eleven miles from the White House. The good news that her sister would settle so close to her revived Martha's spirits, and soon after the

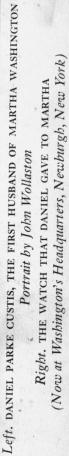

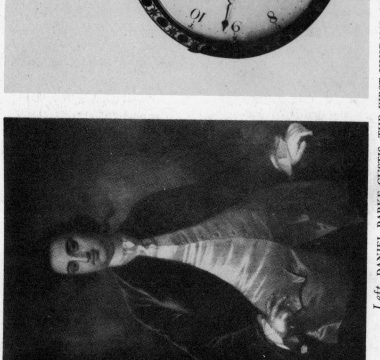

Left. DANIEL PARKE CUSTIS, THE FIRST HUSBAND OF MARTHA WASHINGTON
Portrait by John Wollaston

Right. THE WATCH THAT DANIEL GAVE TO MARTHA
(Now at Washington's Headquarters, Newburgh, New York)

wedding she began to mend.

She was up and about the house just in time to take to her bed again—this time for a happy event. As predicted, when the roses bloomed, she lay in her mahogany four-poster under the white fringed canopy with a tiny daughter in the crook of her arm.

The new baby must be called "Martha," Daniel insisted. And he wanted her to have as a middle name the proud "Parke" the three other Custis children had. Martha smiled and nodded. Already to herself she was calling the baby "Pat," just as she had always been "Pat" to her father.

As the summer of 1757 moved on, Martha regained her health and spirits, but Daniel's health began to worry her. Was he really ill? Never a strong man physically, he had suffered several alarming spells, each attack leaving him weaker and paler. He did not complain, but Martha, stealing worried glances at his white drawn face, noticed the rapid change in him.

"I'm better today," he always said, in answer to her gentle inquiry. But his voice was listless and she was not reassured.

The thing that Martha, sturdy with the vigor that she would enjoy to the last day of her life, could not understand was that Daniel was grieving himself sick. The loss of his namesake, Daniel, had affected him deeply. But no child had crept into his heart as had little Frances, and after her death he gave up the struggle to live.

Invalid that he was—and by July everyone knew it—Daniel Custis insisted on keeping up with his plantation duties. Martha agreed, hoping that such distractions would take her husband out of himself.

But as the weeks passed, he grew no better, and his anxious wife, hopeful of tempting his failing appetite, began to prepare the dishes he liked, chiefly from recipes handed down by her mother-in-law.

Fingering the pages of the old book, Martha wondered how the tempestuous Frances Parke Custis had found time to turn her hand to the preparation of so complicated a mixture as "Oyster Salad" or "Tipsy Charlotte."

Certainly Daniel's mother had never taken the time to learn to spell. These recipes, copied in the lady's own handwriting, bore fearful and wonderful words. "Orringes," "frykasie," "sparragus," and even a Cockney accent, "hartyshoakes"—words which even Martha knew were incorrectly spelled. But on the correct spelling she was as vague as the cooking-expert herself.

Mistress Custis spent the long days of July 1757 pouring over these secrets of the kitchen—spoon bread, Sally Lunn, beaten biscuit, flour wafers called *apoquiniminics*, and even a new recipe for the lowly corn pone. There were wonderful jellies, fancifully shaped and giddily tinted. Spinach produced seaweed green, Martha read; saffron provided bright yellow; the juice of beet roots baked in wine gave a brilliant red. A syrup of violets added to a whipped custard lent it flavor, fragrance and a purple color as well.

Mindful that floating island was Daniel's favorite sweet, Martha could hardly wait to prepare this delicacy, literally floating in a sea of violet custard. When, after a taste or two, he pushed it aside, her heart failed her.

"Daniel," she said, and smiled bravely to keep back the sob in her voice, "let me make some beef jelly. Or take some port after your meal. You are so—so pale . . ."

Her husband returned her smile. "I saw the doctor today, and he told me there was nothing to worry about."

Dear, kindly Daniel! What he had said to the doctor, on

hearing his own death knell, was "Don't tell Martha. She's so young and happy."

Eight years after Martha and Daniel Custis were married in St. Peter's Church, the frail affectionate man, who had found the death of his second child too great a shock to bear, took to his bed, never to leave it again.

When his friend, Governor Dinwiddie, honored him with an appointment of a seat in the Council, a position that was almost an inheritance in the Custis family, the new councillor was too ill to go to Williamsburg to assume his duties.

Through these trying days in the White House on the Pamunkey, Martha used every ounce of her charm and character and sweetness to strengthen and encourage her sick husband.

Coming into his room on a hot August morning in her floating muslin gown, her manner was bright and smiling, her eyes brave. Daniel, his face as white as the pillows beneath his head, watched her moving gracefully about the room, arranging roses in vases, as she urged him to try one of the delicacies on the breakfast tray.

The hot sunshine shone on the glittering river outside. The shade of the tall tulip poplars made flickering shadows on the lawn. And inside, the house remained quiet and hushed, because the master was ill.

Then into his father's room toddled sturdy young Jacky, resembling his great-grandfather, Daniel Parke, in looks, a fact which his mother was forced reluctantly to admit. Standing beside the sick man's bedside, Jacky told him good morning in a high childish voice—a good morning that was to be a good-bye.

Eight brief years of married life, and on that August day in 1757, Martha Dandridge Custis became a widow.

"He takes my life with him!" she sobbed, throwing herself on her knees beside the bed. Daniel was too young to die, only forty-six. Martha could not believe that the kind voice which had cheered and encouraged her for such a tragically short while was stilled.

For days after Daniel's funeral, she sat, broken-hearted and bewildered, in the summer house under the climbing roses and honeysuckle, beside the blue river.

Martha was only twenty-six. But she felt that for her, life was over.

Chapter five　　　　　　*Love at first Sight*

"You're a very wealthy woman, Patsy," Richard Carter Nicholas, Daniel's lawyer and friend, explained to sad-eyed Widow Custis. It was two weeks after the funeral, and Martha, in a black dress without a touch of white, had consented to talk over with Richard the provisions of her husband's will.

Daniel had divided his estate into three equal shares among his wife and children. Martha inherited a hundred thousand dollars, fifteen thousand acres of land near Williamsburg, valuable lots in the city, besides the two homes, the White House and Six Chimneys, and two hundred Negro slaves—a great fortune in Colonial days.

"You'd best engage a manager for the estate, even though he ask very high wages," counseled Richard Nicholas. "To run the White House plantation alone is too much for any woman."

Not too much for Martha Dandridge Custis, as she was quick to tell the surprised lawyer. Sweetly but firmly, the widow declined to employ a manager. She would personally take over the Custis investments, the property in and around Williamsburg, and the running of the White House.

"If I keep busy," continued this remarkable young woman, "I shall have less time for pining."

So for nine months each morning she went to Daniel's desk to conduct her business affairs.

73

She was there on a morning in May, 1758—rather a pathetic little figure in black bombazine, her hair brushed back severely under a plain mob cap, as she figured the amount of tobacco sold that month from her plantation.

Martha's usually rosy cheeks were pale, her eyes heavy. She had been at her desk since seven o'clock, yet try as she would, she could not compute the tobacco figures to her satisfaction. Over and over she did the "reductions ascending" and the "reductions descending," wishing the while that she had paid more attention to the teaching of Thomas Leonard. But the results remained the same. With Daniel gone less than a year, the White House, for the first time, was showing a loss.

What could be wrong? It had been a good tobacco year on other plantations, bumper crops everywhere. She had believed herself capable of carrying on things as Daniel had left them. Wherein had she failed?

Martha's lips tightened. Macon was at the bottom of this trouble, she knew. Since Daniel's death, the once-industrious overseer had slackened his pace. Quick to sense the lack of authority, the Negroes spent their time idling in the tobacco fields. If the situation continued, a manager would have to be employed, as Richard Nicholas had advised. And this would be an admission of her failure.

With a discouraged sigh, Martha flung down her goose-quill pen, rose, and went to the window. The familiar view —the placid river, the wooded bank on the opposite shore— dissolved in a mist of tears.

She could hear the shrill voice of three-year-old Jacky calling to his puppy out beyond the tulip trees. And there was good, brown-faced Molly carrying baby Patty, bundled in a pink blanket, into the summerhouse. These blessings she had, and more. Then why was she worrying herself sick over losing a few hundred pounds on her tobacco crop? Why was she so restless and unhappy?

It had all started on the Sunday before, when Martha's neighbors, Colonel Richard Chamberlayne and his wife, stopped to greet her as she left the services at Saint Peter's.

"What do you do with yourself these days, Patsy?" asked Mistress Chamberlayne, linking her arm through Martha's soberly-draped sleeve.

Before Martha could reply, the Colonel, a bluff hearty man in a claret velvet coat, spoke for her.

"She works like a man over estate and plantation matters. That's no life for a charming young woman, Patsy. You need some fun and diversion."

"Yes, dear, you do," agreed his wife. "Why don't you come over to Poplar Grove and spend a few days with us? It will be good for you."

Martha remembered the solemn dignity with which she had declined the Chamberlayne's invitation. Her excuse, "The children, I can't leave them. Baby Pat isn't very strong. Jacky needs disciplining."

But today, the more she thought of it, the less shocking seemed the notion of joining these friends for a quiet visit. She was fond of Richard Chamberlayne and his wife. Richard's mother had been Wilhelmina Byrd, sister to Evelyn, and Daniel's first cousin. If she left home for a while, she might see her plantation problems in a clearer perspective.

So it happened that a note was sent to Poplar Grove by Martha's faithful slave, Cully, and within the hour the mistress of the White House herself was stepping into the Custis chaise.

Already the young widow felt a little better for having

made the decision to visit her neighbors. Her sense of well-being had extended to the donning of a lace collar on her black mourning dress—not very festive, but the first bit of white Martha had worn since Daniel's death. The May sunshine was sparkling. Her cheeks were becomingly pink by the time she reached Poplar Grove, a two-story brick house on the south bank of the Pamunkey, still standing today.

Richard Chamberlayne and his wife greeted their pretty neighbor warmly. And seated in their parlor, Martha, who was talkative by nature, found herself chatting as she had not done for many months.

After a while the Colonel excused himself to go down to his wharf. The Chamberlayne house, situated at a public river crossing on the highway between northern Virginia and Williamsburg, afforded a good view of the Williams's ferryboat, crawling to and fro across the Pamunkey. Awaiting the dinner hour, Martha and Mrs. Chamberlayne sat at the parlor windows, watching the awkward old craft as it meandered over to the northern shore. Martha had seen this boat many times in her twenty-seven years. How then was she to know that on its return journey the ferry was to bring to her side the man destined to be the most important influence in her life?

Back the boat came, swaying from side to side on the smooth waters. As it touched the New Kent shore, Martha saw two passengers on board—Colonial soldiers, she could tell by their blue uniforms. One of the soldiers was very tall. Even in the distance, he towered over his companion, who seemed to have charge of the horses.

Martha rose from her chair and stood at the parlor window to get a better view. The tall traveler stepped quickly onto the ferry landing, and after greeting Colonel Chamberlayne, walked with him across the lawn to the house. As they came nearer, the heart of Mistress Custis began to pound with an odd feeling of excitement. Soon the two men were in the room. Her host was introducing the officer in the blue coat with scarlet facing of the Virginia troops. In his big hand he held a cocked hat.

"Colonel Washington . . . Mistress Daniel Custis."

The stately young soldier bent rather stiffly over Martha's small, plump hand. The lady was a stranger to him, that was apparent. But Martha, who had not seen his face in two years, recognized the guest at once. Who could forget that commanding presence? That handsome head, poised on broad shoulders? That face with the rather large nose, ruddy skin, firm lips and chin? It was George Washington, now commander of all the Virginia forces.

And so they met at last; the brown-haired young man, whose six feet of superlative strength made Martha feel small and helpless, and the hazel-eyed widow who was strangely elated as she had not been in months. They smiled, and in their eyes was mutual admiration. Then, blushing deeply, Martha turned to listen to her host's explanation of Colonel Washington's unexpected visit.

Richard Chamberlayne had recognized the traveler as soon as he stepped from the ferry, and offered him the hospitality of Poplar Grove. But George Washington had no time for visiting. He was hurrying to Williamsburg to see the Governor, who awaited his report on affairs in the western wilderness.

"The Colonel was about to ride on, Patsy, when I thought of an inducement." Richard smiled at his guest. "I promised him an introduction to the prettiest and wealthiest young widow in all Virginia."

George Washington's blue eyes, the stern eyes of a military man, crinkled with mirth. Martha had the grace to hide hers behind her fan as she bowed low to acknowledge the compliment.

"I have surrendered, Madam, but only conditionally," the Colonel said in his slow, deliberate voice. "I agreed to remain and dine—only dine—and then I must go on to Williamsburg. Bishop, my servant, will stable our horses, with the order to have them ready early this afternoon. By borrowing of the night, I can be in Williamsburg early tomorrow morning."

Long hours they lingered at the table, laden with the choicest dishes from the Chamberlayne cookhouse: fried chicken and beaten biscuit, jellies and custards. The best of everything for an honored guest, the twenty-six-year-old commander of the Virginia forces.

Later in the drawing-room, over Madeira and sweet biscuits, Richard Chamberlayne asked Colonel Washington about the ill-starred Braddock expedition against the French. "Your hairbreadth escapes, Colonel . . . tell us about them!" Richard begged.

Ever obliging, yet modest withal, Washington told how during the battle of Monongahela, as the surprise attack on the British by the Indian allies of the French was called, he had had two horses shot from under him. He had received four bullets through his coat.

Behind Edward Braddock, the British General, were forty years' experience on the battlefields of Europe, yet he knew nothing of fighting in the wilderness. The General had forced his twelve hundred redcoats to march through the forest in close formation, although George Washington had repeatedly warned him of a surprise attack by the Indians.

On July 9, 1755, the British and Virginia troops had forded

the Monongahela and were within seven miles of Fort Duquesne, the French fort they were to attack, when a wild
war whoop split the air. Bullets whizzed from every direction,
as the hidden enemy shot down the long line of redcoats
from behind logs and trees and bushes.

Shouting at the Britishers to break ranks, George Washington showed them how to screen themselves behind rocks and
trees, as the Indians did. But General Braddock flogged them
back into line with the flat of his sword, thus making them
an easy mark for the enemy's bullets.

General Braddock, himself a perfect target in his red coat,
had four horses shot from under him. From his fifth he fell
mortally wounded. His servant carried him back to a wagon.

"That left me in charge of a losing fight," said George
Washington, and his eyes sought those of the Widow Custis,
who was listening eagerly to every word of his story.

Mounted on his third horse, the young Virginia Colonel
had tried to rally his men. More than half of them lay dying,
their brave red coats stretched like pools of blood on the
forest floor. The rest were running around like animals
trapped in a fire.

Martha's eyes were soft with sympathy as the Colonel told
of their frightful retreat from the wilderness. The wounded
Braddock was carried in a baggage wagon that jolted his life
away. But before he died, he tried to make up for his neglect
of the "beardless youngster's" advice. He gave George Washington his horse, as well as his servant, Thomas Bishop, an
English soldier who had accompanied the General to America.

Now for hours the same Thomas Bishop had been waiting
impatiently before the door of Poplar Grove. There was a
puzzled expression in his eyes as he held the bridle of the
big chestnut horse from which General Braddock had fallen

in the battle of Monongahela.

"It's strange," thought Bishop. "The Colonel ordered me to have the horses ready after dinner. He said his mission in Williamsburg was urgent. What can be the trouble?"

The "trouble" was the charming young widow seated on the couch in the Chamberlayne parlor beside George Washington. The hour he had set for his departure had long since come and gone. Darkness was falling over the plantation.

"No guest of mine leaves Poplar Grove after sunset," Colonel Chamberlayne announced. Washington laughed, and sent an order to Bishop to stable the horses for the night.

Delighted with the romantic turn of affairs, Chamberlayne excused himself in order to attend to pressing business. His wife murmured something about picking roses. Would the guests entertain one another? When the host and hostess left the room, smiling slyly, their departure was scarcely noticed by the engrossed pair on the sofa.

Now there was no more talk of war. It was the lovely Mistress Custis about whom George Washington wished to hear.

Flattered by the tall soldier's interest, Martha described Chestnut Grove and her family. She spoke of Daniel—and tears came to her eyes—and of her two children.

"But enough about me, Colonel," she said demurely, waving her fan to cool her hot cheeks. "Let's talk about you. I know nothing, really—except that you are Virginia's greatest hero."

What a delightful speech!

It was the Colonel's turn to flush and to protest that he was not a hero. But he was enchanted with the little widow, and only too pleased to sit beside her and tell her of his life.

His home was north, in Fairfax County, Virginia, he said;

his plantation, called Mount Vernon, was on the banks of the Potomac. But he had been born at Wakefield in Westmoreland County. At the age of sixteen, he had gone to Fairfax County to live with his half-brother, Lawrence, who had called his home Mount Vernon, after Edward Vernon of the British Navy, under whom he had fought at Carthagena in the West Indies.

"My Uncle William Dandridge fought at Carthagena," Martha interrupted eagerly. "He commanded the *Wolfe*, the *South Sea*, and the *Ludlow Castle*."

The Colonel nodded with pleasure. He had heard of Captain William Dandridge—a brave man, a fine officer.

Lawrence Washington had been a good brother to him, George said. And when Lawrence became ill, he knew the first real sorrow of his life.

The Colonel touched the pock marks which dotted his handsome face. "I was trying to get my brother cured when I caught smallpox."

It seemed that Lawrence had developed a weakness of the lungs, requiring life in a milder climate. His wife, Anna, with a baby less than a year old, could not take her husband to Barbadoes, where it was hoped Lawrence would recover his health. George, a youth of nineteen, had offered to accompany his invalid brother. And in Barbadoes he had caught smallpox, and only recovered in time to bring Lawrence home to die at Mount Vernon, six years ago.

Lawrence had left a life-interest in the plantation to his wife, and after that, to their daughter. Sarah outlived her father only a few weeks. Lawrence's widow remarried, and with her new husband, George Lee, went to live in Westmoreland County. Colonel Washington had purchased her life-interest in Mount Vernon, and thus when barely twenty-one, had come into possession of the plantation of twenty-five hundred acres along the Potomac. He had lived there ever since, except when away fighting.

"Which has been most of the time," he said ruefully. "I'd like to settle down and make Mount Vernon the finest plantation in the colonies."

Martha looked at George Washington with renewed interest. She had thought of him as a soldier; now she saw him as a Virginia planter. His fields grew tobacco, just as the White House did.

The Colonel had divided his land into five farms. Over each was an overseer, but he personally supervised every operation. "You must see to things yourself to make a plantation pay," he declared.

"To make a plantation pay . . ." echoed Martha forlornly. And soon she was telling her new friend about one that did *not* pay—perhaps because he was so big and understanding; perhaps because it was easier to tell her troubles to a comparative stranger.

"What is the matter with me?" Martha asked, such a pretty picture of helplessness that the Colonel longed to embrace and comfort her. "I never have trouble with house slaves. But I cannot manage my field laborers."

"They're tough men, not like house servants," he told her. "No woman could handle them. A man should be in charge."

Martha's big hazel eyes, lifted to his gray-blue ones, thanked him. He had restored her self-respect. It was not that she was incompetent to manage the White House plantation; it was simply that she was a *woman*. And it was not a woman's business.

The sun was high in the sky the next morning before George Washington took his departure. And when he rode off down the lane of poplars, and turned in the direction of Williamsburg, his mind was not on the important report he would make to the Governor. It was back at Poplar Grove with the Widow Custis. Never before had he seen a young woman so dignified and well-poised, yet so adorably small and feminine. An ideal hostess for Mount Vernon. *Mistress Martha Custis. . . . Mistress Martha Washington.*

Home at the White House, Martha Custis stared at her face in the mirror and then looked away quickly, a little ashamed of the radiant vision. Twenty-four hours away—and she had changed from a sober, dull little creature into a starry-eyed, blithe young woman, who, to her shocked amazement, found it almost impossible to keep from skipping a step or two as she moved about the house.

The reason for this strange behavior was a secret in her heart. Although he had not said so definitely, Martha thought that on his return from Williamsburg, Colonel Washington might call at the White House. And the look in his eyes had told her that when he came, it would not be just the friendly visit of one who wished to be of assistance to a helpless young widow. He might have a question to put to her . . . a very important question.

Since it involved her own future, as well as that of her children, Martha knew she must weigh her heart and mind before she gave her answer.

Locking herself in her room, she threw herself down on the chintz-flounced tester bed, and buried her hot face in the pillows.

George Washington.

What did she know of this man, she asked herself? The name of the colonel of the Virginia troops was on everyone's lips. A favorite with the ladies, people wondered why he had not married. Gossip had it that in his early youth, when poor and shy, he had been in love with several girls who turned him down and married other suitors.

"What if he has loved other girls?" she found herself asking. How could one expect a man so gallant and handsome to reach the age of twenty-six without having been in love? The answer was that neither could Martha Custis give George Washington her first love. *She* had loved Daniel, loved him dearly, and mourned his memory for nine long months.

Daniel was her first, her girlhood sweetheart. But in Colonial times, a widow was expected to remarry. Here she was, a widow of only twenty-seven, with two small children to bring up, a plantation badly in need of oversight, and a large fortune to manage. How pleasant it would be to place all her affairs in the capable hands of George Washington; to return to her needle-point and to her musical selections on the spinet!

Colonel Washington, experienced in running a tobacco plantation, would put the White House back on its feet. He would be the "manager" that Richard Nicholas had urged her to hire. If she remarried, could she hope to do better than George Washington? Such a man—handsome, a noted soldier, and experienced planter—would not come her way twice.

Martha's heart had told her what her answer would be to that important question. And she set about figuring the date of his return. One day to Williamsburg. One day to see the Governor. Then business over as quickly as possible—her heart beat faster—and one day back to the Pamunkey.

On the fourth day Martha sent her slave Cully to a stream that she knew Colonel Washington must cross, with instructions to row him across in the Custis boat. "Fetch a certain gentleman that is expected" was Martha's modest way of referring to her famous guest.

In her room, Mistress Custis arrayed herself for George Washington's arrival. For the first time since Daniel's death she selected from her clothes-press a frock other than her drab mourning gown. It was a lavender satin, that matched the Custis amethysts gleaming at her throat and on her arms, and decorated with fine cream lace.

The sun was setting over the pines when Martha, in her lavender gown, heard the beat of hoofs down the lane of lindens that led to the house on the river bank. With an answering beat of her heart, she hurried to the door and flung it open.

Before the white-columned porch, George Washington reined in his big chestnut horse, his servant, Bishop, behind him. Leaping from the animal's back, he paused a moment to view the pretty picture framed in the doorway. Then with the light tread acquired by long service on the frontier, he strode up the steps and caught the lady's hand in his own.

"Your Negro said he had been sent to the river to row me across. I asked if you were at home. He replied 'Yes, sah, and I reckon you'se the man what's 'spected.' " George Washington looked deep into Martha's eyes, as he asked, "How did you know I was coming?"

She smiled at his puzzlement. "Do I have to explain?"

He laughed happily. Then he took her in his arms.

In spite of the fact that early remarriage was common in Virginia, the widow of nine months found herself shy when she came to announce so hasty an engagement to her proper mother.

"Mama, the truth is my plantation is in a bad shape and I need a manager to look after it," she told the surprised Frances. But there was a glow in Martha's hazel eyes, a smile on her lips. She well knew that it was not a "manager" she wanted in George Washington, but a husband.

The engagement, thus far, was going very well indeed. No young mother could have found greater joy than was Martha's when, at first meeting, her fiancé and her two children became fast friends. Before the day was over, Patty was begging to be picked up by the majestic stranger and carried about on his broad shoulders. Jacky, pouting at first, was soon taking the commander of all the Virginia forces to the nursery to show him his new hobby horse.

So the June days slipped by until Colonel Washington's fortnight furlough was over. The French and Indian War was still going on. He must return to the upper Ohio Valley and lead another assault against the French Fort Duquesne. At the front door of the White House, where only two short weeks before their troth had been plighted, Martha told George good-bye with tears in her eyes, and he rode away, accompanied by the faithful Bishop.

Left alone, Martha Custis set about preparing for her wedding. There were new clothes to be bought, plans to be made for the ceremony. But whatever she did, the thought of George was with Martha always. When would she hear from him?

Mails in Colonial times were irregular, even over the well-traveled coastal highways. And to and from the frontier, as anything beyond the Shenandoah Valley was called in Virginia, they were even more uncertain.

It was a joyful day for Martha then, when she finally received a letter from George, dated July twentieth, and written near Fort Cumberland.

She was in her garden when Cully handed it to her. Her heart was beating so, she could hardly break the seal and untie the string. Eagerly her eyes scanned the paper, sprinkled with capitals, after the fashion of the time:

"We have just begun our march for the Ohio. A Courier is starting for Williamsburg, and I embrace the Opportunity to send a few words to one whose life is now Inseparable from mine. Since that happy hour when we made our Pledges to each other, my thoughts have been continually going to you as to another Self. That an All-Powerful Providence may keep us both in safety is the prayer of your ever faithful and

Affectionate Friend,

G. WASHINGTON."

For a moment Martha could hardly believe her eyes. Was this brief, formal note a letter from a man to the woman whom he expected to marry? With the wholehearted fervor of an affectionate nature, she had expected so much more.

Then her common sense reasserted itself. What if George Washington's first letter was cold? Self-possession was characteristic of the man whom she had promised to marry—that much she knew. What if his affection for her was not ardent in the sense that Daniel Custis's had been?

Stuffing the coldly polite little note into her pocket, Martha lifted her head and smiled. She was not afraid.

When in the last week of December, Colonel Washington returned from the frontier after the successful capture of Fort Duquesne, now renamed Fort Pitt in honor of William Pitt, the English statesman, Martha said she was ready to marry him. They set the day for January the sixth.

Whom should they ask to the wedding?

There was George's family, of course: his widowed mother, who lived at his father's old farm on the Rappahannock, opposite Fredericksburg; his younger brothers, Samuel, John Augustine, and Charles; his only sister, Betty, who had married Colonel Fielding Lewis, a Burgess and prominent merchant of Fredericksburg.

Next to his brothers and sister, the guests George wished most to have at his wedding were the Fairfax family, whose estate, Belvoir, was next to Mount Vernon. He said that his friendship with the Fairfaxes, when he had first gone to live with his brother Lawrence, had meant a great deal to him. They were people of great wealth and culture; they had opened up to the shy and awkward lad, used to the simple life of his mother's farm, a new world.

There was the old Lord Fairfax, the head of the family, who spent most of the time at Greenway Court, his home in the Shenandoah Valley. There was his cousin, George William Fairfax, and his wife Sally, who lived at Belvoir; George William's younger half-brother, Bryan; his sisters, Sarah and Hannah.

"You'll see a great deal of the Fairfaxes when we go to Mount Vernon, Patsy," George promised Martha, "but I want you to meet them now."

Martha hoped that the George William Fairfaxes would come to the wedding, and told George so. She had heard Anna Nicholas speak of her beautiful elder sister, Sally Fairfax. They were daughters of Colonel Wilson Cary of Ceeleys, a large estate at Hampton.

Now for the first time in many years, Colonel Washington was able to make plans ahead. On his return in December, he had brought Martha good news—

He was leaving the army.

The capture of Fort Duquesne had put an end to the frontier troubles with the French. He could retire to civil life, as he had long wished to do. During his absence at the frontier, Colonel Washington had been elected to represent the County of Frederick in the House of Burgesses. And Martha heard, with satisfaction, that instead of a soldier's bride, she would be the wife of a Burgess of the state she loved.

On January 6, 1759, a year and a half after Daniel's death, Martha Dandridge Custis was married to George Washington.

The wedding took place "at candlelight," not in St. Peter's, where Martha had married her first husband, but in the drawing-room of the White House. She would have preferred a church wedding, but it was winter, and Virginia churches were unheated because of the fear of fire.

Although for many days the house had been astir with preparations, the bride herself bustled around to the last minute, directing the laying of damask and silver on the dining-room table, arranging flowers, and admonishing Jacky to be on his good behavior. Her cheeks were pink as Oney, her maid, laced her into her stays before slipping her white silk wedding dress over her powdered hair.

"Tighter, Oney!" ordered Martha, holding to the bedpost while the maid pulled the laces of her corset. She was growing plump; her mirror told her that. And today she must look her best for George.

Jacky, a gay romp of four, thought her pretty, and told her so, when he came in to kiss Martha just before the ceremony. He also admired the tall figure of Colonel Washington, standing beside his mother while the Reverend David Mossum, who had married Martha to Daniel, pronounced them man and wife.

Having laid aside his uniform when he resigned his commission, the bridegroom was married in citizen's dress of blue cloth and waistcoat of white satin. On his hands were the white gloves still treasured in the Masonic Museum at Alexandria, Virginia, and they are huge. His shoe and knee buckles were of gold. His brown hair was powdered. By his side hung a dress sword.

With what an air George Washington could carry a sword! Not even Governor Francis Fauquier, standing with the members of the Assembly, in his scarlet and gold uniform, could outshine the bridegroom.

In her dress for her second wedding, Martha Custis looked almost as young as the girl who had made her debut at the Williamsburg Court thirteen years earlier. Her quilted petticoat was of embroidered white satin; over it she wore a white silk dress, threaded with silver. From beneath her skirt peeped white satin slippers with bright buckles. And twined in her powdered hair, as a necklace and earrings, were the Custis pearls.

Martha was attended by three bridesmaids in blue, who assisted her after the ceremony in receiving the guests—not the least among them being the old soldier, Thomas Bishop, in his British red uniform.

The first to kiss the bride were her own children, Jacky and baby Patty, carried up in her nurse's arms. Then her family—her mother, Nancy Bassett and her husband, gay William and staid Bartholomew, and to complete the family group, ten-year-old Elizabeth, and Mary, not yet three.

George Washington's family were there, too. The John Augustine Washingtons came from Westmoreland; George's brother, Charles, from Jefferson County; and the Fielding Lewises from Fredericksburg. But not the bridegroom's independent old mother. Mary Ball Washington thought the journey too long for one of her age. Instead she sent her son a message to bring his wife to call on *her*.

Representing the Fairfax family were George William Fairfax and his wife, Sally, a poised and beautiful woman of twenty-nine.

Gowned in satin of a deep blue that matched her eyes, and wearing the Fairfax sapphires, the tall and slender Mrs. Fairfax came up with her husband to wish happiness to the little bride and her big bridegroom. "Yes, she's as lovely as they say . . ." Martha thought, and turned to greet another guest.

There were so many of them thronging the drawing-room of the house on the Pamunkey. Everyone from the Governor down had come to witness the marriage of Virginia's military hero to the rich widow of Daniel Parke Custis.

Married couples in those days did not dash away after a reception of a few hours. Colonial weddings lasted for days, so that all their friends could come, feast on banquets of rich food, and kiss the bride.

The trousseau a girl needed for such a lengthy wedding was elaborate. After a night in the flower-bedecked bridal chamber, the bride appeared before her guests wearing what was known as her "second-day dress"—a costume as important as her wedding gown. It is recorded that Martha's "second-day dress" was adorable: a rustling, flowered thing opening on a lace-ruffled white petticoat.

She was wearing this gown the next day when, descending the stairs, she saw Sally Fairfax saying good-bye to George. Her husband, the dull, stolid George William, was with her, as well as Richard Carter Nicholas and his wife, Anna, Sally's sister.

Slim and regal in her sable-trimmed bonnet and mantle of burgundy velvet, Mistress Fairfax swept up to the bride in flower-strewn silk. "Good-bye, Patsy," she said, "we'll see you at Mount Vernon." As their hands touched, Martha was aware of the perfume that hovered around the exquisite Sally.

Somehow the wedding festivities seemed gayer to the little bride with Mistress Fairfax gone.

It was a week before Martha and George Washington escaped from their friends, and slipped off alone on what we would call a honeymoon. On a clear, cold morning in January, Martha, wearing a traveling costume of maroon velvet and fur, with a bonnet to match, joined her husband, already booted and spurred, on the porch of the White House. The Washingtons were going to Williamsburg. They would stay in the bride's house, Six Chimneys, while George, as Burgess, attended the sessions of the Virginia Assembly.

Gallantly the Colonel handed Martha into the Custis coach. Then he took the reins of his horse from Thomas Bishop. Mounting, he waited beside the carriage that held his smiling lady.

There was a gay laugh from inside the coach. A flutter of the bride's lace handkerchief to her children and the Burwell Bassetts, standing on the porch to bid them good-bye. Then George Washington and his wife, Martha, started off to Williamsburg together.

Chapter Six   Life at Mount Vernon

IN THE CAPITOL AT WILLIAMSBURG, MISTRESS MARTHA WASH-
ington, wife of the new Burgess from Frederick County, was
seated as the State's honored guest. At a special meeting, her
husband was to receive the colony's formal thanks for his
military services in the French and Indian War.

A fitting climax, Martha thought, to the three-months'
legislative session, which had been the happiest three months
of her life—her honeymoon. Radiant in royal blue silk, with
a becoming plumed bonnet, she could do little to control the
rush of color to her round cheeks at the sight of George
Washington's handsome face. She was in love, wholly and
romantically in love, as she had never been with the staid,
middle-aged Daniel Parke Custis.

As the House of Burgesses was called to order, Mrs. Washington's heart swelled with pride. Its leader, John Robinson,
rose before the high-backed speaker's chair, still standing in
the restored chamber. "On behalf of the members," he said,
"I wish to thank Colonel Washington for his Brave and Steady
Behavior from the first Encroachments and the Hostilities of
the French and their Indians, to his Resignation, after the
happy Reduction of Fort Duquesne . . ."

There was a round of applause. Then came George Washington's turn to reply. He stood, tall and a little stiff, determination in every line of his face. What was the matter?

Tensely Martha waited, her eyes fixed on her husband, her hands folded in her silken lap.

George cleared his throat twice. He lifted his head as though to speak. But no words came. Flushing, he began to stammer.

As the crowd listened, politely embarrassed, Martha's nervousness turned to panic. No one was prepared for the sight of Virginia's military hero in confusion, red-faced and struggling to find words to express himself.

Tears rose in his wife's eyes, a lump in her throat. She longed to fly to the side of the embarrassed, faltering statesman. But so reckless a move was not necessary. Speaker Robinson, with great tact, came to his rescue.

"Sit down, Mr. Washington," he said kindly. "Your modesty is equal to your valor; and that surpasses the power of any language I possess."

There was further applause, and George resumed his seat. Martha managed a smile, but her heart was heavy, even later when friends crowded around to congratulate her on her splendid husband. The bride was at such a stage of hero-worship that she could not endure the thought of George in other than a successful role. As an orator, he was far from that.

"The silent member from Frederick" the other Burgesses called him, as the months passed and George Washington made no speeches. With his usual modesty in matters where he was not well informed, the former Colonel had taken his seat in the Virginia Assembly. But he listened carefully. And soon his good judgment was recognized in committee, especially in the drafting of legislative papers.

In April, after three months, the member from Frederick received his first appointment—to draft a law forbidding stray hogs to run at large in Winchester!

Martha rejoiced. Over cups of green China tea in her draw-ing-room at Six Chimneys, she proudly told her friends about "the honor that had come to George." What if they smiled at the little bride's unabashed enthusiasm? Hogs were im-portant members of society in those days before garbage col-lection; the penalty for stealing one was death.

When the Assembly adjourned in April, the Washingtons returned to the White House to wait until the bottomless clay roads of Virginia settled sufficiently to go north to Mount Vernon. And George began spending numberless hours at Daniel's desk, reorganizing Martha's neglected plan-tation. By Colonial law, as her husband he came into posses-sion of her third of Daniel's estate, one hundred thousand dollars. He was also made guardian of her children's remain-ing two-thirds.

Already George Washington was looking after the young Custises as conscientiously as if they were his own. It greatly pleased their mother that in writing and speaking of Jack and Patty, whom George called "Patcy," he referred to them as "the children"; never "your children"; and only when legal formality required, as "my stepchildren."

White House was not the only plantation to suffer from the absence of its owner. Mount Vernon had grown shabby during the years of the Colonel's military career. Now that it was to have a new mistress, alterations were being made, with the help of George's friend and neighbor, George Wil-liam Fairfax. Workmen were repapering the bedrooms under the supervision of Mistress Fairfax, who chose a different color for each—blue, rose, lavender and green—and recovering the chairs and bed-valances to match. The problem of where to place the garret stairs was solved only after repeated letters between George and Colonel Fairfax.

May came with a burst of blossoms, and barges arrived at the White House landing to load Martha's furniture and heavy baggage for the trip out of the York River and up the Potomac. When everything was off, the Washingtons, Jack and Patty, servants and light luggage, set out in the coach on the road to Fredericksburg. They were to stop there on the way north so George's bride could meet his mother, as well as renew her acquaintance, made at the wedding, with the Fielding Lewises.

Proud indeed was George when the carriage drew up before Millbank, the mansion which wealthy Colonel Lewis was building for his young wife on a tract of eight hundred acres in the center of town. Now known as Kenmore, the two-story brick house still stands in Fredericksburg, set as when Martha first saw it, among trees in a walled yard.

Millbank was unfinished when the Washingtons arrived, but the Lewises had made it habitable and were quick to offer brother George and his new family a hearty welcome. Martha felt a sudden rush of affection for her tall, handsome sister-in-law, "Sister Lewis," as George called her. She liked Betty's good-looking, although cross-eyed, husband.

"George, you and Betty are as alike as two peas in a pod!" she exclaimed, comparing the high foreheads and prominent noses.

"Well, I'm fond of my brother and don't mind," cried the exuberant Mrs. Lewis. "Watch, I'll do a George Washington for you!"

Throwing a cape around her broad shoulders, she donned her famous brother's tri-cornered hat, and struck a pose in profile. "If I appeared mounted on George's horse before his troops, wouldn't they present arms?" she asked.

Everyone laughed. The resemblance was so marked that Martha longed for a portrait of Betty in that cocked hat atop her powdered curls.

By the time Martha had been at Millbank an hour, she felt she had known the Fielding Lewises for years. They dined well and talked late in the parlor whose framed mantel decoration, picturing Aesop's fable of the fox and the crow, had been suggested by Brother George, when Betty had written him that their "invention had given out." He had even sent Italians, prisoners of war, to build it.

Next morning, Mr. and Mrs. Washington drove across the Rappahannock to call on George's mother. As they stopped before her humble farmhouse, Mary Ball Washington, a gaunt figure in homespun and calico sun-bonnet, stood in the doorway. In her early fifties, she looked much older.

"Welcome, son," she said, standing as straight as her soldier offspring. There was about mother and son the same dignity that often gave George's wife a sense of awe.

"Welcome," she said, but she did not call Martha "daughter."

She took them into her plain, four-roomed home, where she spent her days knitting, sewing, weaving, and distilling herbs for the sick. She placed George's rich wife in the best chair by the hearth and looked at her approvingly. The girl probably had faults—she couldn't be as sweet and sincere and kindly as she looked—but any flaws in her were overlooked in the light of Martha's one great deed. She had accomplished what George's mother had failed to do. *She had made her son leave the army.*

As her bony fingers clicked her knitting needles, Mrs. Washington told her daughter-in-law how she had spent her life in a vain effort to prevent George from fighting. There was the time when Lawrence and Augustine, his half-brothers, plotted to put her eldest son in the British Navy. Well, she had put a stop to *that!* And the time she had gone to Mount Vernon to plead with George not to endanger his life by accompanying General Braddock to the frontier.

"This fighting and killing, how I hate it!" Mary Washington sighed deeply.

But that was all in the past. George was safe. He had married the rich Widow Custis; he would settle down at Mount Vernon, to be what his mother had always wished, a dignified country gentleman.

As they prepared to leave, George renewed an old argument. Wasn't his mother unhappy living alone? Why wouldn't she move into Fredericksburg? He would buy her a house near Betty, where her daughter could care for her.

Mary Washington bristled. "I don't need to be taken care of. My wants are few. I can care for myself."

So they rode away and left her—a self-denying, diligent and frugal woman, who took pride in living simply and independently.

The coach seemed rolling faster, now that they were actually off for Mount Vernon.

"Oh, Patsy, I hope you'll like it!" George kept saying, as they neared the end of their journey.

Across Belmont Bay on Colchester Ferry they went, down Reagen's hill, through another valley with three streams to ford, up the slope to the west of Colonel Fairfax's lands. And, as the road dropped again, with the Potomac in sight at the right, before them appeared a white house, three miles to the east.

"There's Mount Vernon!" cried George, his voice choked.

Martha's eagerness matched her husband's. Leaning from

the coach, she saw for the first time the house that was to be her home for forty years.

The people of the estate had lined the driveway to greet her. Their hearts were warmed when the new mistress waved her hand at them and smiled.

"It's all that you said it to be—and more!" whispered Martha to her husband, as the carriage stopped before the house on the river bank.

The Mount Vernon Martha saw then was a small building compared with the elegant white frame mansion, flanked by outbuildings, one sees at Mount Vernon today. There were no colonnades on the ends; no piazza on the river front. If you detach the banquet hall on the north and the library wing on the south, a two-story house remains with but four rooms on each floor. That was the original house. Not a large home for a Colonial gentleman, but to the excited new mistress, quite perfect.

As trunks and bandboxes were unloaded, Mrs. Washington stood looking at it, Patty half-asleep in her arms. Jacky, somewhat abashed by so many strange faces, clung to her skirt.

Her home! Her new home. . . .

"Sally!" Martha turned at George's glad shout. Standing in the entrance hall, under the iron lantern that had been given Lawrence Washington by Admiral Vernon, was Mistress Fairfax in a gown of cream satin.

She came to greet them, her hands outstretched in welcome, a smile on her red lips. Her black hair was parted on the side, above a high forehead. The proud way she held her head made her a queen.

"What a tiny waist she has!" thought the squarely-built little bride as the two women met.

And there, hovering in the background, was George William Fairfax, dull and heavy, but one of the most important men in Virginia, as heir to the Fairfax title and agent of Lord Fairfax's Northern Neck property.

Looking at Mistress Fairfax, cool and exquisite in gleaming satin, Martha grew conscious of her dusty garments. She longed to escape to her room, to bathe and change her dress. But Colonel Fairfax held her with tiresome details about the repairs at Mount Vernon . . . of course, she must step out and see the view of the river.

Walking across the lawn shaded by stately trees, beside the tall, slender Sally, Martha was acutely aware of the difference between them. Mistress Fairfax was a gay, poised woman of the world, mentally keen, vivacious and fascinating. Beside this sparkling creature, Martha felt plump and dull. Tears came to her eyes. Sally Fairfax had spoiled her homecoming by just being present. Why hadn't she stayed at home?

But when Martha reached the high bluff on which the lawn ended, and saw below the shining river, all troublesome thoughts were forgotten. Before the house swept the Potomac in a twelve-mile stretch of water, and opposite lay the low gray shore of Maryland. To the right, the river curved out of sight behind the high green point on which stood Belvoir, the Fairfax home, separated from Mount Vernon only by Dogue Creek.

It was an hour after her arrival before Martha reached the room Sally had ready for her. In this dainty bower, with its white ruffled curtains, dark mahogany furniture and shining brass andirons, the tired bride longed to rest. But there was no time for it. No sooner had she washed off the dust of travel, changed into a silk gown and hurried to the nursery to pick up the children, than guests began to arrive for the "infare"—the faring of the bride into the bridegroom's home.

JOHN PARKE CUSTIS (JACK)

MARTHA PARKE CUSTIS (PATTY)

George Washington's marriage to the richest woman in the state had caused great excitement in the neighborhood. Everyone wanted to see her.

The guests found the owner of Mount Vernon at his hospitable best, glowing with pride, and, for once, almost talkative.

They found the new Mrs. Washington a young woman of twenty-eight, bright-eyed and earnest and accustomed to making visitors feel at home.

"She has the qualities the wife of Colonel Washington should have—charm and character and graciousness" was the verdict of all.

"Did you see her boy, John Parke Custis, a handsome lad, but with a mischievous spirit . . . ?"

"And the little one, Patty, like a gypsy with her dark hair and eyes. A sweet child—but do you think she looks quite healthy?"

Thus the gentry of Fairfax County gossiped as they sipped their punch and ate fruit cake and took the bride into their hearts.

A thin-faced young man of twenty-three and his demure wife came up to Martha.

"I'm another Cary—Elizabeth," the girl introduced herself. "You know my sisters, Sally Fairfax and Anna Nicholas and Mary Ambler?"

And, of course, Martha knew of Bryan Fairfax. He was the son of William Fairfax's third wife, the Massachusetts Deborah Clarke; and so he was George William's younger half-brother. Only that year he had married Colonel Wilson Cary's youngest daughter.

Martha liked the unpretentious Bryan Fairfaxes. The soft-spoken Elizabeth was neither so clever nor so worldly as her older sister, Sally. She was a sweet girl, with frank gray eyes, whom Martha liked at once.

"Come to see me again—soon," she said to Elizabeth.

Within a fortnight the George Washingtons had adjusted themselves to a pleasant pattern for living at Mount Vernon. We can see them there on a typical day of their early married life.

Both were early risers. George was up at four o'clock each morning for a few hours of bookkeeping before his breakfast of hoe cakes, honey and tea at seven-thirty. Of this he ate frugally, to keep his slim figure. Martha was up, too, bustling about the house in a crisp morning gown, her brown hair in a mob cap, unlocking doors, issuing orders, passing out supplies to the slaves.

After breakfast George rode off on a tour of inspection of his five farms—the Mansion House, Muddy Hole River, Dogue Run and Union—where a small army of laborers, black and white, were at work in the tobacco and wheat fields. Martha usually retired to her room for an hour of Bible reading, an unfailing custom her life long, which she felt strengthened her for the day. Then she was ready to plunge back into her household duties, fortified by a second breakfast with the children of Virginia ham and hoe cakes and buttered Sally Lunn, with quince jelly and a pot of tea. For Martha, as her increasing curves showed, was *not* careful of her figure.

This being the fruit season, with the Mount Vernon orchards spilling their bounty of red cherries, peaches and plums, Martha had planned many weeks of preserving. Eight hundred jars of jellies, jams and dried fruit must be in her larder by winter. She checked the supplies in her lavender-scented linen closet, attended a sewing class for young women slaves, and went to the cabin of the ailing laundress to leave food and medicine.

At a quarter to three, the master of the house rode up in his blue coat, black knee breeches and boots. Changing for dinner, which was served at three, George made his appearance in a clean shirt and white silk stockings, his hair powdered and tied in a queue.

It was Martha, pink-cheeked and smiling, who remembered that George liked pickled pork, boiled turnips and a dumpling made of dough and apples, cinnamon and sugar. What if the heavy meal brought on a headache? His wife could cure him with a home remedy called "Angelic snuff," pleasant to take and smell.

After dinner, Martha gardened for a while and then rested in the cool of the shady veranda with her needlework. In his study, George inspected the reports of his overseers, wrote up his accounts in a neat hand, or read his growing library of books on farming.

A light supper of tea and toast; and on the rare evenings when they were alone, Martha seated herself at the spinet and George listened, with pleasure, to the tinkling tunes. He was not musical himself. He had a flute (it is still in the music room at Mount Vernon), but he had never learned to play it. Nor did he care for games, although cards were played when there were guests. And there usually were. Now that Mount Vernon had a mistress, the guest rooms, bright with flowered chintz, were seldom empty.

Martha enjoyed planning meals and making visitors comfortable, although she sometimes complained that she seldom passed an evening alone with her husband. And, mused George, would anyone believe it, although Mount Vernon's dairy boasted a hundred cows, he had to buy butter for the family! But no one was prouder than he that rich cakes and puddings and custards, calling for dozens of eggs, quarts of cream and pounds of butter, graced the Washington table, when the Masons, Diggeses, Fairfaxes and other neighbors dined at Mount Vernon.

The Fairfaxes were at Mount Vernon for dinner and the night about twice a week. And at least that often, the Washingtons dined at the Fairfax's two-story brick house, Belvoir, pronounced "Beaver," two miles down the Potomac.

At Belvoir, Martha found a different household from any that she had ever known; it puzzled her as much as it had the young, impressionable George Washington, fresh from his mother's farm. The house was handsomely furnished, and well it could be, for George William received a large salary for handling Lord Fairfax's property. "But there's dust on everything!" thought the good housekeeper from Mount Vernon. And what astonished her most was that heaped on every table at Belvoir, and on shelves along the walls, there were hundreds of Sally's books.

Behind Mrs. Fairfax's smooth forehead, and revealed by her alert blue eyes, was a mind keener than those of most men of her acquaintance. Seated at her dinner table, Martha listened, not to the usual talk of horse-racing and cockfighting, but of books and plays and ideas fashionable in England—conversation in which George Washington could join, but not his wife.

Martha sighed, and wished the visit would end. No one cared to hear that Patty seemed stronger today or that Jacky was quick at learning to read. What were they laughing at? Sally Fairfax was possessed of a wit that left Mrs. Washington tongue-tied and subdued.

Hearing Martha's sigh, Sally turned to her and smiled. "This isn't very interesting for you, *cheri*. How is your canning coming along?"

Only half listening to Martha's reply, she was off in a spirited discussion of the slavery question with the men, sprinkling her conversation with strange French phrases.

Martha was impressed with Mrs. Fairfax's ability as a hostess. But as a housewife, no! The whipped cream in the gooseberry fool was sour; the roast dry and over-done. Such culinary catastrophes would have mortified the mistress of Mount Vernon. But the mistress of Belvoir seemed not to notice them as she chatted briskly to George Washington, seated beside her.

After seeing Belvoir, Martha knew what her husband meant when he said this cultivated English household had opened a new world to him. To the sixteen-year-old George Washington, a lean, ignorant youth with big hands and feet, meeting such people had been a revelation; and Mistress Fairfax, two years his senior in age, and ten in education and sophistication, was the finest lady he had ever seen.

Sally had written cheerful letters while George was away at war. She had made his shirts—in those days before haberdashers, the women of the best families took pride in making the men's ruffled shirts. She had taught his big feet how to dance. She had shown him how to be gallant with the ladies; how to bow and kiss their hands—things the astounding *Rules of Civility and Conduct*, written by young Washington at fourteen, had never told him.

Certainly for beauty, liveliness, and social position, Mrs. Fairfax was without a superior in all Virginia, Martha acknowledged. But *why* did she have to live next door at Belvoir?

The Washingtons' marriage was a happy one from the start.

Writing to a relative in England at this time, George said: "I am now I believe fix'd at this seat with an agreeable Consort for Life. And I hope to find more happiness in retirement than I ever experienced amidst a wide and bustling World." Then, referring to his dream of some day visiting London, he admitted he was "now tied by the Leg and must set Inclination aside."

When Martha read that letter, she laughed merrily. She knew that George did not feel tied either to herself or Mount Vernon. Rather, he had dropped anchor in the harbor of his heart's desire.

The Potomac was the scene of much rivalry among the rich planters whose estates bordered the river. Each house owned a barge made to order in England; the Negro crew rowing it was dressed in the family livery. These boats seemed forever in motion, sweeping up and down the river, freighted with ladies and gentlemen going to Mount Vernon, Belvoir, Gunston Hall, the home of the George Masons on the point below Belvoir, and other mansions on the Potomac.

For all this social life, the Washingtons needed numerous changes of clothes; and the year after their marriage saw George writing to a relative, Richard Washington, concerning purchases to be made in England and sent by the first ship bound for the Potomac.

It gave George pleasure to see his young wife fashionably dressed. He ordered for her a coat of salmon-colored tabby velvet; a cap of Brussels lace or Point to cost £20; two flowered lawn aprons; eight silk and cotton hose; two pairs of satin shoes with high heels "of the smallest fives"; twelve pairs of kid gloves and mitts; a fashionable hat; a black mask to guard Martha's complexion; a silver tabby velvet petticoat; perfumed powder, scissors, pins and hairpins and sugar candy.

And "a very good spinet to be made by Mr. Plinius, harpsi-chord maker, in South Audley Street, Grosvenor Square."

On an afternoon, nearly a year later, Patty and Jack were seated with their mother in the summerhouse overlooking the river, when they saw a boat come up the Potomac and stop at their dock. *It was the ship from England.* The sight of it took Martha back to her own childhood, when a similar ship had come up the Pamunkey with goods ordered by Colonel John Dandridge.

The slaves rapidly unloaded the spinet, clothing and books. The heavy boxes were carried up to the house. Martha and the children could not wait for the servants to unpack them. Memories of her own first ball gown from London came to Martha with the awed look on Patty's face, as she lifted a small "Persian quilted" coat from the box and told the little girl to put it on.

There was a hat called a "Capuchan" to match the coat, and four lawn and two cambric frocks, daintier than any Patty Custis had ever owned.

In another package were "a fashionably dressed" doll; six pairs of white kid gloves; six egrets for the hair of a four-year-old child; and, unfortunately for the health of one so frail, a pair of pack-thread stays.

For Master Custis, there was a suit of winter clothes, and one for summer. A "light duffel Cloak with silver frogs." A silver laced hat. Six pairs of cotton stockings. Four pairs of strong shoes, and one pair of "neat pumps." A pair of gloves. Two "hair-bags." Toys, and "6 little books for a child beginning to read."

When Martha unwrapped silver shoe buckles and sleeve buttons, and then a suit of livery for the fourteen-year-old Negro servant assigned him, the Custis heir danced around with delight. Eagerly he begged that he might have his young friends come in and see these gorgeous things from England spread out on the four-poster bed and the chairs and tables of the room. And smiling happily, his indulgent mother agreed.

All too well, Martha knew her reputation for being over-fond of her children. She could not bear to let Patty and Jack out of her sight. She took them with her when she went down with George to Williamsburg for the legislative sessions, when they drove to Annapolis and Alexandria to the races. Going with her husband to visit his brother, John Augustine, Martha once tried the experiment of leaving Jacky at home. But, as she wrote to her sister Nancy, it was with such anxiety to herself that the boy probably accompanied his mother on future visits.

"I carried my little patt with me and left Jacky at home for a trial to see how well I could stay without him though we ware gon but wone fortnight I was quite impatient to get home. If I at aney time heard the doggs barke or a noise out, I thought thair was a person sent for me. I often fancied he was sick or some accident had happened to him."

While George attended the meetings of the House of Burgesses at Williamsburg, Martha's days were filled with shopping. There were music books and instruments, dresses and trinkets to be purchased. And, alas, doctor appointments for frail Patty to be made. The child, to Martha's deep concern, had inherited delicate lungs from her father.

Mrs. Washington, who was vain of her small feet, bought quantities of tiny slippers with high heels in the Williamsburg shops, as well as bright colored stockings, which she laundered herself. She put them "through three lathers . . . lett them dry on the wrong sides" and ironed "them smooth on ye wrong side."

Since George was fastidious, and bathed regularly in the Potomac, Martha was careful to keep herself equally dainty. Because he admired pretty women, noticed their gowns and how their hair was dressed, she dressed fashionably and was always very neat. She was faultlessly clean, which was not always the case, even with the rich, in those days when bath tubs had not been invented. Perfume was relied upon to do the work of soap. Garments and hair powder were highly scented.

There still exists a recipe in Martha's own handwriting, on how to make "A Perfume to Stand in a Roome":

"Take three quarts of rose buds & put them in a pot with bay salt, 4 grayns of musk & ambergreece, 30 drops of oyle of rodium, a little benjamin & storeax, & keep it allways close covered, but when you have a mind to have yr roome sweet you must take of ye cover."

Another tells how "To Perfume Cloaths after they are Washed." And how to perfume "ordinary hayer powder." Mistress Washington had a recipe "To keep ye Hayre Clean and Improve it." And this was her substitute for the tooth-brush and paste of today, "To Keep Teeth Clean & White and To Fasten Them":

"Take cuttle fishbone and make it into a very fine powder & rub ye teeth well with a cloth, then wash them after with white wine & it will preserf ye teeth & keep them white & clean & preserf from ye toothach iff it be used every day."

With the coming of the hunting season, Mount Vernon was crowded with guests, none of whom stayed less than a fortnight. It was the custom to hunt three times a week. On hunt days breakfast was served by candlelight, and George took to the field at daybreak, with his huntsman, Will Lee, and his friends.

There were days when Martha put on her scarlet riding habit, and with the visiting ladies, rode to the hounds. But more frequently, as the years passed, she remained at home, arranging the feast to be set before the hungry riders when they returned from the chase.

When the deep notes of the hounds announced that the hunters were near, Martha, in a gown of dainty gauze, hurried to the door to greet them. There was Will Lee, the huntsman, on Chinkling, and George astride Blueskin, an iron-gray hunter, almost as blue as his name indicated. Martha thought her husband the handsomest man in the world, in his blue hunting coat, scarlet waistcoat, boots and velvet cap!

One day when the George William Fairfaxes came over to hunt, they brought with them a short, stout man of sixty and a young stranger.

The older man peered at Martha with nearsighted gray eyes. "Lord Fairfax," Sally introduced him proudly.

The young man was Thomas Bryan Martin, his lordship's nephew.

Lord Fairfax, a renowned fox hunter, had come to Belvoir from Greenway Court, his home in the Shenandoah Valley, for the hunting season. Once more the head of the Fairfax family would ride to the hounds with George Washington, as they had done almost every year since George, at sixteen, had come to live with his brother Lawrence.

At that time the old nobleman had just arrived from Leeds Castle, his home in Kent, England, to spend the rest of his life on the six-million-acre grant between the Potomac and the Rappahannock, inherited from his mother. Staying first at Belvoir, before going to the Shenandoah Valley to live, Lord Fairfax often hunted with George Washington. He liked the boy's boldness in the saddle, his industry and his accuracy. Many a morning he had stood watching while George practiced his surveying. And he was pleased when his cousin and agent, George William, brought the lad to his Shenandoah home, Greenway Court, on a month's trip to survey the property.

After a hard day's tramp, making surveys, young Washington had spent his evenings talking to the cultured old gentleman. Lord Fairfax was a graduate of Oxford. In London he had been a man of fashion, and a contributor to Addison's *Spectator*. He belonged to the great world of which the ambitious youth dreamed.

Martha looked with interest at Lord Fairfax, the only British peer living in America during most of the eighteenth century. When he complimented her, somewhat gruffly, on the feast spread before them, Martha felt herself repaid. She knew his reputation for hating women. Lord Fairfax had fled to America because he was jilted on his wedding day, when the lady he loved had preferred a duke. That was why he had gone off into the Shenandoah wilderness to live, emerging only for a good hunt, a good dinner and some good stories.

After the meal, the men lingered over their port and walnuts to discuss the courage of the leading hound, the pedigree of the swiftest horse. The ladies gathered around Martha in the drawing-room to indulge in a bit of gossip and exchange recipes, of which Mistress Washington's were in great demand. We can imagine her seated on the sofa, her feet in their buckled shoes just reaching the floor, accepting the kind words of her friends on her hunt breakfast, supremely content. Today things had gone well—George had "catched" a fox. But Sally Fairfax and her husband seemed worried about something. They were nervous and short-tempered. Finally they called their carriage and went home.

"What ails our neighbors from Belvoir?" Martha asked George.

They were upset, he explained, because of the presence of the young man, Thomas Bryan Martin, with his uncle. Martin, the son of the old nobleman's sister, Frances, had come to Virginia to live with his rich bachelor relative. Sally and her husband were sure that Martin was trying to influence his uncle to make a change in the property management.

It was all clear to Martha now—the chill in Sally's voice when she spoke to Thomas Martin. For well did Martha know what the loss of the large salary that went to George William as his uncle's agent would mean to the extravagant Mistress Fairfax!

On New Year's Day, 1760, we read in George's diary that "Mrs. Washington broke out with the Meazles." On the fifth day of her illness, Doctor James Laurie came to see her. Also "Mrs. George William Fairfax spent the day with Mrs. Washington, and, the evening being cold and windy, was sent home to Belvoir in the chariot."

Poor Martha, "broke out with the meazles." And on her first wedding anniversary!

Perhaps on this visit Sally told Martha important news— she and George William were sailing to England for a brief trip. The purpose of their journey was sensational. Colonel Fairfax was going abroad to prove to his English relations that he was not a Negro.

Because George William had been born at New Providence in the Bahama Islands while his father, William Fairfax, was there as Chief Justice, the story had spread to England that his mother was a Negress. Ridiculous, of course. His mother was Sarah Walker, the daughter of Major Thomas Walker of the Royal Artillery. But because of the large English estates of the Fairfax family, it seemed advisable to curb the gossip at once.

It was the ambitious Sally who insisted that her easy-going husband go to England to personally deny the slander. *Nothing must ruin her chances of becoming Lady Fairfax.*

So in 1760 George and Sally Fairfax sailed for England, leaving the care of Belvoir to their closest friend, George Washington. Before their departure, Martha honored them with a farewell dinner at Mount Vernon.

We can see her dressed in plum-colored satin and the Custis amethysts, seated at the head of her table, playing the part of the gracious hostess, talking pleasantly to the eccentric Lord Fairfax on one side and to George William on the other.

"Really now, Patsy, why don't you and George come to England with us?" Colonel Fairfax repeated again and again. "We'd like to have you visit us at our home in Yorkshire."

See England, the mother country, that was Martha's dream as much as George's! "How I'd like to come," she sighed. "But we can't leave the children and Mount Vernon."

When the meal was over, George Washington toasted each of his guests. Then Lord Fairfax gallantly suggested drinking to the health of their hostess. And Martha, pleased, forgot the self-consciousness that always beset her in the presence of the haughty Sally and followed a custom of the day. When the old nobleman stretched out his glass to her, Mrs. Washington lifted one petal from the yellow rose she wore and let it fall into his brimming wine.

"Very prettily done, Patsy!" Sally's patronizing tone spoiled completely Martha's little moment of happiness.

Flushing, she wanted to weep with chagrin. But the host was bringing the dinner to a close. Rising to his great height, George Washington lifted his glass high and gave the toast that brought a lump to the throats of the five loyal Britishers:

"To the King and Queen of England!"

Peggy Forsha
+
Bill DeVinney

*M*OUNT VERNON ON A JUNE AFTERNOON IN 1769 HAD A peace about it that Martha Washington would long remember. Over four years after the passage of the Stamp Act, it was still possible to sit in the garden with little thought of the trouble between the American colonies and England. Erect in her basket chair, Martha sat sewing on a kerchief for her daughter.

Dear Patty! Now twelve years old, she was big-eyed, fairy-like, with a feverish flush on her thin cheeks. The slaves, who adored Patty Custis, called her "the Dark Lady," because of her brunette skin and brown eyes. Almost every day she could be seen on her pony, attended by a servant carrying a basket, making the rounds of the Negro cabins to attend the sick and needy.

But the child herself was too frail! Martha sighed deeply. Perhaps the waters of Bath Warm Springs would restore her strength. George hoped to get away for a few weeks there in August.

"Martha!"

Her husband seated himself in a chair beside her. "I want to talk to you about something."

Martha's heart contracted. "Patty is worse?"

George shook his head. "Not that," he said, unfolding a sheet of paper. "I've been writing to our agent in London."

115

Robert Cary & Company, the Washingtons' English agent, was receiving notice not to send the household any of the articles unfairly taxed under the laws made by Parliament against the American colonies. The master of Mount Vernon was determined to carry out the terms of the non-importation agreement passed by the House of Burgesses.

"In future, Patsy, you must get along without the British goods we've agreed not to import," he explained.

Martha nodded, instantly ready to join hands with her husband and his friends in a plan which they hoped would compel the mother country to change her attitude.

"No more imported silks and satins for your dresses. Can you get along without them, my dear?"

"Of course, Papa. My women slaves can weave all the fabrics we need. We'll not miss a thing."

"Not even your cup of tea? It'll be hard for us, but no more tea must be served at Mount Vernon."

"*No more tea!*" Martha could not conceal her dismay. Doing without nice clothes was easy, but *tea!*

No fragrant, scalding tea at her morning meal, flanked with golden batter bread, dripping with butter and spiced grape jelly. No tea and fresh muffins in the evening when George joined her and the children for a light supper.

Colonel Washington, too, liked his cup of tea. But, as he explained to his wife, they must set an example to the neighborhood by banning the taxed beverage at Mount Vernon.

"Of course," sighed Martha, turning, in her mind, the pages of her fat book of recipes. Hot apple cider was stimulating. Ground chocolate mixed with milk made a fragrant, frothy drink. Cambric tea, milk and brown sugar with a touch of cinnamon, was a delicious brew.

"But they are not *tea*," Martha confessed to herself, after

George returned to his study to finish his letter.

Sitting alone in the twilight, she tried to remember back four years earlier, to the passage of the Stamp Act in February 1765, when all this trouble between England and the colonies had begun.

At first there had been mysterious talk of Parliament's threat to tax the American colonies by forcing them to put stamps on imported articles. But it was "man talk" over port in the dining room while the ladies gathered in Martha's sitting room to exchange recipes and discuss the bonnets and sacks that Sally Fairfax had brought back with her from London.

Mistress Fairfax herself had almost nothing to say to the ladies. Watching her, Martha could see Sally's blue eyes cloud over with boredom, could hear the impatient tapping of her satin-shod foot.

Once the men had filed into the room, Mistress Fairfax was herself again. Ardently interested in politics, she was more sparkling than ever during these troubled times. She liked to talk about the colonies' quarrel with the mother country— from the English angle, of course—and talk she did, until the sleepy George William took his wife's arm and escorted her out to their carriage.

The idea of taxation for revenue, so new and puzzling to Martha and the other sheltered ladies of the neighborhood, was an old story to Sally Fairfax. She had come back from London fully informed on the plan of the British government to pay off the debt of the Seven Years' War by placing taxes on the American colonists. And at the social functions which followed the Fairfax's return, she had long and spirited conversations with the men on the crisis. Would the King succeed in passing the Stamp Act? Or would his Prime Minister,

William Pitt, who had denounced the harsh measures against the Americans, win their cause for them?

That the colonists had a "cause" came as a surprise to Martha Washington, whose whole life had been spent in social and domestic ways.

"Yes, it's true," George replied to her questions. "The Americans are prepared to resist these unfair taxes, unless we're given representation in Parliament."

But taxed the colonies were, and without representation. George the Third managed to get rid of America's defender, William Pitt, and to force the Stamp Act through Parliament.

Martha remembered the first stamps which had come from England, with the royal command that they be purchased and attached to every newspaper, almanac or pack of playing cards. Business papers were taxed, too; bills, bonds, licenses and deeds of property.

"Monstrous!" George Washington had cried.

Martha, alarmed, sought to soothe him. A little more of this, and her husband's outbursts would be as rash and undignified as those of Patrick Henry, the young back-country lawyer who had dared to speak out against the British policy one May morning of 1765 in the House of Burgesses.

The fact that following Patrick Henry's speech Governor Fauquier had dissolved the Virginia Assembly as a rebuke had further served to shake Mistress Washington's safe and ordered world.

With a heavy heart, she began to wonder who was right. The Tories, who were English sympathizers? Or the Patriots? The Washingtons had friends in both factions. The Fairfax family, staunch Tories all, were their dearest companions. On the other hand, George had known many of the Patriots since boyhood. And these grim-faced men, determined to resist the unfair taxes England was forcing on the colonies, began coming to Mount Vernon to ask Colonel Washington's advice.

Over her dinner table, Martha had listened to stormy talk while the green turtle soup cooled in the tureen and the servants whispered that the wild turkey was growing dry and tasteless on the spit.

"Any person using the stamp paper is a traitor!" shouted Richard Henry Lee. And the loud-talking men, promising to find and punish such weaklings, pounded on the table until the wine glasses danced.

George, for once, had lost his sedate demeanor and was as red-faced as his companions. He was joining the others in agreeing, at the risk of their lives, to protect anyone who should be arrested for having defied the new law.

Treason, indeed!

It was all Mistress Washington could do to calm the noisy debate by hastily serving her bountiful meal. These irate men were hungry men, and soon the talk grew less heated, until, with the whipped cream syllabub, smiles and compliments were exchanged around the candlelit table.

But what if the Tory Fairfaxes had been present? What if Lord Fairfax or George William had heard the threats of the bitter Patriots? No, in the last four years, entertaining at Mount Vernon had not been easy.

A year ago a British frigate, the *Boston*, had anchored in the Potomac off Belvoir, and there was the usual exchange of courtesy between house and ship. The Washingtons and Fairfaxes were invited out to inspect the warship, and that night Colonel and Mrs. Fairfax gave a dinner to welcome Sir Thomas Adams and his officers to an American harbor.

It had not been a happy meal, Martha recalled.

There was a tension about Sally Fairfax which her neighbor in those days did not understand. All through dinner she talked to Sir Thomas Adams in a low voice. Her fine brow was puckered, her eyes dull with anxiety.

Things had not gone well for the Tory Fairfaxes. While George William and his wife were in England, Lord Fairfax's nephew, Thomas Bryan Martin, had persuaded the old man to transfer the land-office from Belvoir to Greenway Court and place it in his hands. Thomas Martin became the agent of the Fairfax properties. Sally and her husband came home to Virginia to find their income greatly reduced.

Now Martha Washington folded Patty's kerchief, sighing softly. What was ahead, she wondered? But as yet no one gave serious thought to a separation of the colonies from the mother country. This spring of 1769, the House of Burgesses had again been dissolved, this time by Lord Botetourt, the English governor, for a protest against the British Revenue Act. The legislators, refusing to stay dissolved, had marched from the Capitol to the Raleigh Tavern to draw up an agreement of non-importation by which the colonies agreed to stop importing articles from England and until the taxes they complained against were repealed. Yet that day, Martha, who had accompanied George to Williamsburg, sat in her lodging busy with her embroidery, with no more thought of the proceedings at the Raleigh Tavern than if her husband had been attending a regular meeting of the House. No one whispered the terrible word "Revolution."

Had not the rebellious Burgesses, gathered in the Apollo Room of the Raleigh, after signing the Non-Importation Act, drunk toasts to the England they had defied in silver mugs of ale? "The King!" "The Queen and the Royal Family!"

That night, at the ball at the Governor's Palace, Martha

Washington had twirled her silk flounces in the figures of the minuet, happy and reassured. George was dancing; his smile was constant, his grace in the minuet a marvel of dexterity. Shutting away unpleasant thoughts, she had told herself then that the incident at the Raleigh Tavern was no cause for panic.

In the coach driving back to Mount Vernon, George Washington had little to say. His face was stern, his thoughts far away. He had been one of the signers of the protest against the British Revenue Act. Far ahead, down the years, he could see what it might mean to every person in America.

Their return home had marked the end of the old carefree life at Mount Vernon, Martha thought, as she gathered up her sewing and strolled back to the house. Following the visit to Williamsburg, George spent hours alone in his study. His wife had waited, docilely, for him to take her into his confidence.

Today, the letter to the agent in London indicated the seriousness of the trouble with the mother country. This was more than a petty quarrel over taxes. Martha suspected that the Washington household would have to do without English importations for a long, long time.

It was characteristic of Martha Washington that by the next day she had packed away her imported finery, her quilts and brocades. She had also sealed up her precious stock of tea, and would henceforth regard with scorn any woman who continued to indulge in the banned luxury.

Additional spinning wheels were set up in the workhouse at Mount Vernon. Women slaves took their places beside them, working with fresh spirit under the direction of their mistress, who walked among them, carrying a spinning wheel under her own arm.

As a member of "The Daughters of Liberty," sworn not to use British goods, Martha Washington set to work on the coarse homespun cloth of which she was to become so patriotically proud. From it her plain, practical dresses were made, dresses very different from the rich imported silks she had once worn.

There were no more embroidered muslin tuckers, velvet gowns and mantles, plumes and frilled bonnets in Martha's clothes presses. But how she longed for delicate stuffs to set off the fragile beauty of her lovely Patty! It was the mother's pleasure to gaze at the girl's too-slim figure, her big dark eyes, her brown silky curls. Long after the imported dresses were gone, there was thin, carefully-fashioned homespun for Patty and silk ribbons for her hair.

Patty Custis was growing into a beauty, but it was the beauty of invalidism. The girl was too ill to blossom into healthy good looks. Her pallor increased. Part of each day she spent on her couch, eyes closed.

Patty's lungs were delicate, as her father's had been. Her mother was reconciled to that. But the year before the child had suddenly suffered epileptic seizures. In a panic, Martha had called in all the regular doctors. And when their "fit drops," at a pound a bottle, had done no good, she had turned to a quack named Joshua Evans, who placed on Patty's finger an iron ring as a talisman.

Frequently, this summer of 1769, Martha looked at her daughter, her eyes heavy with anxiety. If only the iron ring would have the miraculous virtues they claimed! So far there had been no improvement.

In these trying days, Martha did not even have the comfort of her husband's presence. So strained was the situation between England and America by July that Colonel Washington was in Williamsburg weeks at a time, leaving his wife to manage the plantation and nurse Patty, who, patient and uncomplaining always, seemed to be wasting away.

Tears falling, Martha wrote George of the girl's condition: "Would your duties permit you to return home? Patty is asking for you." Dropping his work, the loving stepfather hastened back to Mount Vernon. It was August now; Patty lay back on her pillows, pale in the sultry heat that had settled down on the banks of the Potomac.

They took her to Bath Warm Springs in West Virginia then, traveling by wagon, a trip of six days. It was cooler in the mountains, and there were pine trees. Patty drank the famed waters and insisted that she was better, proving her renewed strength by joining in some of the milder gaiety of the Colonial resort. But Martha, remembering how Patty's father had pretended improved health almost to the hour of his death, was not greatly encouraged.

As though she had not enough grief over Patty, Martha Washington faced a second problem in her son, Jack, now grown into a handsome, headstrong youth. No worry about *his* health. Jacky had lived up to the promise of his buxom, boisterous babyhood. And he was his mother's pride.

Young John Custis had too much spending money. He had horses and servants and pedigreed dogs with which to play, and a great amount of fashionable equipment, which he carried with ease and grace, for his stepfather had taught him to ride hard after the fox and his mother had seen to it that he attended the balls and races at Williamsburg and Annapolis.

There had always been too much attention for Jack. It had made him thoughtless and unsettled; at times, even wayward. But popular always. And he was, outwardly at least, a pleasant generous youth, who took eagerly to the gay side of life.

It was only when Jacky's high spirits turned to defiance of all authority that George Washington decided to remove the boy, for his own good, from his mother's side.

Walter Magowan, who had been tutoring the Custis children, had returned to England, so, in 1769, George Washington decided that his stepson must go away to school.

Martha cried a little, pleading with George to be more lenient of boyish pranks and let Jack stay home. But her husband had made up his mind. Young Custis was packed off to Annapolis, to study under the Reverend Jonathan Boucher, an Episcopal clergyman who had several young gentlemen under his charge.

To the new instructor, George Washington wrote:

"I will cheerfully pay twelve pounds a year to engage your watchful eye to him, as he is a promising boy and will possess a very large fortune. Add to this my anxiety to make him fit for more useful purposes than horse racer."

The Reverend Mr. Boucher hastened to accept the flattering commission, saying: "Ever since I have heard of Master Custis, I have wished to call Him one of my little Flock."

"The right tutor for Jack," George Washington assured his wife. And lonely though she was without the boy's laughing presence, Martha was forced to agree with him when a second letter came from the Annapolis clergyman, commenting on Jacky's "peculiar innocence and sanctity of manners . . . teeming with all the softer virtues."

Of George Washington's desire to save his wife from the truth about her son's behavior there are many proofs. He did not show her the disturbing letter he received shortly thereafter from the Reverend Mr. Boucher: "I must confess to you I never did in my life know a youth so exceedingly indolent, or so surprisingly voluptuous. One would think Nature had intended him for an Asiatic Prince."

In vain, the tutor tried to instill some learning in the Custis heir. But Jacky was not a student. He preferred fox hunting, shooting, and fishing to books. And he had formed a liking for the theatre—The Players had come to Annapolis—and for Sarah Hallam, the actress.

"Jack has a Propensity to the Sex," wrote Mr. Boucher to the boy's distressed stepfather. "I took such steps as I judged most likely to wean him in time."

His efforts must have been unsuccessful, for Jacky turned his gallant attentions to a Miss Galloway, the sister of a wild student, whose father was an Annapolis wine merchant. This brought a sharp reprimand from Washington, "I have your well-being much at heart," following which Jack promised "to apply close to his studies," adding, "But time slips of a pace." Excursions to horse races, oyster parties and play-houses around Annapolis occupied many of Jack's days and nights. After two years, he was not much further in Latin than when he left Mount Vernon. He knew little arithmetic, and less Greek.

It was in 1771 that the Reverend Mr. Boucher, despairing of ever making a student of Jacky, suggested the idea of sending him on a European tour.

But his prudent stepfather said no. The Custis estate was a good one, but not profitable enough for a European jaunt for a mere schoolboy. Nor did Jack himself wish to go, for he had fallen seriously in love.

From Annapolis, Jacky had made frequent visits home. His route lay past Mount Airy, the home of Benedict Calvert of Maryland, son of the fifth Lord Baltimore. The attraction there was their second daughter, the fifteen-year-old Eleanor —as merry and bright a brown-haired miss as ever led her lover a brisk chase over the hunting field.

Martha was charmed with the match. And to her credit, let it be said that she felt no motherly qualms over sharing her beloved son with another woman. In fact, she started to dream of the elaborate wedding festivities. An alliance of the prominent Custis and Calvert families was almost a union between Virginia and Maryland!

But there was a break in the mother's pleasant reverie, a rude jolt for the happy young couple. George Washington would not give his consent to the marriage, for Jack was not yet eighteen, had been "fickle, and might wound the young lady."

In the spring of 1773, polite letters passed between Mount Vernon and Mount Airy. Washington's note to Eleanor's father, so difficult to compose, and yet so courteous and flattering to the charms of the young lady, began:

"I should think myself wanting in candor were I not to confess that Miss Nelly's amiable qualities are acknowledged on all hands, and that an alliance with your family would be pleasing to Jack's, but as his guardian, I consider it my duty to endeavor to carry him through a regular course of education."

He concluded with a dignified statement of his young ward's advantages in land, slaves and moneys, and proposed a two-year postponement of the marriage.

The Calverts, sensible people, agreed to the terms. But Jack, who could not bear to be thwarted, argued and scolded, and threatened to elope without his stepfather's consent.

Martha was very unhappy. "There's truth in your letter, of course," she told her husband. "But Jacky is so much in love, marriage may be just the responsibility he needs."

George Washington had his way. Jack's education was continued; not in Annapolis—that was too close to Mount Airy—but at King's College, now Columbia University. To prevent any hitch in the arrangements, Colonel Washington himself escorted the blustering young man to New York.

Back at Mount Vernon again, he found Martha too concerned over Patty's condition to listen to his account of her son's safe arrival. The girl's attacks, now more frequent, left her exhausted. Her days on earth were few, the doctors knew, yet when Colonel Washington received an urgent call to Williamsburg, they told him it was safe to go. And Martha, much as she needed her husband's strength, bade him goodbye with composure, promising to write every day.

Patty failed rapidly. As Colonel Washington was leaving Williamsburg to accompany the new English Governor, John Murray, Earl of Dunmore, on a tour of western Virginia, Martha's message came. He reached Mount Vernon on the nineteenth day of June, 1773, just in time to dine with his dear stepchild, who seemed "in better health and Spirits than for some time." But soon after "she was seized with one of her usual Fits." George carried her to a couch. Patty Custis smiled weakly, laid her thin hand in his, and closed her eyes. . . .

The trip with Lord Dunmore was canceled. The summer sun shone over the blue Potomac, but the chill of winter had fallen on the stately house. George and Martha Washington sat in the garden, mutely aware of the loss of the child who had been their pride for too few years.

A letter to Martha's brother-in-law, Burwell Bassett, reveals

George's own heartache, and his tender consideration for Martha's even deeper sorrow.

"It is an easier matter to conceive than to describe the distress of this Family; especially that of the unhappy Parent of our Dear Patcy Custis, when I inform you that the Sweet Innocent Girl Entered into a more happy & peaceful abode than any she has met with in the afflicted Path she hitherto has trod. This unexpected blow has reduced my poor Wife to the lowest ebb of Misery; which is encreas'd by the absence of her son whom I have just fixed at the College in New York and want of the balmy consolation of her Relations . . ."

He begs that Martha's "dear Mama" come from Chestnut Grove to make her home at Mount Vernon. Mary Dandridge had died ten years since; and Betty had married John Aylett in April. Frances Dandridge was alone at Chestnut Grove. But she could not be induced to leave her own home.

The loss of her only daughter left Martha stunned for many weeks. But her recovery, once it began, was more rapid than that following the death of Patty's father. The one-time rebellious and exuberant young woman had learned to accept sorrow and disappointment. Good health and a cheerful disposition, as always, sustained her. Within a few months we see Martha Washington, again firm and resolute, going about the house at Mount Vernon, inspecting the larder and issuing orders to her slaves.

With Patty gone, her motherly affection and hopes centered even more intensely in her son. She insisted that Jacky should return home from college. She needed him, she wept. And, his own heart aching with the loss of Patty, George could not refuse his wife's plea. So back to Mount Vernon came the spoiled heir, after an absence of only three months, instead of the two years he should have spent at King's College.

Jacky was eighteen now, tall and slender, with black curly hair and a humorous smile. The house rang with his laughter and that of pretty Nelly Calvert, who tried to take Patty's place during her visits to Mount Vernon. Martha watched the happy pair, her eyes tender. The sense of loss was easing. Friends were calling. There were a few small dinners, a barbecue, as George Washington recorded, "of my own giving."

There was also another event in the neighborhood, dated July 8, 1773, in his diary, less than a month after Patty's death:

"At home all day, Colonel Fairfax and Mrs. Fairfax came in the afternoon to take leave of us."

The leavetaking of Sally and "her Fairfax," as she called her husband, was no short journey. The neighbors at Belvoir were again sailing for England to be gone at least a year. Colonel Fairfax had inherited Towlston Manor, in Yorkshire, from his Uncle Henry; he was going to England to take possession of it.

Ambitious Sally, untiring in her desire to become Lady Fairfax, had again urged this trip on her husband. Now that they had lost the income that went with being Lord Fairfax's agent, they must make sure of this English property.

So one July morning in 1773, Sally and "her Fairfax" sailed from America, this time not to deny a slander, but to proudly take possession of Yorkshire estates that would bring Sally one step nearer to the coveted position of Lady Fairfax. And as their ship traveled up the River Thames on their way to London, it passed three boats going to America with a cargo of tea, three boats that would change the lives of the Fairfaxes, the Washingtons, and all Americans.

Back at Mount Vernon, Martha Washington knew nothing of the ill-omened tea ships then approaching. She only knew that she was happy for a while to be rid of the sense of defeat that Sally's brilliant presence always brought her. The knowledge that for a year or two Belvoir would be closed, and George's diary bare of references to fox-hunting and dining across Dogue Creek, could not but give a lift to her spirits.

Martha's happiness was further increased when her husband, agreeing to Jack's marriage to Eleanor Calvert, set the date for the third of February, 1774. She still felt the loss of Patty too keenly to attend the ceremony at Mount Airy. But Martha sent by Colonel Washington this tender, motherly greeting to the young bride:

"God took from Me a Daughter when June Roses were blooming—He has now given me another daughter, about her Age when Winter Winds are blowing, to warm my Heart again. I am as Happy as One so afflicted and so Blest can be—"

There is a portrait of the sixteen-year-old Eleanor, painted just before her wedding; a slim, graceful figure in a riding habit, rather boyish looking with her open jacket and tricornered hat. But she had character and pluck, for all her youth. She did not fuss over Jack Custis. She treated him, for the first time in his life, as an adult.

The change in the spoiled boy was miraculous. It appeared that he had only needed a wife to anchor him. And as Eleanor and Jacky settled down contentedly at Abingdon, a plantation of several thousand acres four miles up the Potomac from Alexandria, Martha was human enough to say to her husband, "I told you so." That she had been criticized for her indulgence in taking her son out of college and approving so early a marriage, she knew well. She also knew a good match when she saw one.

Mistress Washington joined in the pleasant task of helping her new daughter-in-law furnish Abingdon. She had lost Patty, but she had gained another daughter in Eleanor. Nor was Jack wholly lost. A large portion of his and Nelly's time was spent at Mount Vernon, only eighteen miles away. And it was said that "if any horse escaped from the Abingdon stable, it would be found in due time at Mount Vernon."

Poor Martha!

Just as she was expressing her gratitude for her new serenity of soul, another blow fell. News of the closing of the port of Boston by the British on June 1, 1774, was received. George Washington, stern-faced and tight-lipped, left at once for Williamsburg. The dissatisfaction against England, first caused by the Stamp Act, and smoldering ever since, burst forth again.

On a stormy day in the previous December, the three ships laden with tea that the Fairfaxes had passed on the River Thames appeared in Boston harbor. A band of sturdy young colonists in Indian costumes had boarded them, ripped open the chests of tea with their hatchets and dumped the taxed cargo into the water. As punishment, the British now closed the port.

In sympathy for the Bostonians, the House of Burgesses ordered a day of fasting and prayer. This act Governor Dunmore considered rebellion; the House of Burgesses was again dissolved and its members sent home in disgrace.

The hot-headed Virginia squires, reddening with anger over this indignity, had scarcely made plans for their homeward journeys when a dispatch threw hospitable Williamsburg into a state of excitement.

The family of Lord Dunmore had arrived from England.
Of course, there must be a ball given for the Countess of
Dunmore! The Apollo Room at the Raleigh, which still
echoed with Patrick Henry's eloquence, was hastily made
ready. And the men who had been most bitter in their de-
nunciation of the Port Bill bowed low to the Governor's
Lady and led her through the stately figures of the minuet.

But after that things changed quickly. As a first step toward the union of the colonies, a meeting was called for
September 1774 in Philadelphia. The Continental Congress,
it was to be named, and advocating it, along with aid for
Boston, was George Washington.

At a session of the Virginia Assembly he said publicly: "I
will raise one thousand men, subsist them at my own expense,
and march myself at their head for relief of Boston."

Brave words. And dangerous ones in a country poorly
equipped for waging war.

Martha Washington showed her own courage and perfect
confidence in her husband's judgment by writing, with much
warmth and a touch of her old temper, to a relative who
mourned George's "folly" in joining with the rebels:

"Yes; I foresee the consequences; domestic happiness sus-
pended; social enjoyments abandoned; property of every kind
put in jeopardy by war; neighbors and friends at variance, and
eternal separations on earth possible. But what are all these
evils when compared with the fate of which the Port Bill
may be only a threat? My mind is made up; my heart is in
the cause. George is right; he is always right."

The day appointed by the Patriots for fasting and prayer
had been strictly observed at Mount Vernon. Martha, who
might have been sitting beside the river these days sewing

Left. SALLY FAIRFAX (MRS. GEORGE WILLIAM FAIRFAX OF BELVOIR)

Right. ELEANOR CALVERT (MRS. JOHN PARKE CUSTIS)

or idly dreaming, was to be found in her workrooms directing the weaving of rough flax into homespun, the stitching
of shirts and blouses and dresses. These clothes were no
longer for the use of the servants alone, but for the Mount
Vernon family as well.

One August morning Edmund Pendleton and Patrick
Henry, on their way to the Continental Congress in Philadelphia, arrived to spend a day and a night.

"I am ready to make any sacrifice," Martha told her guests,
"but I feel very anxious."

However, during their visit she talked to them "like a
Spartan mother to her son on going to battle," Edmund
Pendleton wrote. And he told how he and Patrick Henry
left for the Congress with George Washington, inspired by
his wife's courage.

On the morning that the three men set out on horseback,
Martha accompanied them to the door.

"God be with you, gentlemen," she said. "I hope you'll
stand firm. I know George will."

With these brave words on her lips, Martha Washington
watched the three determined Patriots ride off to do their
part in securing justice for the colonies. With Colonel Washington was Will Lee, his huntsman, as body servant, now
that Thomas Bishop had grown old and infirm.

Mistress Washington saw George and his friends set forth
on a dangerous errand which, if successful, meant a long and
bitter war; if unsuccessful, the possible loss of life and con-
fiscation of such large estates as Mount Vernon. Yet Martha,
as always, was enthusiastically in agreement with whatever
her husband thought. "My mind is made up; my heart is in
the cause," she had written. And she had added, "George is
right; he is always right."

For all her bravery, Martha Washington had her moments of doubt. War clouds were gathering . . . for weeks the stalwart Patriots of the neighborhood had been saying "It's the only way left for us . . . we must fight." And her heart tightened with fear.

George Washington's return to Mount Vernon in late October was reassuring enough on the surface. He had even found time for shopping in the fine Philadelphia stores—a sword chain for himself, a cloak for his mother, and for his wife, a handsome pocketbook.

Smiling with pleasure at this surprise gift, Martha listened to her husband's report of the Continental Congress. Sitting in Carpenter's Hall, the delegates had adopted a Declaration of Rights. They had served notice on George the Third that the colonies would resist what they considered any unconstitutional acts.

The modest Colonel did not tell his wife how his soldierly bearing had impressed the other delegates. But his standing could not long be concealed. All over Virginia militia companies were being formed and drilled. And because of his experience in the French and Indian War, it was being said that in case of trouble George Washington would lead the Virginia troops.

One April afternoon in 1775, the Washingtons sat in their sitting room, conversing gravely with their Tory friend, Bryan Fairfax. The conflict had reached their own Virginia. Lord Dunmore had seized the powder belonging to Williamsburg. Patrick Henry had delivered a stirring war speech, ending with "Give me liberty, or give me death!"

With these words ringing in her ears, Martha put aside her knitting to greet a white-faced messenger just arrived on the gallop from Alexandria. He brought the news no one was prepared to hear: *Blood had been shed at Lexington and Concord, and the British driven back onto the Boston peninsula.*

Mutely the Washingtons and their guest stared at one another. "This is serious," said George sternly. "It may mean war."

Bryan turned pale. "You wouldn't fight against the mother country, George?"

"If I have to—" Washington answered firmly.

All three knew how weak, how unprepared, were the disunited colonies to do battle against England.

The second Continental Congress, called in May 1775, was one in name only. It might better have been called a War Council.

Martha would always remember the soft May morning when George, again a delegate, set out for Philadelphia. Busy with her housekeeping duties, she had seen her husband last at breakfast before he went up to his room to dress for the journey. When he came down the stairs, his heavy sword hitting the bare steps as he came, Martha met him in the front hall.

"George . . ." she gasped, and could say no more.

He was no longer in civilian clothes. *He was wearing to Philadelphia his uniform of a Virginia colonel.*

Always Martha would remember how her husband had come to her and taken her in his arms. "Yes, Patsy, there may be war," he said gently. "You're going to be brave, aren't you?"

She nodded. They walked to the door of Mount Vernon—the tall soldierly man, six feet three, and the small brown-haired woman—his arm around her. But Martha had to bury her face against his uniform and master her tears before she could look up with a smile and kiss him good-bye.

She was busy directing her women slaves at their weaving when George's first letter from Philadelphia reached her. Folding the message, Martha placed it in the pocket of her apron. Then, her heart pounding, she went to her room and stood beside the window to read it.

My Dearest,—I now sit down to write to you on a subject which fills me with concern, and this concern is greatly increased when I reflect upon the uneasiness I know it will give you. It has been determined in Congress that the whole army raised for the defense of the American cause shall be put under my Care, and that it is necessary for me to proceed immediately to Boston to take upon me the command of it. You may believe me, my dear Patsy, when I assure you, that, so far from seeking this appointment, I have used every endeavor in my power to avoid it, not only from my unwillingness to part with you and the family, but from a consciousness of its being a trust too great for my capacity, and that I should enjoy more real happiness in one month with you at home than I have the most distant prospect of finding abroad, if my stay were to be seven times seven years. But as it has been a kind of destiny that has thrown me upon this service, I shall hope that my undertaking is designed to answer some good purpose. You might and I suppose did perceive that I was apprehensive I could not avoid this appointment, as I did not pretend to intimate when I should return. That was the case. It was utterly out of my power to refuse this appointment without exposing my character to such censures as would have reflected dishonor upon myself and given pain to my friends. This, I am sure, could not, and ought not to be pleasing to you, and must have lessened me considerably in my own esteem. I shall rely, therefore, confidently on that Providence which has heretofore preserved me, not doubting but that I shall return safe to you in the fall. I shall feel no pain from the toil or the danger of the Campaign; my unhappiness will flow from the uneasiness you will feel from being left alone. I therefore beg that you will summon your whole fortitude, and pass your time as agreeably as possible. Nothing will give me so much sincere satisfaction as to hear of it from your own pen."

Martha's world crashed around her as she read the message that George Washington had assumed command of all the colonial troops. The sacrifice was hers. In less than two years she had borne loss after loss. Patty, lost by death. Jacky, by marriage. And now her husband, lost to the Continental Army.

Yet, strangely, Martha Washington's face was radiant. The mood of George's letter, which for tenderness had never before been equaled by him, rested in her mind above the news it brought. Remembering his cold, stiff note written during their engagement, happy tears rushed to her eyes.

"I should enjoy more real happiness in one month with you at home than I have the most distant prospect of finding abroad, if my stay were to be seven times seven years. . . ." Martha repeated the words, and her heart flooded with joy.

Chapter Eight   "Lady Washington"

THE BITTER SUMMER OF 1775 FADING INTO FALL BROUGHT Martha no promise of George Washington's return to Mount Vernon.

For a time after her husband's departure she found comfort in the assurance in his letter "not doubting that I shall return safe to you in the fall. . . ."

But as the October chill turned the maples to red and gold, that happy reunion seemed less and less a possibility. The army at Cambridge was holding the British imprisoned in Boston; and General Washington, commander of the Continental Army, as the American forces were called, was absorbed—heart, brain and body—in the struggle for freedom.

At Mount Vernon, Martha waited impatiently for news from Cambridge. Her plea that she be permitted to join her husband at camp had been firmly rejected. To stay at home and "pass the time agreeably" was George Washington's idea of the proper war-time status of a Virginia lady.

Staying at home was pleasant enough, for Martha loved Mount Vernon, and this year, with her world rocking under the impact of war, it had never seemed lovelier or more peaceful. But "the passing of time" under new and painful circumstances, was far from agreeable. Martha Washington had never been more lonely in her life.

Her eyes were sad, her cheeks pale, one October day as she sat at her desk writing to George. If he would only let her come to camp! She shut her eyes to keep back the tears. A wife's place was at her husband's side, even in war time. If she wrote him more urgently, would he change his mind?

She had begun her letter when into the room rushed Lund Washington, a distant cousin of George's, who had come to Mount Vernon as estate manager during his absence.

Lund! Of course, he could run the plantation without her. She was not even *needed* at Mount Vernon. But why was his face so white? And what was he saying? *Danger* . . . how could she, Mistress Washington, be in danger? And in her own home, too, where George had thought her so safe.

"You must leave Mount Vernon at once, Patsy," Lund kept repeating. "The British are coming!"

Martha rose to her feet, spilling ink over her desk. "Lund, have you lost your mind? What do you mean?"

"Lord Dunmore is coming up the Potomac with gunboats. Because Mount Vernon belongs to the leader of the American forces, the British intend to burn it. And because you're George Washington's wife, they're eager to capture you!"

For the life of her, Martha could not take this threat seriously. True, since his attempt to disarm the colonists by seizing their powder at Williamsburg, Lord Dunmore had been regarded as a dangerous enemy. But remembering the dull statesman with whom she had so often played cards, Martha wanted to laugh. She could not be afraid of him. Nor of "Montague's boiled crabs," as the colonists called the redcoats. It was too absurd, and she told Lund Washington so. Was he joking?

No, Lund was not joking. He had heard the report in Loudoun county, where the people, alarmed, wished to send a guard of soldiers to conduct Mistress Washington inland to Berkeley.

"You see, Patsy, you must leave at once," he warned. "Get as far back from the river as possible. Hide there, where the British cannot find you. . . ."

Little Mrs. Washington drew herself up to her full height. "Run away from my home? Never!"

In her husband's absence, Martha had been lonely, but never afraid. Nor was she afraid now. No doubt Lord Dunmore, the pompous fool, had begun raiding expeditions up Chesapeake Bay. But that did not prove he would dare to harm her. Lord Dunmore would not presume to come to Mount Vernon in any role other than that of an invited guest!

It was not until a messenger arrived with a note from Martha's neighbor, George Mason of Gunston Hall, begging her to flee from the British almost at her door, that she agreed to leave her home.

At that, she was away less than forty-eight hours. A brief carriage ride back country, a night's sleep in a safe home, and Martha's curiosity began to temper her anxiety. What was going on at Mount Vernon? Had Lord Dunmore actually arrived? She had to know.

Summoning her coach, Mistress Washington gave orders to drive back to the plantation on the Potomac. Of course, she promised her host she would use caution. Of course, she would return if the home situation proved serious.

But Martha did not return. The alarm at Mount Vernon had subsided before she reached there, as did others later. And so little did she think of the Dunmore scare that she did not even write of it to her husband.

Lund, however, related the facts to George Washington. And George Mason wrote to his friend:

"Dunmore has come and gone and left us untouched except for some alarm. I sent my family back in the country, and advised Mrs. Washington to do likewise. At first, she said 'No, I will not desert my post,' but finally did so with reluctance, rode only a few miles, and, plucky little woman she is, stayed away only one night."

The husband of "the plucky little woman" read this note with mixed emotions—admiration for her bravery and irritation at her failure to protect herself. Yet her behavior innocently succeeded where her carefully worded pleas had failed. George decided his wife would be safer at his side, and wrote her to join him in Cambridge.

His letter found Martha visiting her sister, Nancy Bassett, in New Kent. In company with the young John Custises, a happy family gathering was enjoying a wild turkey dinner when the "invitation," as Martha called George's decision that she might go to Cambridge, arrived. She was jubilant. At once she began to lay plans for the journey north, as did Jack and Eleanor, who would not dream of allowing their Mama to travel so far alone.

Martha was as happy as a bride. The trip would be long and uncomfortable, but the "plucky little woman" was no more afraid of the inconveniences of travel than of Lord Dunmore. At the end there would be the tall, commanding figure of her "Old Man," as she called her husband. She could not leave soon enough.

The morning of her departure, Colonel Bassett drew Martha aside. "I hate to tell you, Patsy," he said kindly, "but you may run into trouble on this journey. There are nasty rumors about—that you're . . . a *Tory*."

Martha drew back stiffly. "*A Tory!* How could I be—with George in command of the American forces?"

"They don't doubt George's loyalty, but yours. Look at this gossip the British are circulating about you—that you've left your husband because of his treason against the Crown!"

With trembling fingers, Martha took the newspaper clipping her brother-in-law handed her:

"Mr. Washington, we hear, is married to a very amiable lady, but it is said that Mrs. Washington, being a warm loyalist, has separated from her husband since the commencement of the present troubles, and lives, very much respected, in the city of New York."

Face scarlet, Martha tore the paper into shreds. They might attack her loyalty to the cause of the colonists, and she would deny it, coolly and objectively, but to attack her *marriage*—

"You see, Patsy. Do you think it wise now to undertake this trip?" asked Burwell Bassett in a worried voice.

"Now more than ever!" Martha answered, firmly. "I shall join George in camp, if for no other reason than to disprove such lies."

Immediately Mrs. Washington ordered her trunks loaded onto the baggage wagon. Then she, Eleanor and Jack, climbed into the coach. The Bassett family waved good-bye. And as the carriage rolled off on its long journey to Cambridge, Martha settled back, ready to face whatever awaited her.

Ahead lay a life very different from the sheltered existence she had known. With George Washington's acceptance of the command of the Continental Army, his wife had become a public figure. Every move she made, everything she did and did not do, was held up to criticism by those all too eager to find fault with her.

As the coach swept northward through the towns of Mary-

land and Pennsylvania, curious people stood in their door-
ways to catch a glimpse of Mistress Washington. There were
cries of "Tory! Traitor!"—cries bitter enough to tear the
heart of a woman less prepared for them than the brave little
lady in the carriage.

But with only a few hours' warning, Martha's tact and
good sense had made her equal to the situation. No matter
how cold and tired she was, she smiled at the jeering people
and waved her handkerchief. She persuaded Jack and Eleanor
to smile, too, although Jack, furious at the insult to his mother,
was in a mood to scowl blackly.

"Tell everyone that it is Mrs. Washington who rides to
join the General," Martha instructed her coachmen. "Her
son and daughter-in-law accompany her."

Then with utmost composure, she faced the window and
smiled. As the coach trundled by they caught a glimpse of
her, these worried men and women of the colonies, and what
they saw surprised them. Here was no haughty English
beauty in silks and satins, but a pleasant-faced woman, apple-
cheeked and smiling, wearing the kind of clothes they, too,
had learned to wear—stout homespun. Her bonnet was plain,
her hair unpowdered. Her children, also, were quietly dressed,
sensible-looking young people.

So this was the family of the new commander! After the
carriage had passed, the cry of "Traitor" changed to more
friendly talk.

Neither Martha nor her children had ever been north of
Alexandria. They knew nothing of the distance or of the
roads, muddy and furrowed now in November. But George
Washington, furiously busy with the building of fortifications
around Boston to hem in the British, took time to map
precisely the route his wife should take, and his thoughts were

constantly with her.

The Tories, loyalists of the Crown, were as numerous in Philadelphia as the Whigs, or supporters of the Continental Congress. Because of this divided state of feeling, few ladies ventured to call on Martha Washington when she arrived.

The Whig element, however, wishing to honor the wife of their commander, announced plans for a ball at the New Tavern. And a social storm broke over the head of the innocent Mrs. Washington. Many, even in the Whig Party, thought it bad taste to entertain elaborately at such a critical time, when Congress had asked people to abstain from "vain amusements."

A committee called on "Lady Washington," as they addressed Martha (here her title of the Revolution is used for the first time), and begged her to discourage the ball by refusing to attend.

"The desires of your committee are agreeable to my own sentiments," Lady Washington told the gentlemen sweetly, but not without some regret.

No one enjoyed a ball more than Martha Washington, and with feelings hurt by the behavior of the crowds on her journey north, it would have been pleasant to tell George that in Philadelphia, at least, his wife and her children had been politely received.

But she saw that to attend the ball would bring on a crisis that might turn the people against their new leader. So putting aside her own wishes, Mistress Washington let it be known that she would not attend the ball. Plans for it were dropped. And the Washington coach left Philadelphia a few days later with an escort of soldiers.

So divided was the feeling between the Loyalists and Patriots in New York that George Washington warned his wife to come north "by all means, avoiding New York." Prudent Martha crossed the Hudson at King's Ferry, forty miles up the river. And on December eleventh, two weeks after leaving Philadelphia, she reached Cambridge.

Due to bad roads and winter weather, no one could predict the time of Mrs. Washington's arrival. For days one of the General's aides had been waiting at an inn on the road she would travel, to watch for her carriage and guide her to headquarters. But somehow the weather-beaten coach and tired horses slipped past unseen. On a bleak December day, Martha made her entrance into Cambridge, unescorted.

She did not remain unwelcomed long. Seeing her alight from the carriage, Jack Custis on one side and Eleanor on the other, George Washington, his dignity forgotten for once, rushed to her side and clasped her in his arms. And Martha returned her husband's embrace until her cheeks were crimson, her bonnet askew.

Everyone in the camp wanted to meet Mistress Washington. This devoted wife, who had braved the perils of a thousand-mile journey in winter to join her husband in a camp on the outskirts of a city filled with the enemy, was indeed a heroine!

But writing to a Virginia friend, Martha described her trip with typical modesty:

"—I arrived hear safe . . . I dont dout but you have seen the Figuer our arrivel made in the Philadelphia paper—and I left it in as great pomp as if I had been a very great some body— Some days we have a number of shells from Boston and Bunkers Hill, but it does not seem to surprise any one but me; I confess I shuder every time I hear the sound of a gun . . . to me that never see any thing of war, the preparations are very terable indeed, but I endevor to keep my fears to my self as well as I can."

As she settled herself at her husband's headquarters in the Vassall house, Mrs. Washington looked over the place which would later become the home of the poet, Henry Wadsworth Longfellow.

It was a large house, with a wide hall and spacious rooms; the one to the right of the front door was the General's office, with his staff quarters opening behind it. On the left were large parlors, the front windows overlooking a lawn planted with young elm trees.

A comfortable headquarters, and yet not a happy one. Sensitive to her environment, Martha saw that all was not well. George had aged many years from the ruddy country squire who had ridden away from Mount Vernon, seven short months before. For the first time, his wife, eight months older than he, felt herself the younger.

What was worrying General Washington?

Awaiting the right moment, Martha asked him one morning as they sat at breakfast.

To her surprise, his usually slow speech poured forth in a flood. Under the veil of military glory, George Washington was a very worried man. Authorized by Congress to attack the British at once, he found it impossible. "How can I, unless my men reënlist?" he asked, desperation in his voice. *"Patsy, I haven't the men."*

Instead of reënlistments, there had been constant cases of desertion. At this critical time, hundreds of soldiers, dissatisfied with their pay, were leaving the thin ranks of the Patriot army, giving the cowardly excuse that their term of enlistment had expired.

The winter was passing, and by spring the British would receive reinforcements from England. Now was the time for the Americans to attack.

But how could they? The morale of the army was low; the orderly books were filled with trials of privates who had knocked their officers down and pulled them off their horses. Had the lack of discipline come about because the soldiers were without uniforms? The crowd of thin, hungry farmers and clerks were still in the scarecrow garments they had worn away to war.

He had done what he could, George Washington told his wife. He had written Congress, begging for equipment, at least for uniforms, to give his motley ranks the feeling of union that a uniform gives. But Congress had no money. The colonies refused to allow themselves to be taxed.

Martha listened, her heart sad. It was not fair that George should add army morale problems to his military responsibilities. But what could she do to help him? Her eyes strayed across the hall to the parlors. Suddenly she knew—

Rising, she came around the table to where he sat, and laid her hand on his broad shoulder. "If you want your men to reënlist, Papa, you'll have to lift their spirits by inviting them to some gay parties. Fortunately, we've got this large house, just the place for a ball—"

"A ball!" George looked up in amazement. "Patsy, we're at war. We can't be making merry."

"You want your men to reënlist, don't you? Then give them a good time—say a Twelfth-Night party."

Washington shook his head. "Patsy, I'm afraid I must refuse you. A dance would take the men's minds off their task."

"Fiddlesticks, Papa! A little amusement would give them

strength . . ." She leaned down and placed her cheek against his. "Let's give a dance on Twelfth Night! Not only for the officers, but the men, too . . . Jack and Nelly will help us. Please, dear, it's our wedding anniversary."

His eyes softened. Sixteen years since that January day at the White House when the girlish figure in satin and pearls had stood beside him to take her vows as his wife. And a good wife she had been. His arm went around her waist. How could he refuse her?

The Washingtons and the young John Custises celebrated Twelfth Night with a dance. Eleanor wore a simple white gauze; Martha a cerise petticoat under a dress of cream damask—a costume ordered long ago from London and thrice re-made since the Non-Importation Act. It was the only evening gown in her Cambridge wardrobe—far too simple for the wife of the General, some of the ladies whispered behind their fans. The war raged about them, they were making their own sacrifices. But woman-like, they had hoped to feast their eyes on Lady Washington's rich garments.

Aside from this disappointment to a few, the Twelfth-Night party, and the Washingtons' other parties that followed, were a great success. It was noticed, too, that with the coming of the General's wife to camp, an improvement occurred in the morale of the troops. There were no smart uniforms. Yet the "rebel rabble," as the trim redcoats called the ragged Americans, marched past headquarters singing *Yankee Doodle* . . . the tune the soldiers of the King had hurled at them in contempt.

> "Yankee Doodle, keep it up,
> Yankee Doodle dandy;
> Mind the music and the step,
> And with the girls be handy. . . ."

MOUNT VERNON MANSION *(The River Front)*

WEST FRONT OF MOUNT VERNON MANSION
*(Taken from the Bowling Green within the Serpentine Drive.
Showing the Colonnades, the Lodgings for White Servants on the
left, and the Kitchen and Servants' Hall on the right. The Sundial
stands in the centre of the Circle)*

The troops were still whistling *Yankee Doodle* when it came time for reënlistment. The gay tune had become the battle song of the Revolution. General Washington made an appeal to the militia of Massachusetts and New Hampshire to take the places of the troops which had deserted, and to everyone's relief, it was well responded to. The regiments were finally filled.

There was yet another crisis at Cambridge; one which the harassed General admitted to his wife perplexed him "more than the siege of Boston." In Washington's staff, there were jealousies, petty but dangerous. Questions of social etiquette, quarrels over dinner invitations to headquarters; all these came to George Washington for solution. Sometimes after a day of hazardous field maneuvers, he had to go back to his office, tired and hungry, to struggle with these bickerings.

Happy to be of help, Mrs. Washington stepped into the situation and took charge. She was well prepared for her task. As would always be the case when she was at camp, the house of the commander became another Mount Vernon —a gathering place for his young officers and their wives, with whom Lady Washington became instantly popular.

Surrounded by new friends, Martha's thoughts were seldom far m her beloved family in Virginia. Her brother William of the Royal Navy was "suddenly drowned" on January 22, 1776; and now she worried when she did not hear from her people. She wrote her sister, Nancy:

"—I am really very uneasy at not hearing from you and have made all the excuses for you that I can think of, but it will not doe much longer, if I doe not get a letter by this night's post, I shall think myself quite forgot by all my Friends."

George was also writing letters. Coming into his office one morning, Martha found him at his desk, finishing a letter to George William Fairfax in England.

The Atlantic Ocean separated the Fairfaxes and the Washingtons, but the war was an even greater barrier. When would Sally and George William return to America? Certainly not until peace was declared. Colonel Fairfax had had smallpox on going to England. His illness had continued until the war made his return impossible. And could he come back now, his Tory convictions would not make living in America very agreeable.

Knowing this, the Fairfaxes had written George Washington to continue to look after Belvoir for them, and to auction off some of their furniture; for Sally expected to bring back more elegant pieces from London. Also he was to have the Fairfax initials put on their pew at Pohick church.

Martha stifled a sigh, as she turned away from George's desk. Some day the war would end, then the Fairfaxes would return, and the intimacy between Mount Vernon and Belvoir resumed. With Sally next door at Belvoir, could she ever be really happy?

Meanwhile, these letters would continue to pass to and fro across the ocean, keeping the friendship warm. The Washingtons had had a message from Sally—pages of witty London gossip in her tall, artistic handwriting—telling them how "her Fairfax" would never lose his interest in Virginia and was doing all he could to help American prisoners in London.

All through this cold winter of 1775-6, while the siege of Boston continued, alarming rumors were coming from Mount Vernon; rumors which made George glad that Martha was by his side. Lund Washington wrote that Lord Dunmore was still raiding the shores of Chesapeake Bay:

"Plantations are being closed. Women and children have fled to the interior, and are stowing themselves in every hut they can find, out of reach of the enemy's cannon. . . . I am packing up your china and glass in barrels, and other things into trunks, and I shall be able at the shortest notice to remove them out of the way. . . . Everybody tells me, they would come and defend your property so long as they have life."

During these troubled times, George had moved his mother, against her will, from her farm on the Rappahannock to a white cottage near Betty Lewis in Fredericksburg. Each morning Mary Washington walked up the box-bordered walk to see her daughter at Millbank. Each afternoon she rode out in her chaise, driven by "old Stephen," to her farm across the Rappahannock, which she still managed.

Mary Washington needed to keep her mind occupied these days. Again the country was at war. Again George's life was in danger. And her opposition to her son's fighting *against* the English Crown was as great as her opposition had been to his fighting *for* the Crown in the French and Indian War.

The Fielding Lewises, on the other hand, were heart and soul in sympathy with the Revolution. At Millbank, now completed, Betty had a room where she and her women friends made cartridges. Not strong enough to go to war, Colonel Lewis was fitting out three regiments at his own expense, and building a ship, the *Dragon*, for the Virginia Navy. He had also opened a factory in Fredericksburg to make small arms and ammunition for the Continental Army.

So stood the affairs of the Washingtons at home. In Boston, they were moving rapidly to a climax. Aided by the arrival of Colonel Knox with reinforcements from Lake Champlain, General Washington decided to attack the British. During the night of March 17, 1776, he captured Dorchester Heights, a position which commanded the town, and from which his cannons could bombard every enemy ship in Boston harbor.

At headquarters, Martha waited anxiously for news of the conflict. Sir William Howe knew he was check-mated. What would he do next?

One can appreciate her joy when word came that the British commander would evacuate Boston, provided the Americans did not molest him. As the last English soldier was rowed out to the packed transports, to sail away with two thousand fugitive Loyalists to Halifax, the Continental Army, with General Washington at its head, marched in triumph into the deserted city.

That was the night when a small woman in a brown home-spun gown stood beside her soldier-husband and gave thanks for a military miracle. The siege of Boston was over! New York would be the next objective of the British, General Washington was sure, but for a night there was time for cele-bration and thanksgiving.

With a lull in the fighting, Martha could turn her thoughts to other things. Eleanor Custis's "delicate health," much dis-cussed in Cambridge that winter, gave Mrs. Washington no cause for worry. The approaching birth of her first grand-child was as yet a happy family secret. Jack and Eleanor would return to their Virginia home for the great event anticipated in August, at which time Jack, just come of age, would inherit the Custis fortune and settle down as a country squire at Abingdon.

George Washington's guardianship was ended. And the fidelity of the trust placed in him is shown by the fact that during the seventeen years of his administration he had doubled the value of his stepson's inheritance. John Parke Custis found himself the richest young man in Virginia.

Mrs. Washington and Eleanor, who had spent some of the most anxious hours of the late winter in knitting and stitching a layette for the expected heir (Martha prayed for a boy as bonny and strong as her Jacky had been), now began to pack for the journey south. General Washington had gone to New York City with his troops. His wife and her children were remaining in Cambridge until spring thaws made the roads passable.

Before their departure in April, they were kept busy with a stream of visitors, coming to bid kindly, gracious Martha Washington good-bye. Nor were the guests all of high estate. The poor came, too. There was, in fact, the first of the American Negro poets, Phillis Wheatley, who brought a poem she had written in praise of George Washington, and left proudly bearing a gift from the General's wife.

There were many gifts for the Washingtons crowding the trunks that accompanied them when their coach departed for New York. Jack Custis rode along holding a weeping-willow twig, given him by an English officer who had brought the slip from Pope's villa at Twickenham, intending to plant it on the confiscated lands he would get when the rebels were defeated. With the evacuation of Boston, the Englishman saw his mistake. Giving up all idea of settling in America, he presented the willow twig to young Custis, who carried it back to Abingdon, where it would become the ancestor of all weeping-willows in the United States.

Traveling by way of Hartford and New Haven, Martha and her children reached New York. At the General's headquarters, a brick house on Pearl Street, Martha joined her husband, while Jack and Eleanor continued on to Virginia.

It was a panicky New York in which Martha Washington found herself. There was smallpox among the troops. And many civilians were being inoculated in fear of catching the disease. Although she dreaded it, Martha decided to undergo the ordeal. She was inoculated by Doctor John Morgan, the head of the army hospital, before she accompanied George to Philadelphia, when he went there in May to attend the Continental Congress.

While her husband attended the meetings that drafted the Declaration of Independence, Martha awaited the outcome of the inoculation. He wrote to his brother, John Augustine:

"Mrs. Washington will, I expect, have the smallpox favorably. This is the 13th day and she has few pustules. She would have written to my sister, but thought it prudent not to do so, notwithstanding there could be but little danger of conveying the infection in this manner."

John Hancock, president of the Congress, had invited the Washingtons to stay with him. "Mrs. Hancock will esteem it to have Mrs. Washington take the smallpox in her house." But Martha had the tact not to put the hospitality of Dorothy Hancock, a young bride, to so severe a test. The Washingtons went to an inn, where Martha could be ill, if ill she had to be, in private.

Fortunately, she had "the smallpox favorably," to quote her husband. When in June the General was forced to return to New York to face Sir William Howe's army, he was able to leave his wife out of danger and eager to be off to Mount Vernon.

But her departure was delayed. Lord Dunmore was making one more attempt to invade the Virginia coast. It was said that the house he most desired to burn was Mount Vernon, the prisoner he would most cherish, Martha Washington.

By the time he was routed by the Prince William militia

and driven off for good, there were other things on Martha's mind. News had come of the poison plot against Washington's life in New York, concocted by ex-Governor Tryon, mayor of the city.

The plot failed. But it brought home to Martha the fact that George's life was constantly in danger. And frantic with worry, sick and weary of war, she wrote from Philadelphia to her sister, Nancy:

"I am still in this town and no prospect of leaving it. The General is at New York; he is well and wrote me yesterday, and informed me that Lord Dunmore, with part of his fleet was come to General Howe, at Staten Island; that another division of Hessians, is expected before they think the regulars will begin their attack on us.

"I doe, my dear sister, most religiously wish there was an end to the War that we might have the pleasure of meeting again. My duty to very dear mama, and tell her I am well. I don't hear from you so often as I used to do at Cambridge. I had the pleasure to hear by Colonel Aylett, (Betty's husband) that you were well, and should have been glad to have had a line from you, by him. I hope Mr. Bassett has got the better of his cough. Please to present love to him, my dear Fanny (Nancy's daughter) and the boy, and accept the same yourself."

Martha reached home in August and found a new happiness which served to curb her worry over the fate of George Washington and her country. *She was a grandmother.* A daughter, Elizabeth Parke, had been born to Eleanor Custis. Martha's elation knew no bounds. She had hoped for a boy, but one touch of the curling fingers of baby Eliza, and the wish for a male heir was forgotten. The baby was adorable. Eleanor was an admirable mother and wife. And Jack was talking of following his stepfather's example by becoming a member of the Virginia Assembly.

Now Eleanor and baby Eliza were at Mount Vernon for longer and longer visits; Jack, too, when his political career permitted it. That this companionship for his wife had been arranged by the ever-thoughtful George Washington is shown by the letter he wrote to his stepson when he assumed command of the army:

"My concern upon this occasion is, the thought of leaving your mother. It is unnecessary for me to say that I am always pleased with yours and Nelly's abidance at Mount Vernon, much less upon this occasion, when I think it absolutely necessary for the peace of your mother; a consideration which I have no doubt will have weight with you both, and require no arguments to enforce."

To Burwell Bassett, he wrote:

"I must entreat you and Mrs. Bassett to visit at Mt. Vernon, as also my wife's other friends. I wish you to take her down, as I have no expectation of returning till winter & feel great uneasiness at her lonesome situation."

It was hard work for Martha to refrain from imploring: "Let me be with you, George! You're the one I want . . . these others, kind though they be, do not take your place."

Mount Vernon was the loveliest home in Virginia, Jack and Eleanor devoted, baby Eliza Martha's solace when life looked darkest, yet she was determined to follow George to his next encampment. Although she knitted and sewed from dawn until twilight, she never quite felt she was doing enough to help win the war. Sixteen spinning wheels under her supervision turned out material to clothe the ragged American troops. And as she worked and worried and waited, she followed every scrap of news that came from the front.

One courier brought good reports; the next, the story of a defeat. She heard of the battle of Long Island, the seizure of New York by the British, the disasters of Harlem Heights and White Plains. Martha tried to keep calm, as the Americans' fortunes ebbed and flowed, as Washington's army was driven in flight back across New Jersey to the Delaware River, and then on Christmas Eve he turned on the Hessians at Trenton—a victory soon followed by another at Princeton on January 3, 1777.

The British then gave up the chase and retired to spend the cold weather snugly in New York; Washington withdrew his battered army into winter encampment at Morristown, New Jersey. There was so much smallpox in the camp that even the churches had to be turned into hospitals.

When she heard of it, Martha wrote George, inquiring anxiously after his health. The months of worry and fighting had told on him. Word came to Mount Vernon that the commander was ill of an attack of quinsy, so sick that he feared he was dying and had asked General Greene to succeed him as leader.

Instead of crushing her, this news acted as a challenge to Martha Washington. She wrote her husband that if she did not hear at once of his recovery, she would leave for Morristown. "And if no carriage is available," she added, "I'll come on foot!"

True to her word, Martha went north. In Jack Custis's chariot, she reached Morristown in the middle of March. By that time George was well enough to go to Pluckamin, some distance from camp, to meet his wife.

A Mrs. Eliot, at whose house he waited, saw a carriage

stop at the door and a plainly-dressed little woman step out
of it. Sure that this could not be Lady Washington, and
believing it to be her maid, the General's hostess made no
move to greet the newcomer. What was her astonishment
then on seeing him rush out to the tiny stranger and take
her in his arms!

Martha and her husband had been separated for nine
months. Anxiously she looked up at him—tall, straight and
slender still at forty-five, without any of the stoutness of
middle age. Her brown eyes searched his handsome stern
face, his large nose, and firm mouth. They had been apart
for so long. Was everything all right with George? Had he
changed?

"Are you well, Patsy?" General Washington asked in his
direct way. "Was your journey comfortable?" Then the
blue eyes under his weary brows lighted up. "How are Blueskin and Ajax? Why, what's the matter?"

For Martha had begun to laugh, clinging to her big husband, hysterical with relief. The long months of their separation rolled away like a cloud. He had not changed a bit. He
was the same George, her "Old Man." For even as he in-
quired after her welfare, in the same breath he asked—far
more anxiously—about his horses back at Mount Vernon.

Wɪᴛʜ ᴛʜᴇ ᴀʀʀɪᴠᴀʟ ᴏꜰ ᴍᴀʀᴛʜᴀ ᴡᴀsʜɪɴɢᴛᴏɴ, ᴄᴏɴᴅɪᴛɪᴏɴs in camp changed with a speed that made the careworn General breathe a sigh of relief. Martha was alive to the needs of the cold, half-starved soldiers, ill from disease and homesick for their families. She knew about the necessity for fresh clothes and bedding, for medicine, for soap and water and brooms; the need of doctors and nurses and the touch of a friendly, feminine hand.

Within a week she had made her plans, and set them in motion. Barracks were scoured and fumigated. Sick wards were staffed by competent nurses, clean blankets provided, and the best food reserved for the ill and undernourished.

Mornings Martha spent in the rooms quarantined for smallpox cases. Was she immune from her inoculation? Probably, but Martha gave it little thought; she was fearless. She seemed to blossom under vicissitudes. Encountering his wife in a starched stuff coverall, head bound in a white cloth as she bustled through the hospital corridor, George Washington stopped to remonstrate, "Patsy, you shouldn't be here . . . you'll be ill."

Her head full of lists of linen bandages, orders for gruel and junket for the sick trays, Martha was too occupied to answer. But she patted her husband's arm as she trotted beside him down the hall.

"We need more orderlies here, George. Can you spare us three?" Then her expression changed. "Never mind. You've enough to do. I'll find them myself." At the door of the quarantine room, she smiled her good-bye.

"God bless you, Patsy, and thank you for coming to camp," he said. "You're what we all need."

The Washingtons lived that second winter of the war in the cramped Freeman Tavern at Morristown. There the first callers, curious ladies who had heard of Lady Washington's wealth and Virginia ancestry, were greeted by a squarely built, round-faced matron wearing a brown homespun gown, no jewels except her gold wedding ring and—"Would you believe it?" they whispered among themselves—"a checked apron."

Worse than that, she was knitting.

The ladies of Morristown, dressed in their made-over silks and hoarded jewels, gasped in surprise. Obviously Mrs. Washington was a lady, used to the ways of society. Yet after greeting them, she settled down in a chair and resumed her knitting. No servants were about. No refreshments—not even a biscuit and a glass of sherry—were served. There languished the flower of New Jersey society, without a stitch of work, and highly embarrassed, while the wife of the commander of the Continental Army made woolen stockings for the soldiers.

It cannot be said that Martha Washington's famous tact was in evidence that afternoon. Blame it on her absorption in the pitiable needs of the sick soldiers. Blame it on her contempt for the smug; well-fed ladies who sat so comfortably before her. At any rate, Martha did not hesitate to remind her callers how important it was that American women should realize that the country was at war. They should take their place, figuratively at least, in the battle line with the soldiers.

"Our break with England has cut us off from many of our necessities," she said briskly, finishing off the heel of a long, brown stocking. "We women must make ourselves independent. Or—" and her eyes swept the imported costumes of her visitors—"learn to do without the things we cannot make at home."

Red-faced and chastened, the ladies took their departure. Extravagantly-gowned, frivolous idlers—and in a time of great peril! That is what they were. . . . Lady Washington had as much as said so.

Talk spread around Morristown, and soon these ladies, as well as others, offered themselves for war work. Some were sincerely impressed by the General's wife and tried to copy her. Others—and these Martha was quick to spot and to deal with ruthlessly—were the shallow-minded gadabouts, with no real interest in the cause, who saw a chance to better their social position by claiming a place at Lady Washington's side.

There was no Red Cross in those days. The nearest things to it were the knitting and sewing groups formed by Martha Washington to make clothing for the ragged American soldiers and to roll bandages from cast-off linen. Petticoats and kerchiefs were pulled from orris-scented chests; table cloths and napkins piled up for boiling and fumigating and cutting into soft lengths of white stuff to staunch wounds.

Under patriotic Morristown women, canteens were organized where hot food was available, day and night. Of Mrs. Anna Kitchel, the wife of a farmer of Whippany, it was said that her soup kettle was boiling twenty-four hours a day to feed the hungry troops.

When the women grew to know Lady Washington better,

they ceased to be shamed by her magnificent energy. As in Cambridge, a circle formed around her, and despite the discouragement and hardship of the colonies' fight against England, life in camp was almost pleasant. There were small dinners, horseback rides and even dances. Twice a week, there was open house at headquarters where, according to an old diary: "The General's lady seemed in perfect felicity by the side of her 'Old Man,' as she was heard to call him."

April came to the Jersey hills. And with the spring of 1777, war began again. The British raided the shores of the Hudson River and Long Island Sound. The Americans broke camp and prepared to resist. And Martha Washington, aware that field duty offered no living quarters for the wife of the commander, returned to Mount Vernon.

That was her life throughout the eight bitter years of the Revolution. Summers at Mount Vernon, working and waiting for news from George. Winters in camp, sharing with him the hardships of army life.

Not once was she heard to complain of the poor food, insufficient heat, rough buildings and hard work. Instead Jacky and Eleanor Custis found it difficult to quell her impatience when summer drew to a close and the time came for the General's aide to journey down to Virginia to escort Lady Washington to headquarters.

There was always a hearty welcome for her. The arrival of the Washington chariot, bringing a plump little lady, usually dressed in brown, lifted the gloom that hung over the American forces during most of the war.

As for the traveler herself, one glance at the tall, granite-faced General in buff and blue, scanning the horizon for the approach of the carriage, and memories of the lonely days at Mount Vernon were instantly erased. She was with

George once more. And that meant home.

The summer of 1777 there were two grandchildren at Mount Vernon—Eliza, bright-eyed and active, and a new baby to fondle, this time her namesake, Martha Custis, another "Patsy." If George could only see them, Mistress Washington thought, bringing out the silver mugs and rattles that her own babies had played with long ago.

Yet even as Martha taught Eliza her first steps, leading her by her rose-leaf fingers, and rocked sweet baby Patsy to sleep in her arms, her thoughts were on the battlefield with her husband. Would there be a letter today—tomorrow?

The war was progressing. There was news of the British invasion of America from Canada under "Gentlemen Johnny" Burgoyne. Then on October 17, 1777, Burgoyne was defeated by the Americans at Saratoga. Sir William Howe, the British Commander in New York, who had been expected up the Hudson to meet Burgoyne, thus separating New England from the middle colonies, had gone off on his own to capture Philadelphia.

And George Washington's troops were defending that city.

Martha Washington was frantic with worry. Eliza, climbing on her lap to bid her good night, was kissed absentmindedly and hustled off to bed. Patsy cried, unheeded by her grandmother. News when it came was bad. Howe had sailed up Chesapeake Bay, defeated the Americans at Brandywine Creek, and again at Germantown. When the British took Philadelphia, Martha despaired.

Where was George? Dead? A prisoner?

Her head swam with fear, and she managed only with great effort to carry on through those autumn days, so golden on the banks of the Potomac, and so bleak in her heart. Philadelphia was in the hands of the British. Congress had fled.

Anxiety possessed the habitually stable Mrs. Washington. Jacky and Eleanor tried to comfort her. The children were adorable. But Martha shut herself in her room and wept.

Then in November a message came. General Washington was safe and well. He was taking his men into winter headquarters at Whitemarsh, fourteen miles north of Philadelphia.

Rereading the dispatch as she sat at breakfast with Jack and Eleanor, Martha's cheeks glowed with happiness. She saw between the lines an answer to the question uppermost in her mind—soon she would be with her George!

This winter his headquarters would be the Elmar House. Surely so large a mansion could accommodate the wife of the General. Long before the "invitation" came, Martha had packed her trunks and was ready for the journey.

It was a trying one. The General's wife made her entrance at Whitemarsh in a rude sleigh belonging to an innkeeper at a ford of the Brandywine Creek, where her own carriage had sunk to the hub in a snowdrift. She left it without a qualm and continued on in the borrowed vehicle. Numb with cold and exhaustion, she nonetheless greeted her husband with a smile. And he—well, he was so glad to see his "dear Patsy" again that he picked her up and carried her across the threshold of the Elmar House as though she were a little girl.

The tattered American army encamped on the hills north of the village had never had greater need of Lady Washington's help. Its men had fought fierce battles a short while before. And there were the same long rows of ill and wounded, the same need for food and surgical instruments and medicine as at Morristown.

This was the scene of misery Martha saw on her first day at camp—Mistress Washington who might have been living comfortably at Mount Vernon, surrounded by her loving family. And with all the vigor of her superb health and spirits she plunged in to do what she could to help, aided by jolly, plump Lucy Knox, wife of the equally plump general of artillery, Henry Knox, the only other officer's lady at White-marsh.

Their work was not to be carried on that winter from the Elmar Mansion. The night of Martha's arrival, the British marched out from Philadelphia and attacked the Americans. Warned in advance, they stood their ground and little harm was done. But the audacity of the raid worried General Washington. Whitemarsh was too near the enemy to be a safe winter quarters. He would have to withdraw his troops. And Martha—why had he ever let her leave Mount Vernon? —must return home or move with the army on its wintry march to Valley Forge.

"Of course, I'm going with you, Papa," announced Mrs. Washington, when she heard his plans. In the rush of departure, there was no further talk of her returning home.

A heavy snow was falling as they set out on the long, cold journey, George riding his big bay horse, Martha behind him on a pillion. Ahead, the bareheaded, ragged troops plodded through the snow. Because of lack of shoes and stockings, many were barefoot. Their path could be traced over the frozen ground by the blood from their bruised and cut feet.

Ragged, footsore men ceased to be an unusual sight as the Washingtons passed along the line of march. Blowing on their cold hands, their despairing faces bowed against the sleet, long muskets slipping from gaunt shoulders—Martha could not look at the suffering men. She heard George groan, "Poor fellows!" Yet, frightful as were the hardships of this march, their fate at Valley Forge would be worse. There were no blankets for the soldiers, no straw, perhaps no meat, no bread.

Tears froze on Martha's cold cheeks. "George, can't you do something . . ." she begged. "Get them shoes, at least."

"If I only could, Patsy," he answered bitterly.

Nineteen long miles and the Washingtons reached Valley Forge. It was a dreary hollow, containing a few houses huddled around an iron forge and along a frozen creek emptying into the Schuylkill River.

On the bleak hillsides, in an icy wind that left their hands raw and bleeding, General Washington set his ragged men to work building log huts in which to house themselves. Day and night, they worked. And through it all, their commander remained beside them, eating and living in a tent, just as they did.

Only when the last hut was finished would George Washington move into a small stone house where Martha had been living with the family of Isaac Potts, a Quaker preacher.

The house was frightfully crowded and uncomfortable. The Washingtons could be spared only two rooms on the ground floor. The rest of the cottage continued to be occupied by the Potts family. One room George used as an office; the other was their bedroom. But like a good soldier's wife, Martha's thoughts were on the progress of the war her husband was fighting, not on the inconveniences of her surroundings.

These days at Valley Forge—one of the most bitter periods of George Washington's life, when he was attempting to keep together an army, wretchedly armed and clothed and paid, forgotten by a people whom they were trying to protect—were not the "lost days" of her life Martha was to refer to later. They were too full of the work she loved to do—

the unselfish care of others. And it was her sincere and un-tiring personal service for the soldiers that caused them to shout when the sweet face of their General's wife appeared before them, "God bless Lady Washington!"

Never was a woman so busy as was Martha Washington at Valley Forge. The camp was full of smallpox and dysen-tery. There was little food, mostly salt beef and pork. Any day the small, round figure of the General's wife, dressed in brown homespun, might be seen, basket in hand, going among the huts, seeking the most needy invalids, and giving them what fresh food she had.

In a dark, miserable room, she found a dying sergeant and his frightened young wife. Death was no novelty to Mrs. Washington. Not a day passed that she did not close the eyes of some soldier, cover him decently, and say a word to the weeping relatives. But this young sergeant touched her deeply. The frail, dark-eyed girl beside his straw pallet reminded her of Patty.

Martha Washington tried to comfort the young wife. She attempted to feed the sick man the beef broth she had herself prepared, but he was too weak to swallow; his eyes were glazing over. Putting aside the cup, she knelt on the straw where he lay and prayed for his recovery. When she rose, the General's wife was weeping.

She cried so much these days . . . whenever she thought of her darling sister Nancy, who had died in December at only thirty-eight, leaving broken-hearted Colonel Bassett and a large family of children. Pretty blond Nancy! It seemed only yesterday that she had sat before the tutor, Thomas Leonard, with her Horn Book. Martha had loved her so. Her other sister, Betty, a young widow now, John Ayette having died of pleurisy a year before, could never take

Nancy's place in Martha's affections.

But she kept her personal sorrows to herself. And no matter how sore her heart was, Mistress Washington always managed to present a smiling face to her harassed husband when they met for dinner.

A log dining room had been built onto the Potts house, and here the Washingtons entertained twice a week George's "family," as he called his staff officers and their wives.

There was a party on George's birthday, February 22nd (the first recorded celebration). From his account book, we learn that the army band serenaded him and he gave them fifteen shillings.

Every morning, except Sunday, Martha invited in the wives of the officers to knit socks for the soldiers, to patch and make shirts for them from such material as could be found. Lucy Knox's pretty laugh rang out. She told a story or two. One could not be gloomy for long with Lucy around. Soon the knitting and sewing societies took the place of the balls and receptions of Cambridge.

In the long winter evenings, Martha encouraged the young men on Washington's staff to come in and call on the General. The entertainment was simple. No dancing or card playing. "Just conversation over a cup of coffee," to quote a French officer, "and singing. Every gentleman or lady who could sing was called upon in turn for a song."

A nineteen-year-old French nobleman, the Marquis de Lafayette, who had enlisted in the American army, was liked by both the Washingtons. George was flattered by the admiration in young Lafayette's eyes; Martha respected his modesty.

"I hesitate to show a Frenchman my ragged soldiers," Washington had said, when the Marquis came to camp.

"I am here, monsieur, to learn and not to teach," he had replied.

The Washingtons did not speak French; Lafayette's English was feeble. But they had an interpreter in their adjutant, Alexander Hamilton, who having been born in the West Indies, spoke the language fluently. And the enthusiastic young French nobleman greatly cheered the gloomy American camp.

The month of February was the hardest of all at Valley Forge. More than three thousand men were ill in their huts. Over a thousand had deserted to join the British. And three times as many would be gone by spring, unless they were paid.

Day after day George Washington sat at his desk, portfolio open before him, his jaw moving as though biting back the angry words he was writing. Martha, knitting by the window that looked out over the bleak hills, knew he was composing another of his vain pleas to Congress for money and food and clothing for his ragged, unpaid soldiers . . . telling Congress that spring was coming, and his men were unfit for service. How could they fight, naked and half-starved?

Martha's heart ached for her husband. To add to his troubles, he had been deeply hurt by the intrigue of his fellow officers. General Gates had played but a small part in the Battle of Saratoga, yet in a letter to Congress he had taken all the credit for Burgoyne's defeat. Now some of Gates's friends—a man named Conway, and others—were trying to have the command of the Continental Army taken from George Washington, who never won any victories, and given to Gates, the hero of Saratoga.

George is so sincere, thought Martha, turning to the window to hide her tears, so eager to do his best. Sensitive, too, and hurt by disloyalties. Certainly no one tried harder to be a leader.

Knowing these things about her husband, Martha Washington remained at his side. Quietly, but with warm assurance of her belief in him, she nursed him, fed him, cared for him. If ever a woman earned the right to share in her husband's triumphs in later life it was she, who bore with George Washington his troubles during that terrible winter at Valley Forge!

About this time, their old friend from Virginia, Bryan Fairfax, came to see the Washingtons; and George and Martha welcomed him warmly.

Since the outbreak of the Revolution, Bryan had been in trouble. A mild Tory, he had opposed the separation of the colonies from the mother country. A pacifist, he had refused to take up arms against the Crown. A few months earlier he had started for New York, some vague hope in his mind that he might bring about an end to the war by talking with the British. He had been arrested at Lancaster, Pennsylvania.

When General Washington heard this, he secured Bryan's release and allowed him to go ahead into the British lines on his word of honor not to give the enemy any helpful information.

But in New York Bryan found he could not conscientiously take the oath required by the English. And, giving up hope of settling the war, he was on his way back to Virginia to rejoin his family.

It was the first time that George Washington and Bryan Fairfax had met since the war began.

Martha's heart glowed as George strode up to his shamefaced neighbor. "Old friend . . ." he said, grasping his hand.

"There are ties between the Fairfaxes and the Washingtons too strong for even a war to break!"

Nor had George's friendship for the Fairfaxes in England wavered. Colonel Fairfax was a Tory, but a liberal one. There was no doubt that he loved Virginia. But ambitious Sally was determined to be Lady Fairfax, and only a staunch Englishwoman could become Her Ladyship! So there was no question of their returning to America.

And what had the Fairfax's loyalty cost them?

Their Virginia property had been confiscated. No longer would they receive any revenue from their American estates —Belvoir in Fairfax County, Shannondale in Frederick, and Piedmont in Loudoun.

It was all very sad, thought Martha. She pitied the Fairfaxes, but at the same time she could not help being pleased that their link with America was broken. With the Virginia property gone, there would be less reason for Sally's return to America after the war.

Spring came at last. The ice thawed in the frozen creek; the bitter winds subsided. The soldiers, too, were in better spirits. They had food to eat, because General Washington had scoured the countryside to bring in provisions. And they had a new German drillmaster, Baron von Steuben, a blue-eyed officer from the army of Frederick the Great, who had come to train them. Every morning Von Steuben had the troops out on the parade ground going through their maneuvers. Martha liked to stand at the window and watch them.

In May the Americans' spirits were further lifted. *A treaty had been signed with France.* Impressed by the victory at Saratoga, the French had joined the Americans and declared war on England. When the good news reached Valley Forge, the Marquis de Lafayette, overjoyed, seized General Washington and kissed him on both cheeks. At last, the struggling colonies had a friend!

When Lady Washington left Valley Forge that spring, the scene of the war had shifted to New York. Sir Henry Clinton, who had replaced General Howe as commander of the British forces, marched the English out of Philadelphia and started for New York. The Americans came after them. The battle of Monmouth was fought, but the enemy escaped. Washington then moved his army further into New Jersey and along the Hudson, where for the next three years he kept the British imprisoned in New York.

Meanwhile, Martha spent a quiet summer at Mount Vernon, enjoying the growing family at Abingdon. Under the watchful eye of his stepfather, who was never too busy to look after his family, Jack had been elected to the Virginia Assembly. But the rich young husband and father had not changed so very much from the lazy, pleasure-loving boy who had been too fond of hunting and fishing to study his lessons.

He began staying away from the sessions of the Assembly "out of disgust," so he said, which brought a sharp rebuke by letter from his stepfather.

Privately, George Washington thought Jack belonged in the army; the discipline might do a lot for such a gifted but unreliable young man. But young Custis did not wish to enlist. He had not liked school. He did not like politics, really. The demands irritated him.

Only his mother understood him, so Jacky muttered to himself as he crumpled one of the General's stern letters and threw it away. And now, as always, Martha stood ready to defend him. There was nothing irregular, so she wrote

GEORGE WASHINGTON
Painted on bed ticking at Valley Forge, by C. W. Peale

her husband, in the wish of a Virginia gentleman to remain with his family during war-time, to protect them, and manage his estate.

Martha longed to talk the matter over with George. Letters were unsatisfactory. If she could only explain to him! She was delighted when her "invitation" came to spend the winter at Middlebrook, New Jersey. Within three days, a small woman in a brown bonnet and cape was rocking along the rough roads in the Washington coach, eyes straight ahead, heart pounding—a woman who knew where the road led her, and was glad.

General Washington came to Philadelphia to meet her. They were honored at a ball at the City Tavern, with the French minister as one of the guests. Martha must have smiled, recalling the snub that city had given her at the beginning of the Revolution. Then she had been the wife of a traitor to his king. Now George was the ally of the King of France. And she was Lady Washington.

Headquarters at Middlebrook that winter were in the house of an Ephraim Berry; a two-story wooden dwelling, its upper floor unfinished. Anxious to give his wife comfortable accommodations, George Washington had engaged two carpenters to fix up a room for her private use in the uncompleted attic. .

One of the workmen told how Lady Washington arrived before the work was begun. She came into the room, a plump, pleasant woman, and said to the men, "I care for nothing but comfort here, and want you to fit me up a closet on one side, some shelves and hooks for hanging clothes on the other."

Every morning about eleven o'clock Mrs. Washington came upstairs with a glass of spirits for each of the workmen.

And after she and the General had dined, the men were called down to eat at the same table. They worked hard, nailing smooth boards over the rough floor, and stopping the holes in the walls.

"We tried to do something to please so nice a lady," one said.

On the fourth day, when Mrs. Washington mounted the stairs to inspect their work, they had made the shelves, put up the pegs in the wall, built the closet, and converted the rough garret into a comfortable room.

As she stood looking around, one of the men said, "Madam, we have tried to do our best. I hope we've suited you."

She smiled. "I am astonished. Your work would do credit to skilled workmen, and you're mere lads. I'm not only satisfied but highly pleased with what you've done for my comfort."

In February, the anniversary of the alliance with France was celebrated in the American camp with fireworks and dancing. Chubby, bowlegged General Knox and his artillery were hosts at a banquet and ball that followed the fireworks.

General Washington opened the ball by dancing the minuet with bright-faced Lucy Knox, one of his favorite partners. As a girl, the brunette Lucy Flucker had been a belle. Now she and her Henry, a former Boston bookseller, had grown as "round as their own mortars." But there was nothing heavy about Lucy's feet. And her mind was as agile as her steps.

We find no mention of Martha Washington having danced with her husband or any other gentleman at these "pretty frisks." Forty-eight and twice a grandmother, Martha thought herself too dignified for even the minuet, although George could dance for over three hours without sitting down, as he did with Mrs. Greene.

With General Greene, who was asthmatic, Mistress Washington sat out the dances, while the fiddles squeaked and Lucy Knox's light laughter filled the air. The Greenes had named their new baby "Martha Washington"; their first had been called "George Washington." So Martha and Nathanael Greene had plenty to talk about.

It was a beautiful spring, after a mild winter, a sharp contrast with the year before at Valley Forge. There were frequent visitors at camp—even delegations of Indians—and each guest must be given a review of the troops. Thirteen cannon greeted the French minister. General Washington reviewed the troops on his big bay horse, and was "incomparably more majestic" than the foreigners. The ladies sat on a raised platform to watch. Martha was thrilled when her own regiment, Lady Washington's Dragoons, in white uniforms with blue facings, marched by, led by Lieutenant-Colonel Baylor.

Then came May. The army marched to the Hudson Highlands to defend them against the British. And Martha was bundled off home again.

For once, she was quite content to return to her son and his family. In March a new baby girl had been born at Abingdon, and christened Eleanor after her mother. Jacky had written, happy at the arrival of the third little daughter, yet expressing alarm over the health of his wife. Would his mother hasten home as soon as she could and assist with the care of the baby?

When Martha reached Abingdon, she found Eleanor very ill indeed, too weak to assume the responsibility of rearing her husky namesake. So Martha took the baby "Nelly" with her to Mount Vernon, to be nursed by Mrs. Anderson, a healthy young Englishwoman who had lost her own child.

It was like having a baby of her own! Day and night,

Martha and "Mammy" Anderson hovered over the child's crib, loving the baby girl and spoiling her.

All too soon the fall of 1779 came. Baby Nelly was returned to her mother, now well and strong again, at Abingdon, but not before her doting grandmother gained the promise that the following summer she could once more "borrow" the precious child.

To Morristown, New Jersey, traveled the Washington coach, bearing the wife of the General to his side. But this time she was housed in more comfortable quarters than the old Freeman Tavern. Martha found George living in the home of the widow of Colonel Jacob Ford, on the Newark road, nearly a mile out of town.

The General and his suite occupied the entire building, except two lower rooms, which were reserved for Mrs. Theodosia Ford and her family. On the right side of the hall running through the house was the General's dining room. Over it, the Washingtons' bedroom. George had two log additions built, one for a kitchen, the other for his offices.

In this large house, surrounded by lawns and gardens, it would seem as if the Washingtons, used to restricted quarters, might have found space enough even for George's official "family." Yet from his letters it appears that the place was crowded. Mrs. Ford and her family lived in the house. The General's staff had to be accommodated. And Martha had brought eighteen servants from Mount Vernon, for whom there was no lodging until the two log buildings were added.

It was a worried circle that gathered around the Washingtons' table this dreary winter of 1779-80—the darkest days thus far of the Revolution. No victories had been gained. Food and supplies were low. Soldiers deserting. The cold was severe. Around Morristown the snow lay six feet deep, thus preventing the bringing of food into camp.

From Morristown the Americans kept a worried watch on the British in New York. An alarm gun was stationed on one of the Short Hills, ready to signal in case the enemy made a move toward Philadelphia or West Point. In a meadow, close to Washington's headquarters, fifty log huts had been built for the General's Lifeguard. In case of trouble, this picked body of men, all over six feet, were to rush to the General's assistance until the main body of the army, encamped two miles away, could arrive.

That winter Martha was often awakened in the middle of the night by an alarm that the British were coming. The guns on the hill went off. The Lifeguard rushed into the General's headquarters, barricaded the entrances and threw up the windows. Five soldiers placed themselves at each window, guns loaded and cocked. There they remained until troops from the main camp reached the house to investigate the cause of the alarm.

At the first sound, George would leap from his bed, don his uniform and hurry to his office.

Under strict orders, Martha remained in bed, the winter wind from the open windows sweeping through the drawn curtains, the silhouettes of the soldiers ranged against the moonlit sky. In after years she often laughed as she told how she and Mrs. Ford shivered under their blankets until the alarm subsided, the windows were shut and the soldiers withdrew.

The ability to laugh under conditions that would have frightened most women was Martha's Dandridge heritage. Her father's hearty laughter had roared through the house on the Pamunkey, come good news or bad. Now his daughter's cheerful smile put heart and hope into the harassed leader of the American forces. His "dear Patsy" was beside him, going through the war with him; it gave him strength.

Were the Americans to lose the war?

Horace Walpole thought so. And he expressed himself in behalf of the English nation, now aware of the pitiful state of the Continental forces, when he wrote: "We look on America as already at our feet."

On hearing this statement, Martha tossed her head and said: "Stuff and nonsense!"

The bright flame of his wife's courage helped George Washington to ward off all thought of defeat.

Chapter Ten   The Hardest Years

It WAS THE SPRING OF 1780, AND AS YET THERE WAS NO RE-lief for the American forces. Martha, who had stood beside her heart-sick and weary husband with unfailing cheerfulness and willing hands, found her own hope slowly dying. The situation was alarming. General Washington had less than ten thousand men, not enough to attack the British. But in the enemy camp were signs of activity. Soon the war must be resumed.

At moments Martha's imagination went ahead to the fury of battle—she could picture George, riding his horse, directing the troops, always in grave danger. She heard the pitiful cries of the wounded, and fear clutched her heart.

But Martha, being Martha, could not despair forever. One purpose had brought her to her husband's side, to aid him. Surely before long there would be a gleam of hope.

It came in May with the return of the Marquis de Lafayette, who had gone to France to persuade the French King to help the Americans. With high spirits, Martha welcomed "the French boy," always one of her favorites. Kissing Mrs. Washington, young Lafayette then threw his arms impulsively around the shoulders of the haggard General Washington and delivered his message:

French aid was on the way! Louis XVI was sending a fleet and an army of six thousand troops under the Count

179

de Rochambeau, who would place themselves under Washington's command.

Although these reinforcements were not to arrive for some months, the news of their coming worked as a miracle on the morale of the discouraged American soldiers. Less than ten thousand, they mustered the strength of twice that number.

Later that night before the fire at headquarters, Lafayette whispered to Martha news that delighted her. A son had been born to his wife, the Marquise. They had christened him George Washington de Lafayette.

That summer at Mount Vernon, Martha, who had been longing for her beloved family, and for a rest, now longed even more for something else—help for the Continental troops. If only she could rouse the interest of the colonies more actively in plans to prevent sickness and hunger and lack of clothes! It might mean—it *must* mean—a strong, well-equipped army, ready to join forces with Rochambeau's Frenchmen and march against the British. It could bring the end of the war.

November found Mrs. Washington riding north to join her husband at New Windsor, in New York State. This time she did not travel straight to camp, stopping only to rest the horses. Each day she paused along the way to encourage people to organize committees for the relief of the soldiers.

In Philadelphia she was pleased to find the ladies already absorbed in war work. Plunging in with her customary energy, she showed them how to start a fund to carry it on. Women sold their jewels. Martha herself gave generously, as the entry from her husband's account book shows: "Oc-

WASHINGTON'S HEADQUARTERS AT NEWBURGH, NEW YORK

tober 10, 1780. Mrs. Washington's bounty to the soldiers,
£6,000."

At New Windsor, a Hudson River town two miles below
Newburgh, Martha made her home with George in a Dutch
farmhouse built by the DeWitt family.

"Lady Washington is back in camp!"

The joyful news spread like wildfire. And the ragged
soldiers, finding their hardships more endurable because of
the presence of the smiling little lady, recaptured some of
the faith with which they had begun the long fight for
freedom.

That winter the story of deprivation repeated itself. The
French troops had landed at Newport, Rhode Island, but they
would not be ready to fight the English until the following
year. Meanwhile, American supplies were low; the soldiers
discouraged and hungry. Their struggle against England
seemed almost hopeless. Again Martha set to work to cheer
the forlorn troops, carrying baskets of food to the sick, returning to her own cramped quarters to knit and patch torn
clothing and band together the officers' wives in sewing
groups to make new garments.

As in other years, it became Martha's duty to see that the
staff was entertained, as well as prominent families of the
district. Some days as many as thirty guests dined at headquarters. Finding food for them was a problem which taxed
their hostess's ingenuity.

Through the account of Uzal Knapp, one of the Washington Lifeguard, we learn of the party given by the General
and his wife on Christmas Day, 1780. There were twenty
people at table, among them two French officers of Rochambeau's army; Governor Clinton and his family; and Molly
Clinton, the mother of DeWitt Clinton. On the rough

wooden table were platters of meat and vegetables, pies and puddings, bowls of apples and the hickory nuts of which George Washington was fond. Will Lee, the General's servant, waited on the table and saw that everyone had plenty of cider.

During the meal, the Lifeguard band, stationed in the hall, played lively tunes, under the direction of their sergeant, Uzal Knapp. In the evening the girls of the village were invited in to dance with the officers of the Lifeguard until nine o'clock. General Washington watched the young people, his quiet smile showing his enjoyment of the gaiety.

There is a story told of Martha's exquisite tact on that Christmas Day which came straight from her warm heart and had nothing to do with social training.

To her surprise—because an invitation to headquarters was almost a royal summons—a young girl of the community had declined to dine with the General and his Lady at their Christmas feast.

Curious as to the reason, Martha found that the girl, still in her teens, was a dwarf, less than three feet high. She had thought Mrs. Washington's invitation was given for the purpose of gratifying the curiosity of her guests concerning so small a creature. Shyness had made her decline.

Later Martha prevailed upon the girl, whose name was Anna Brewster, to visit her. She found her pretty, and perfect in form; the smallest woman ever seen in America. When the midget arrived, she was greeted by Martha Washington and her other guests—very little girls, as small as Mistress Brewster, before whom she could not feel inferior. They all sat on the floor, Mrs. Washington included. And they had their tea on doll-size china.

The life of Martha Washington at New Windsor was not

unlike what it had been at other camps, except for increasing anxiety, shared by everyone from the General down to the drummer boy, over the success of the American cause. The French fleet was in the West Indies. Rochambeau and Washington did not dare attack the British in New York until naval help arrived.

Meanwhile, Lord Cornwallis was planning to conquer the southern states. Of the American forces in Virginia under the Marquis de Lafayette, the British nobleman was contemptuous. "The French boy cannot escape me," he boasted.

Thus the war had reached Martha's beloved Virginia. But in spite of the danger, when June came and a meeting of the American and French armies was planned, she journeyed down to Mount Vernon as usual.

That eventful year of 1781—destined to bring freedom to America—brought double sorrow to the Washington family. Samuel, George's five-times-married brother, died in Jefferson County. And, in January, Fielding Lewis passed away.

Martha's first act on reaching home was to invite her widowed sister-in-law and her six children to Mount Vernon to spend the summer. Fielding Lewis, a wealthy man at the outbreak of the war, had lost his fortune helping the Patriot cause. He had equipped three regiments, had lent $35,000 to the state, and as the great gunmaker of the Revolution, had run at his own expense an arms factory in Fredericksburg. After borrowing thousands of pounds to lend to Virginia, the Colonel was unable to pay his taxes. He died leaving large debts and a mortgage on Millbank. Betty found herself so poor that she was forced to turn beautiful Millbank into a girls' school. This she did early in September, after a restful summer under her brother's roof.

One evening, a week after her departure, Martha was

seated before the fireplace in her sitting-room, knitting. Jacky and Eleanor were with her. Their three little girls, and a new, six-months-old baby boy, were upstairs asleep.

Jacky had just glanced at the clock and said, "Mother, we should go to bed," when a knock was heard at the front door.

Martha sprang to her feet. In such troubled times, any visitor might be an enemy. Tensely she watched as Old Cully hobbled to the door, unbolted and opened it. For a moment Martha stared at the tall, uniformed figure in the doorway. Then with a glad cry she rushed forward to be caught in a pair of strong arms. George Washington, who had not crossed his own threshold since May 1775, when he accepted command of the American army, had come home!

The General was accompanied only by his aide, Colonel David Humphreys, and his servant, Will Lee. They had left the Count de Rochambeau at Alexandria, the Marquis de Chastellux at Georgetown, who were to follow them in the morning.

Quickly the whole household was astir. The news flew over the plantation—"The master is home!" Next morning the slaves flocked from every cabin to greet him, including Thomas Bishop, his servant of the French and Indian War, now a family retainer. All looked lovingly at George Washington's face that had grown lined and stern during the war.

When the debonair Frenchmen, Rochambeau and Chastellux, arrived, Martha saw to it that they found rest and relaxation at Mount Vernon. But much as her heart yearned for it, she could not do the same for her tired husband. George spent long hours with Lund Washington over important estate matters. He wrote to Lafayette, who had the British cornered in Yorktown with their backs to the sea, that help was on the way; he must hold Cornwallis at all cost and not let him escape. But George's moments alone with his "dear Patsy" were few and hurried. It did not seem to Martha that, on this visit, she and her husband passed a whole hour together!

General Washington and Count Rochambeau had given up the plan to attack New York. With the help of the French fleet, finally arrived from the West Indies, their troops were on the way south to attack Lord Cornwallis at Yorktown.

There was time, however, on the four-day visit, for George Washington to become acquainted with his stepladder of four rosy grandchildren, all born to the John Parke Custises during his absence—Eliza, now five; Martha, four; Nelly, two and a half; and the six-months-old boy, George Washington, who was being nursed by "Mammy" Anderson.

There was also time for a talk with the children's father, closeted in Washington's study, where often, as a boy, Jacky had been scolded by his stern, though loving, stepfather.

At twenty-six Jack Custis was the same spoiled child, handsome and unreliable.

"Do you think it right to spend so much of your fortune on hunters and pedigreed dogs and fine clothes?" his stepfather asked him. "When will you settle down and realize that only hard work makes a plantation a success? Do you think it just that Eleanor should have the responsibility of running Abingdon while you enjoy yourself?"

To General Washington's surprise, Jack answered humbly: "I know I've been a disappointment, sir, and I want to make amends by doing what you've long wished me to do—enlist in the army. If possible, I'd like to be on your staff."

Was Jack Custis serious? As Washington surveyed his tall figure, every inch that of soldier, he pictured him in uniform, riding at his side. He loved Martha's son. It would be a comfort to have Jacky with him at Yorktown in the dark days ahead.

So Jack joined the army, suddenly obsessed with a violent patriotism, largely because of the dashing Frenchmen, the Count de Rochambeau and the Marquis de Chastellux, whom he admired and who were going to fight the British. When General Washington left Mount Vernon, his stepson rode beside him as an aide.

As for Eleanor, she was used to giving way to her gay young husband's wishes. She helped him pack, her hands a bit unsteady, but her sweet mouth set in a smile.

Giving up her son was not that simple for Martha Washington. She had had six years of war; she was fifty years old, and suddenly grown tired. Jack was her only child, and to see him go into battle for the first time wrung her heart. Added to her anxiety over George's safety would be the question: Is Jacky in danger, too?

But time was short, and George's face too stern to remonstrate with him over Jack's sudden enlistment. Before Martha realized it, the four days were over, her husband and son were gone, and a strange quiet settled over the white house on the Potomac.

Martha and Eleanor were sleeping one cool dawn six weeks later when an excited soldier galloped to Mount Vernon to bring Mrs. Washington a letter from her husband. It told the news that was being rung across the fields by church bells. "Cornwallis is taken!" The Americans had won a great victory at Yorktown!

The British general, attacked on land by the Americans under Lafayette, Washington and Rochambeau, and unable to escape by sea because of the French fleet under De Grasse, had surrendered.

"Praise be!" Martha cried, rousing the sleeping Eleanor to read her the news. "Now Papa and Jacky can come home."

But close on the heels of the first welcome rider came another. "Your son is very sick, Madam," he told Martha. "You must go to him at once."

Their joy instantly forgotten in fear, the anxious mother and wife plied the boy with questions. To their anguish, they learned that Jack lay ill at the Bassett home, Eltham Hall, in New Kent. He had caught dysentery in the trenches before Yorktown. And realizing he might be dying, he had expressed one dramatic wish—to see Cornwallis surrender his sword!

No one could refuse him. Dr. James Craik, Washington's old friend and physician, and the surgeon general of the army, had Jacky carried to the scene of the surrender so that he might witness the British handing over their flags. Then from the rejoicings at Yorktown he was taken, dying they feared, to Eltham, thirty miles from camp.

In all haste, Martha and Eleanor started for Eltham. But the roads were bad, and, as in all travel in those days, they must stop often to rest the horses. There were no bridges across the rivers. So there were delays at every crossing as the coach was driven on a flat boat that floated it across the stream. No journey, Martha and Eleanor agreed, ever seemed so long as those four days spent in hurrying to Jacky's side!

At last they reached Eltham, where George Washington soon arrived at a gallop from Yorktown. When Dr. Craik told him that there was no hope for the young man's recovery, the distracted stepfather flung himself on the bed and wept. Jacky had been a son to him. In spite of his faults, he loved him dearly.

The family had assembled just in time to watch Jack die. Eleanor became a young widow with four small children;

Martha, childless. Their grief left them stunned.

Jacky was buried at Eltham Hall, and his sorrowing family returned to Mount Vernon to face a future without the presence of vivid John Custis. It did not seem possible that one so active, so joyous, could lie still in death. Friends who called were shocked at the apathy of Martha Washington, pale, shrunken, too crushed even to speak; and at Eleanor Custis, thin and frail and weeping her heart out.

Eleanor, looking older than her twenty-six years, held with one hand her five-year-old Eliza, a pretty child whom people thought resembled her father; and with the other, Martha, who at four was a solemn little girl with her grandmother's capability. In the nursery, baby Washington cried aloud, and Nelly, still almost a baby herself, joined in the clamor.

It was more than Eleanor could stand. Her harsh weeping pulled Martha out of her own grief and sent her to her daughter-in-law's side to comfort her. Mrs. Washington's heart bled for the girl, so devoted a mother, so fine a wife to Jacky. And the children were bright and well mannered, though the two younger ones were a bit of a problem—

That was what George Washington was thinking, as he watched this painful scene. Crossing to the couch where the stricken young widow had thrown herself, he spoke soothing words to her, and said:

"Nelly, your mother and I want to adopt your two younger children. You'll have enough to do in rearing Eliza and Patsy."

This was no sudden impulse on Washington's part. He and Martha were a childless couple who loved children. Ever since the birth of Nelly and baby Washington, their mother had been in delicate health, and to give her rest, the children had lived at Mount Vernon. Adoption could easily be arranged without a break in their lives. They would simply continue to live on with their grandparents and be taken care of by "Mammy" Anderson.

Smoothing Eleanor's rumpled hair, Martha smiled for the first time since her son's death. How wise George was, and how good. And how sweet it would be to honor Jacky's memory by rearing his son and favorite daughter, Nelly, under the roof of Mount Vernon—a spot Jack had loved.

In the end, Eleanor Custis accepted the Washingtons' offer and left her two younger children to brighten their grand-parents' home. It was easier somehow to go back to Abingdon with only her two older daughters to look after. There would be no babies crying, no confusion. There she would be able to rest and sleep.

No mother who ever lived loved her son more than Martha Washington. And it was ironic that the American victory at Yorktown, for which she had been praying for years, should cause his death.

There was never a word of blame against her husband, who had accepted Jack's enlistment and taken him on the campaign from which he did not return. George Washington, seeing Martha's white face and dull eyes, wished with all his heart that she would show some of her old fire. She was sad, but not bitter; crushed and docile . . . and that was not his Patsy.

The Peace Ball at Fredericksburg on November twelfth, a week after Jack's death, was the last touch. George Washing-ton, the country's hero, was forced to go. He attended the dance with his eighty-year-old mother on his arm. But his thoughts were back at Mount Vernon with his sorrowing wife.

Besides Martha, another person had been saddened by the

battle of Yorktown, over which the nation was rejoicing. Thomas, Lord Fairfax, of Greenway Court, had given the sixteen-year-old George Washington his start in life; he continued to like him as long as he fought for the Crown. During the Revolution, the old nobleman remained a staunch Loyalist, frank and open in allegiance to England. And he was dumbfounded when he heard that his young friend had captured Lord Cornwallis and the British army.

"Come, Joe, carry me to bed. It's high time for me to die," he told his Negro servant—which he did the following year, at the age of ninety-two, bitter at George Washington for having "turned rebel."

The surrender at Yorktown ended the fighting of the Revolution. The Americans' French allies—even the Marquis de Lafayette—were going back to France. But the British still held New York, and General Washington did not dare disband his army.

Nearly eighteen months of camp life at Newburgh, New York, lay before weary disheartened Mrs. Washington.

George and Martha spent the spring and summer of 1782 in the Hasbrouck House, a stone cottage with a sloping roof, which stood in an apple orchard overlooking the Hudson, a half mile outside the village of Newburgh. In this one-story Dutch farmhouse Martha lived with her husband longer than in any other camp; it became the most noted of Washington's headquarters.

Martha liked Newburgh. From the Hasbrouck House, she could look across the Hudson to where on the Fishkill hills stood the warning beacon, ready for lighting should a British ship be sighted. It gave her a feeling of safety. It was also reassuring to know that an enemy fleet would be stopped by the iron chain stretched across the river.

George Washington was glad he had brought his wife with him to Newburgh. The acute stage of her grief had subsided. She could be bright and cheerful again. The children at Mount Vernon were well and happy, so Nurse Anderson reported. Eleanor Custis was improving. She had visited Jacky's grave at Eltham and planted violets from Abingdon.

Tears filled Mrs. Washington's eyes as she read her letters, but there was no more sobbing. When guests came to the Hasbrouck House, Martha greeted them with a smile.

The largest room, which was used for callers and as a dining room, had seven doors and only one window. The fireplace was a part of the room, the space beneath a wide chimney being large enough to roast a whole bullock. There was a big round table in the center, a few chairs—that was all. Yet this half-bare room was a gathering place for General Washington's "family" about which he and Martha were sentimental all their lives.

In the evenings the staff officers would assemble around the fireplace to smoke their pipes and talk. Martha, attracted by their merriment, would come from her bedroom to enjoy an amusing description of a young man's difficulties in finding his way to Knox's quarters to call upon the jolly Lucy, or to hear the others tease Baron von Steuben about the whale he claimed to have caught in the Hudson, which turned out to be an eel!

The quarters of General Knox were in the Ellison house, four miles outside Newburgh, near the artillery camp. There Lucy Knox held many a gay "frisk," at one of which General Washington opened the ball with Maria Colden, and danced with the other belles of the countryside. In tribute to the charms of these Hudson River girls, a young French officer wrote their names on a window-pane with his diamond ring—

Maria Colden, Getty Wynkoop and Sally Jansen.

Life was so different after Yorktown! Martha Washington was now the wife of the hero of America. When she passed through Philadelphia on her way home to Mount Vernon, she was presented by the Pennsylvania Assembly with a coach that had belonged to Governor Penn. Later on, visiting her old home in Williamsburg, she was given a gold medal and the freedom of the city. These gifts made up for another she had lost. A French ship was captured by the British, and among its treasures sold at auction in New York was "an elegant present" from Maria Antoinette, Queen of France, to Mrs. George Washington.

The Mount Vernon summer of 1782, with her grandchildren no longer "borrowed" but her own, was the pleasantest Martha Washington had known since the beginning of the war.

In her sitting room, scented with flowers cut every day in her garden, Martha played with little Nelly and baby Washington. She chatted with Lund Washington, his wife Elizabeth, and "Mammy" Anderson, under whose care the young Custises had blossomed into healthy youngsters, outgrowing their clothes with startling rapidity, and filling the house with the sounds of tears and laughter.

The mail would arrive, with George Washington's letter always on top of the pile. There would be silence in the room while Martha read and reread the carefully written words. George was not coming home. Until actual peace was declared, the American army could not be disbanded. The treaty with England was receding month by month. So the troops had gone into winter headquarters at New Windsor, and Washington was resuming his residence at Newburgh.

There, in November, Martha joined George for a second

winter. And instead of peace, she found restlessness and intrigue.

The soldiers had not been paid for a long time, and by March they were on the verge of mutiny. Letters were circulated among the troops, urging them to overthrow the newly-born republic and set up a dictatorship. They were told that Washington intended to seize the crown, now that freedom from England was won, and make America a monarchy.

When George heard this slander he was very angry, but to his wife's satisfaction, he managed to keep his head. He called a meeting of his officers in the New Building on Temple Hill in New Windsor. As he stepped before them to read his address, he put on his eyeglasses. "You see, gentlemen," he said quietly, "that I've not only grown gray, but blind in your service."

Washington's address begged his officers to have faith in the republic. His first pathetic statement had already touched their hearts, and soon all fear of a mutiny was over.

In this same building, in April, occurred a happier event— George Washington, who had secured money for the soldiers from Congress, read an order announcing the end of the war.

Meanwhile, throughout the spring, Martha had been indulging in her favorite occupation—gardening. A plot of land was set off at the east of the Hasbrouck House for her use, and there she planted a garden of flowers and vegetables. Soon she would wander between beds edged with bricks and bright with the flowers she had raised at Mount Vernon— iris, tulips, jonquils and narcissus. She had an herb garden, too, in which she planted mint, parsley, thyme, and other herbs for flavoring meats and soups.

Any day Mrs. Washington might be seen on the slope

outside the Hasbrouck House, directing a helper on how to dig a flower bed.

"Turn over the sod, lad, and dig deeper," she would say in her rich, Southern voice. And the startled passer-by might see Lady Washington take the spade from the boy's un-skilled hands, and, her quilted petticoat trailing in the mud, the wind playing havoc with her gray hair, show Newburgh how a flower bed *should* be dug.

Gardening kept Martha contented until the middle of August, when she returned to Mount Vernon. Now, almost two years after Yorktown, she was saying good-bye to camp life. She had been a part of it for nearly eight years. She had, as she often said, heard the opening and closing gun of every important campaign in the Revolution.

Her only desire was to get back to Mount Vernon and peace. Lund Washington's letters were filled with accounts of the grandchildren. Speaking of baby Washington and Nelly, he wrote, "I loved the father and I love the chil-dren. . . ." Martha's impatience mounted. She longed to clasp the children in her arms.

Finally she went down to Mount Vernon to get the house ready; George to New York to lead the victorious American forces into the city after the British left on their ships. He said good-bye to his officers at Fraunce's Tavern, and then journeyed down to Annapolis, where Congress was sitting. There he was met by his wife, who had ridden up in the family chaise to bring him home.

In the Maryland State House, before Martha and a packed chamber, General Washington resigned to Congress his com-mission as commander-in-chief of the Continental Army. His work was done, the Revolution successfully over.

Once more private citizens, the Washingtons turned their

faces homeward, escorted by three colonels of the General's staff and the faithful Will Lee. On Christmas Eve of 1783, they reached the entrance to Mount Vernon—home at last.

George's eyes gleamed as he watched for each familiar landmark. Martha, cozy and plump, sat beside him in the chaise, her face smiling. In through the gate they sped and up the drive that led to the white house on the bank of the Potomac.

The carriage came to the cottage of Thomas Bishop. Will had ridden ahead to tell Bishop, now over eighty, of the approach of the master and mistress. Who was this redcoat, this British soldier, standing straight as a pine and saluting? It was the white-haired Bishop, dressed in the English uniform he had worn at the defeat of Braddock twenty-eight years before.

George stopped the carriage. Leaning on his stick, the old soldier hobbled out to grasp the hand of the commander whose youthful triumphs he had witnessed, while Bishop's daughter dropped a curtsy to Lady Washington, who, as her father said proudly, had "as good as brought up the girl."

It was sunset when Martha and George alighted at the entrance to their home.

In the open doorway were their adopted children—four-year-old Nelly standing alone, and her two-year-old brother holding on to "Mammy" Anderson's hand and dancing excitedly on his small, unsteady feet, as his adoring grandmama held out her arms to him.

From every point servants, young and old, rushed out to welcome the master and mistress. The General's officers handed their bridles to waiting grooms. Then holding their beloved children in their arms, Martha and George went into the house to greet George's sister, Betty Lewis, and her daughters, Sally and Betty, who had come for the holidays.

Happily, George Washington gazed around the home he had seen but once in eight years, now handsome in its Christmas dress. The hall was hung with ropes of spicy cedar. Mistletoe and green holly were over each door. And fires of hickory logs blazed in every fireplace.

Christmas had always been a great event at Mount Vernon. But this year of 1783, when the holiday and the master's homecoming were one, it was doubly joyful. All Christmas Eve, the plantation was alight with bonfires, noisy with guns and pistols. From the Negroes' cabins came the sound of fiddle and banjo.

Christmas morning Nelly and her brother woke early. When "Mammy" Anderson had dressed them, they rushed downstairs to inspect the stockings their grandparents had helped them hang at the fireplace the night before. Both little stockings were overflowing with gifts! And there stood their grandparents to watch Nelly and Washington open their packages.

All Christmas Day neighbors and friends from Alexandria called at Mount Vernon to exchange holiday greetings with George and Martha. The slaves from the Washington farms were the first callers. They gathered around the door of the mansion, to "catch a Christmas gift" from the mistress who never forgot them.

"Christmas gif'!" they chorused, as the Washingtons appeared.

Martha laughed. She had known better than to say it first. Then following the ancient Southern custom, each slave would have had to give her and George a Christmas present. Now it was up to them to be the givers.

After a bountiful turkey dinner, the household assembled

around the fireside to sing carols. Martha sat before the yule log, lighted by a brand from last year's log, baby Washington on her lap. Across the hearth was George, with granddaughter Nelly by his side. They were home! And Martha's voice rang out happily in the old English carol:

"Come, bring with a noise,
My merrie, merrie boys,
The Christmas log to the firing.
On your Psalteries play,
That sweet luck may
Come while the log is tending."

When the Christmas holidays were over. Martha began to pack away her husband's uniforms. His coats of blue and buff, with gilt buttons. His silver mounted sword. The writing case on which he had written so many pleading letters to Congress. His tents and camp chest. Only when they were stored in the attic did she feel that George was home to stay!

Nature seemed to sympathize with the Washingtons in their desire for quiet after the fatigue and excitements of the past eight years. After Christmas, Mount Vernon became snowbound. Locked in by frost and snow, through which not too many friends could reach them, Martha and George took up their beloved plantation life.

Their service to their country was over. Nothing would ever again take them from Mount Vernon.

Chapter Eleven   Their Own Vine and Fig Tree

THEY WERE HAPPY YEARS FOR MARTHA WASHINGTON, THE
five following the signing of the peace treaty with England.
She and George were home again, absorbed in the plantation
tasks that reached the very core of their hearts.

With the master away for eight years, there was much to
be done at Mount Vernon—buildings to be painted and
roofed; new farming experiments tried out. The interior of
the mansion, too, bore signs of neglect. Calling for her scissors and dye pots, Martha set to work. Faded streaks on
draperies and chairs vanished, as did the tarnish from copper
kettles, silver trays and pewter platters.

All this was labor that the Washingtons loved. And Martha's contentment is mirrored in one of George's letters:

"I am now enjoying domestic life under my own vine and
fig tree; and in a small Villa with the implements of husbandry
and lambkins about me, I expect to slide gently down the
stream of life till I am entombed in the mansions of my
fathers."

There were changes in the neighborhood, too, since George
went off to war. It had been his sad duty to write Colonel
Fairfax of the destruction of Belvoir by fire a year ago.

The first drive the Washingtons took after their return
was to inspect the ruins. George stood, silent and sad, looking

at the charred remains of the stately brick house, the burned stumps of trees and deserted gardens. What desolation time and the war had brought to this second home of his youth!

The Fairfax fortunes had indeed fallen on evil days during the Revolution. Thomas, Lord Fairfax, had left his land to the two sons of his sister Frances in England; his Northern neck property to Denny Martin; Greenway Court to the scheming Thomas. But Sally and George William Fairfax could get some satisfaction from the fact that this inheritance would do their rivals little good. Most of the Fairfax land had been confiscated during the war.

The Washingtons had heard from George William only recently; a pathetic letter, yet a proud one. Simply he had stated that since he would no longer receive any income from America, he and Sally were leaving their Yorkshire estate, Towlston Manor, and moving to Bath, a fashionable English resort, where he expected to live more quietly.

George Washington was so touched by this letter that he wrote at once to the Fairfaxes, urging them to return to Virginia, now that the war was over. "Your house is no more, but mine is most sincerely and heartily at your service till you could rebuild it," he assured them.

Martha lived in acute suspense as she awaited the Fairfax's reply. How would it be, having the glamorous Sally living at Mount Vernon?

One morning their answer came. Martha and George were breakfasting at a small table, drawn before the fire because George had a touch of rheumatism.

"Patsy," he said excitedly, looking over the mail, "here's a letter from the Fairfaxes!" And he began reading with maddening absorption, leaving Martha, appetite dulled, staring into the fire.

"Are they coming back?" she finally asked.

"No, Patsy," George answered, regretfully. "Fairfax says they cannot return at present. The Court season approaches. They're very much occupied."

Martha bristled. She had begun to pity Sally, had she? Clearly she was wasting her sympathy. The Fairfaxes had lost their Virginia estates, but with Lord Fairfax's death, they moved one step nearer the title. That coveted title had gone first to his brother, Robert Fairfax of Leeds Castle in Kent. The new Lord Fairfax had no children; he was an old man, seventy-eight. In a few years, Sally would achieve her ambition . . . she would be Lady Fairfax.

What was Sally like now? Had the years been kind to her, Martha wondered? And how had she taken the loss of their American income? Had disappointment made bitter her beautiful mouth? Hardened her sparkling eyes? It was strange that Martha did not think of Mistress Fairfax as a woman past her middle years. Even as she smoothed the fichu at her own plump throat and settled her panniers over hips that were far from slender, she remembered her lovely neighbor as a tall and graceful woman, radiant and eternally young.

But there was little malice in Martha Washington's nature. To save her life, she could not harbor resentment, not even against the woman of whom she had always—she admitted it —been slightly jealous.

Martha had so much that summer of 1784 to make her happy. In her adopted grandchildren, she relived the lives of her own son and daughter. History had turned back a quarter of a century, giving her the sweet companionship of a docile little girl, so like the gentle Patty, and a robust baby boy whose laughter re-echoed through the house as his father's had done. Dear Jacky! Martha sighed, and hugged young Washington the closer.

When two years after her husband's death, Eleanor Custis remarried, the adopted grandchildren indeed became Martha's own.

Eleanor had found consolation for her grief in the love of Doctor David Stuart, the son and grandson of well-known Virginia clergymen, and a friend of her childhood. Oddly enough, her twice-married mother-in-law was shocked. Jacky's wife marrying for a second time! Abingdon, the home her son had loved, to be lived in and managed by a young doctor who most likely knew nothing about farming!

For a time the idea made Martha very unhappy, until George, with his customary fairness, passed judgment on the situation. "I never expected you would spend the rest of your days in widowhood," was his message to Eleanor, for whom he had great fondness and respect.

Thinking it over, Martha gradually came to agree. Doctor Stuart was a fine young man of thirty, a graduate of William and Mary, and of the medical college of Edinburgh, Scotland. He was well born, a descendant of the royal Scottish house of Stuart. A good companion for Eleanor, a proper stepfather for Eliza and Martha, the two older granddaughters at Abingdon.

Of the two Custis children who lived at Mount Vernon, Nelly was now a pretty well-mannered child of five, with brown curls; her brother, called Washington, a plump, rosy-cheeked boy of three. When guests arrived, it was a charming sight to see the tall dignified General, his tiny wife, and the two children always at their grandparents' side.

The guests were many, for General Washington, hero of the successful war, was too important a person to slip back into being merely a Virginia farmer.

"A glass of wine and a bit of mutton" was all that he promised the visitors. But it proved tempting to so many people that the house built by Lawrence Washington—his little "Villa" as George called it—soon grew too small to hold them all.

One day Martha found her husband at his desk, engaged, as in his youth as a surveyor, in drawing a map.

"I'm making plans to enlarge our house, Patsy," he told her. "When spring comes, the masons and carpenters will follow my directions."

Many an evening that cold winter of 1784 Martha and George spent working on the plans. Two wings added to the original building would give a graceful balance. On the north they wanted a banquet hall for large parties; on the south, a library for George's books. And there must be a wide veranda across the eastern front of the house, where they could sit and look at the river.

March came, and with it carpenters and masons from England to work on the additions. Ships were tied up at the wharf, bringing stone flagging from Ostend for the veranda. George himself superintended every bit of the work. And how many times a day, Martha, with one or both of the children, found an excuse to hasten to his side to see what was going on!

Soon the house was twice as large. It was the long, elegant white mansion that we find at Mount Vernon today; a wooden building, but paneled in imitation of stone, painted white and sanded. A wide hall had been cut through the house. And graceful colonnades framed its western façade.

With the house completed, Martha and George turned their thoughts to beautifying their grounds and planning new gardens. Again George drew maps. The distances and directions, in feet and inches and by points of compass, of the garden houses, the sundial and the dry-well from the "front door of the mansion" were all marked down with the same accuracy with which he had drawn the house plans.

We can see the General measuring off distances with his long strides; Martha, a trifle breathless, trying to keep up with him; and the two children trotting after their grandparents as fast as their short legs will carry them.

When George Washington stopped to drive a stake, the others stopped, too; and Nelly, always a curious little girl, stood big-eyed and wondering as Grandmama explained that wherever a stake was put, a tree or shrub would some day grow.

Over the lawn the family walked, measuring for the drive that would lead from the Alexandria highway, nearly a mile away, to the house. It was to be shaded by weeping willows, grown from the slip that Jack Custis had brought from Boston years before. It would be called a "serpentine" driveway, because it wound like a snake around the oval plot of grass before the front door, with the sundial in the center. And beyond the sundial a bowling green was to be laid out.

Martha remembered another bowling green at Williamsburg, thirty-five years earlier; the children's grandfather, the gentle Daniel, in velvet coat and silken breeches; and herself in striped muslin, lifting the boxwood bowl to send it down the lawn toward the jack. Daniel's father—why was she thinking of him now? The sound of baby Washington's voice, crowing over George's stake driver as it marked a spot for a new locust tree, gave her the answer. The child was the image of the crusty old Colonel! Would he inherit Colonel Custis's position, as well as his looks? Martha wondered. Nelly, bless her, was no trouble at all. But already she was sometimes perturbed by the infantile tantrums of her grandson.

Following the family into the woods to pick out young trees, Martha caught up with little Washington and took his hand. He was only a baby. How foolish to worry! And putting aside her fears, she joined in the selection of magnolias and laurel to be transplanted to the lawn.

The dogwoods had just been set in a circle near the seed house, when the Marquis de Lafayette arrived for a visit, after a thirty-four day crossing of the Atlantic. He came alone, his young wife being too timid to risk an ocean journey.

As boyish looking as ever, the slim French nobleman stepped from his coach at the door of Mount Vernon, flung his arms around his old commander and kissed him on both cheeks.

Never was a guest more welcome! Martha Washington, wearing her best mauve silk, and a lace cap with black velvet ribbons on her graying hair, greeted him with such warmth that Lafayette wrote his wife that he had never felt so at home in any family except his own.

Little Nelly curtsied prettily and led the Marquis to a wing chair in the parlor, under his portrait by Charles Willson Peale. While young Washington leaned against his silken knee and listened, the young Frenchman told about his son, George Washington de Lafayette, who was just Nelly's age, an older daughter, and the baby, Virginia, named after their own state.

A good night's rest in the bedroom on the second floor, still known as the Lafayette Bedroom, and then the Marquis must be shown all over the plantation.

Martha took "her French boy" to see her new kitchen and washhouses—her dairy and dry-well and spinning house. He

WASHINGTON AND LAFAYETTE AT MOUNT VERNON, BY ROSSITER AND MIGNON

Metropolitan Museum of Art

went to the pasture where a chestnut horse with a white face came at his call—Nelson, the horse General Washington rode when Cornwallis surrendered at Yorktown.

The children even dragged the obliging Frenchman up to the octagonal cupola, built on the top of the house, from where they could look out over the sloping roof to the river boats below.

And, of course, Lafayette must see Martha's new gardens, enclosed in high brick walls. To the north of the bowling green was her flower garden, called "the high garden" on George's map, with its beds of fragrant bloom neatly edged with English box. To the south was Martha's vegetable or "low garden," with its grape arbor, its terraces of vegetables and fruit, its fig trees trained against the wall like a vine, all within easy access of the kitchen.

The flower garden was to carry a mark of the Marquis's visit. Before he left, he planted a tree there that would forever bear his name.

One afternoon the Washingtons and their grandchildren stood around a freshly dug hole, while Lafayette placed in it a magnolia tree and threw the first shovel of earth over its roots. We can see him lift his head, and with Continental grace, make a pretty speech of dedication. And if we go to Mount Vernon today, we can find the Lafayette Magnolia, still growing where he planted it.

On Christmas day of 1785, George and Martha Washington opened their enlarged house to friends and neighbors at a housewarming.

In return for their hospitality, gifts from all over the world began to arrive at Mount Vernon. Admirers of George Washington sent him exotic trees and shrubs. In the flower garden, he built a conservatory to house these rare plants from foreign lands. And he taught his grandchildren geography by pointing to the places of their origin on the globe in his library—the century plant from Puerto Rico; the Sago Palm of the East Indies, from which a starch known as "pearl sago" was made.

A handsome mantel of white Italian marble, with porcelain vases and bronze candelabra to adorn it, arrived from Samuel Vaughan, a London admirer, and was installed in the banquet room. The Marquis de Lafayette sent Martha andirons for the same fireplace, and a pair of bright colored Chinese pheasants which she liked to watch strutting on the lawn. But for "the French boy's" gift to George—a pack of noisy, aggressive hounds—she had no love at all!

One dog, Vulcan, who frequently raided the kitchen, Mrs. Washington especially disliked. On one occasion, with guests at table, she noticed that a ham, on which she had been counting as the main course of her meal, was missing. She was told that Vulcan had entered the cookhouse, seized the ham, and, in spite of brooms and pokers brandished at him by the kitchen force, had run off with it to his kennel.

George and his guests laughed heartily at this—but not Martha Washington. She made some remarks by no means kindly to Vulcan, or to dogs in general, which saddened her grandson, who loved the naughty Vulcan, and liked to ride on his back.

Lafayette's hounds could raid the kitchen for all George cared. His hunting days were over. He was older now, and more interested in farming than in riding to the hounds.

The Mount Vernon children were growing fast and ready for school, so their grandparents agreed. Gideon Snow of Boston was asked to come "to initiate two little children, who are very promising, in the first rudiments of education."

Of the two, Nelly was the more "promising" student, as was soon revealed by her lessons recited to Gideon Snow in the small octagonal schoolhouse in the west corner of the flower-garden wall. The little girl learned to write a hand that pleased even her particular grandfather, and (as her grandmother had not) to spell a word, not as it sounded when spoken, but as printed in her spelling book.

Nelly Custis, however, was no bookworm. She was a sweet, gay child, who liked to play. As soon as lessons were over, she and her young brother—who didn't like lessons at all, and told his tutor so—would run off to dig in the garden or race down to the wharf, where there was always a sailboat tied up, loading crops from the Washington farms, or unloading supplies.

Remembering her own girlhood at Chestnut Grove, Martha Washington sympathized with her grandchildren's love of animals and growing things and the blue water dotted with sailboats. But time was flying, and Nelly, at least (Washington was not much more than a baby, and a boy, too), must be taught to cook and sew, to dance and to sing a pretty tune. And to play the spinet, just as her grandmother had learned to play it years ago.

As she had once taken Patty, Martha took Nelly, followed by a servant carrying a basket of food and medicine, to the cabins where the slaves lay ill.

With her grandmother's help, Nelly began to sew and knit and to make her first sampler. Silk was precious, but there was always silk thread at Mount Vernon. This was so because of a thrifty habit of Martha Washington, who, when her silk dresses were worn, had the silk unraveled and rewound on spools for use in sewing.

Nelly went with her grandmother to gather lavender and put the sweet smelling leaves into muslin bags to be laid between the linen sheets. She enjoyed drying rose petals, mixing them with spices, and placing the potpourri in covered jars to scent the rooms. She liked to work at the charcoal fire in the greenhouse, distilling perfume from the garden flowers.

What Nelly did not like were her music lessons. The long hours spent at the spinet were torture to the restless child. But Mistress Washington, determined that her granddaughter should learn to play, made her practice every day. Sheet music was scarce. Martha spent laborious hours copying out with her own hand pieces by Mozart, Scotch songs, marches and dance music for Nelly. Each morning she sat beside the spinet, and her granddaughter cried and strummed and strummed and cried for hours. And many a thimble-thump the child received on her weary knuckles when she made a mistake or begged to stop.

It wasn't fair, Nelly thought, though being a docile little girl, she did not say so. While she was practicing, likely as not, her brother Washington was off playing.

Was the old pattern repeating itself? In rearing her granddaughter, Martha was as strict as she had been with the gentle Patty. But if young Washington failed to recite his lessons properly, perhaps they were too hard for him. Gideon Snow must find easier problems. He was a baby really, and in his grandmother's eyes he was perfect, just as his father had been.

But much as Martha loved her grandchildren, her husband came first. Fanny Bassett, daughter of Martha's sister Nancy, tells how her aunt was always cautioning Nelly and her brother to be quiet and not to run in the house and disturb the General when he was resting or reading. Everything at

Mount Vernon was adapted to the convenience and comfort of George Washington.

"Your Grandpapa's thoughts are the most important thing in the world," she would tell the children gravely.

But when George was rested and had no serious questions under consideration, Martha encouraged the children to draw him into their pleasures. The man whom the world thought stern and forbidding relaxed with his family in his own home and greatly enjoyed young people.

Mount Vernon was always overflowing with them. Martha's older granddaughters, Eliza and Patsy, were often there, along with David and Eleanor Stuart, who with three young children of their own came over from Abingdon and stayed for weeks in the good old Virginia fashion. There were poor Betty Lewis's children: her daughters, Sally and Betty, her boys, Fielding, Robert, Howell and Lawrence. There were the children of Martha's brother, Bartholomew, and those of her dead sister, Nancy Bassett.

Fanny Bassett was a frequent visitor from Eltham Hall, before her marriage to the General's nephew, George Augustine Washington, the son of his youngest brother, Charles. And after their marriage the young couple lived with their uncle and aunt, George Augustine taking Lund Washington's post as manager of the estate.

Fanny's wedding, which took place at Mount Vernon in the autumn of 1785, was a quiet one because Martha was in mourning for her mother and her brother, Bartholomew.

With Martha, family ties were strong. She had dearly loved her "dear Mama," the proper Frances Dandridge, whose teaching had done so much to form her daughter's character, and who had passed away after a long illness at seventy-five. And she had been immensely proud of the studious Bartholomew, who as Burgess, member of the Privy Council, and Judge of the General Court, became an important man in Virginia. The news of his death at forty-nine and of her mother's passing the week before, which reached Martha by the same mail one April morning, were blows that sent her to bed for a week.

Martha Washington, who loved the festivities connected with a wedding, hardly felt like planning one—even for Fanny Bassett. But life must go on. . . . So she bravely dried her eyes and helped her favorite niece get ready for her marriage, which was celebrated, according to George's diary, "after the candles were lighted."

George had also written in his diary, the June before: *"Dined with only Mrs. Washington, which I believe is the first instance of it since my retirement from public life."*

There were so many guests that Martha, who had always refused to leave any important household responsibility to a servant, finally admitted the need of a housekeeper, and a Mrs. Forbes was engaged.

For large dinners, the table was laid in the new banquet hall, with the service of Sevres porcelain presented to Martha Washington by the Society of the Cincinnati. Each piece bore her monogram—M. W.—surrounded by a laurel wreath, and was decorated with a chain of thirteen links, enclosing the names of the thirteen states.

General Washington met his guests in the hall, usually wearing a dark brown coat and satin breeches, a purple cravat and lace jabot. His powdered hair was gathered behind in a silk bag.

Doctor McWhirr, a well-known clergyman, describes dining with the Washingtons. Martha sat at the head of the table; the General on his wife's left. Mrs. Washington wore a plum-colored silk with a blue sash. Her hair was powdered. But she wore no jewelry other than the locket containing a miniature of "Papa," with a lock of his hair in the back, just as George always wore a miniature of "his dear Patsy" on a gold chain around his neck.

The General called on the clergyman to ask a blessing before the meal, but at the end, he forgot him and offered thanks himself.

Martha smiled and said, "My dear, remember you have a clergyman dining with you today."

"My dear, I wish clergymen and all men to know that I'm not a graceless man," George answered.

Doctor McWhirr concludes by saying that the restraint felt by most people in the presence of George Washington "was relieved by the vivacity of Mrs. Washington, who is of a more lively disposition, always good-humored and cheerful. She is small, but well formed, with a pleasant face and dark hazel eyes. It is plain to see that she adores her husband. They are to all appearances a happy pair."

When there were few guests, or on the rare occasions when they were alone, the Washingtons ate in the old dining room, where the portrait of George's brother, Lawrence, hung over the sideboard he had bought at the Fairfax auction.

A favorite guest at Mount Vernon was dashing young Henry Lee—"Lighthorse Harry," as he was nicknamed because he had won fame as captain of a cavalry regiment during the Revolution. One day the General remarked that he wanted a pair of carriage horses. Did Harry know where he could get them?

"I've a fine pair, General," Lee replied, "but you can't have them. You never pay more than half price for anything."

This saucy reply set Martha off into gales of laughter. Her parrot joined in the merriment. Who but Harry Lee would dare twit General Washington about his well-known bargaining ability?

George laughed, too. "My dear Lee, you're a funny fellow," he said good-naturedly. "Even that bird of Patsy's is laughing at you."

Besides Mrs. Forbes, there was another addition to the Mount Vernon household. Tobias Lear, a young Harvard graduate, had been engaged as Washington's secretary. The letters to his friends, such as George William Fairfax, George would continue to write himself in his precise, beautiful handwriting, but Tobias Lear would manage the bulk of his public correspondence, grown too voluminous for one man to handle.

General Washington did not know it then, but never again would he write a letter to his old friend, Colonel Fairfax.

One August day of 1786 Martha was in her garden, picking figs from the tree trained on the wall like a vine, when she saw George coming down the path, holding a letter in his hand.

She hurried toward him with an agility that belied her fifty-five years. The stricken look on his face told her that someone close to him had died. "George, who is it?" she asked.

In a choked voice, he told her. The letter was from Sally Fairfax, notifying him of the death of her husband in Bath, on the third of April, and his burial in Writhlington Church, Somerset.

Martha touched George's hand, her eyes soft with compassion. "I know . . . you've lost your best friend."

As they walked slowly back to the house, arm in arm, she was thinking: *Now Sally will never be Lady Fairfax.* How

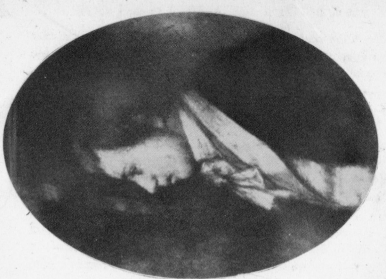

GEORGE WASHINGTON PARKE CUSTIS
AS A YOUNG MAN
By James Sharpless

GEORGE WASHINGTON PARKE CUSTIS
AS A CHILD
By R. E. Pine

she must be wishing that George William had lived just a little longer—long enough for her to be called "Your Ladyship"!

Martha refused to face the fact, but it was true, nevertheless, that for some time an increasing number of people had been coming to Mount Vernon to try to draw George Washington back into public office.

"I'm glad to be of help, and will give any advice I can," he told them all. "But I do not want to mix again in politics."

A convention was called to meet in Philadelphia in May 1787, for the purpose of framing a better government for the United States. George Washington refused to go, although he knew the republic he had helped to create was not doing well under the Articles of Confederation, and it was he who had advised holding this convention.

But Martha thought he should.

A few days before the convention she found him pacing the riverside piazza, his hands behind his back, his head bent in thought.

She stepped in front of him, and seized him by the button of his coat to attract his attention. "Are you going to Philadelphia, Papa? Shall I pack for you?"

George Washington looked down wearily upon his wife. "I'm tired, Patsy. I had some part in bringing the ship into port. It's not my duty to embark again upon a sea of troubles."

Martha knew what she was doing. She was sending George back into public life; threatening her own happiness and his. "Your country needs you, Papa. You must see the people get the freedom for which they fought."

So, reluctantly, "because Patsy thought he should," George Washington went to the convention in Philadelphia.

Martha saw him off with some anxiety. His rheumatism was bad. He was depressed by the illness of his mother, the deaths of his brother, John Augustine, and of Colonel Fairfax.

In Philadelphia, George Washington was chosen president of the body of men who, seated in Independence Hall, framed our constitution. But in four months he was back at Mount Vernon—"Farmer Washington" again, through with politics, he told his wife, and interested only in his home, horses and fields.

There was no reason to fear, Martha told herself, that these quiet days by the blue Potomac would not continue.

In June of 1788, she accompanied George to Fredericksburg to visit his ailing mother.

They found Mary Ball Washington in her garden, as had the Marquis de Lafayette when, on his visit to America, he had gone to see the mother of his old commander. And as she had made the distinguished Frenchman wait until she planted her peas, Mary Washington let her famous son and his wife cool their heels while she plucked the withered buds from a climbing rose. Then she unbent enough to invite them into her white cottage for a cup of tea and a plain biscuit.

She must have been glad to see her son—this eighty-one-year-old woman who knew she had not long to live—but she had not forgiven George for disobeying her and going to war again.

Mary Washington still hated war. And proud as she no doubt was of her son during the Revolution, she had refused to show her pleasure at the honors paid him. When people praised him, she would merely shrug and say, "He always was a good boy. George always does his duty."

She said it now, seated drinking tea with her son and daughter-in-law, as Washington tried to explain to her why he had fought: "Yes, George, I know . . . you always do your duty."

This last visit to her mother-in-law left Martha depressed. As she strolled in her garden and through the quiet rooms of Mount Vernon, the voice of Mary Washington echoed in her ears: "*George always does his duty.*"

There was no use denying the fact that their days at Mount Vernon were numbered. America needed a leader—a *president*. And General Washington, the hero of the recent war, was the man the people wanted.

George knew it, too, that this pleasant life of a Virginia squire might not be his much longer. He said little about it, even to his wife. But quietly he was putting his plantation in order so that he could again leave it.

One April morning in 1789, a tall, gray-haired visitor arrived at Mount Vernon with an important message. He was received by Martha with her usual cordial welcome, for he was Charles Thomson, the Secretary of Congress. He had been appointed to inform George Washington of his election as the first President of the United States.

"Farmer Washington" was riding over his farms that spring morning, superintending the fencing of some fields. It was dinner time before he returned to the house.

He must have been prepared for the news that Secretary Thomson brought him, for he replied calmly, "I am touched by this proof of my country's trust in me. I hope they will have no reason to regret their choice. All I can promise is to do my best."

Martha's reaction was one of complete surprise. She had known, of course, that this might happen. But when the summons came, all she could do was bow her head and murmur a prayer.

She knew how much George's answer would cost them in the years to come. It meant leaving Mount Vernon. "America's First Lady," that would be her title. How little it mattered to her!

Nevertheless, pride stirred in Martha's heart, too, and an appreciation of the qualities in her husband that had made him the country's leader. "*George always does his duty.*" She found herself repeating Mary Washington's words. And when she lifted her wet eyes, Martha was smiling.

There was so much to be done before George left for New York. A hasty visit to his mother in Fredericksburg— the last time he would see her—and then back to Mount Vernon, where Martha had packed his satin breeches, ruffled shirts and long white stockings.

Next morning, the carriage was at the door. Secretary Thomson and Colonel Humphreys, George's aide, were seated in it, ready to leave. But George still paced the piazza, staring unhappily out over the Potomac.

Martha's heart ached for him. They had had so little time at Mount Vernon. The house enlarged, gardens and a few trees planted. And before they could enjoy it all, they must leave home again.

"I've been a soldier, Patsy," George said, heavily. "Now I must learn a new trade, that of a statesman. Do you think I can do it?"

At the doubt in his voice, her round chin rose. There was firm belief and immense pride in her voice, as she answered, "Of course you can, Papa."

Cheered by these reassuring words, George Washington drove off to New York to be inaugurated the first President of the United States.

After his departure, Martha's courage ebbed. Could George be the wise, strong statesman his country expected? He was fifty-seven, and tired of public life. He had steered America through en eight-year war, refusing to take any pay for his services. He was badly in debt, and must borrow money to meet his expenses. Yet his country was asking him to sacrifice himself further. Hadn't he done enough?

Three weeks later, another coach set out from Mount Vernon. In it were Martha, her grandchildren, and a maid. Robert Lewis, who was to be one of his uncle's secretaries, escorted the carriage on horseback.

There was a stop at Abingdon, so Nelly and Washington could say good-bye to their mother, sisters, and the Stuart babies. Then they were off on a journey so exciting that the Custis children, who had never been further than Abingdon, forgot about the sad partings.

All the way to New York, it was a triumphal procession, with honors due the President's wife. At Chester, Pennsylvania, Martha was met by troops of cavalry and the Governor of the State. The soldiers formed into two columns, and Martha bowed graciously as the coach drove between them.

On entering Philadelphia, the streets were lined with cheering people. Thirteen cannon shots (in honor of the number of states) announced her arrival. When the procession stopped at the Robert Morris house, where Martha was to stay, she rose in the carriage and made the only public speech ever recorded of her. With charming modesty, she thanked the people of Philadelphia for their courtesies.

A reception was held in Mrs. Morris's drawing-room next day so Philadelphians could greet the wife of the new President. Then on Martha went to Liberty Hall, the home of Governor Livingston of New Jersey at Elizabethtown. Mistress Washington arrived rosy and smiling. The welcome she received as she passed through New Jersey, she had been told, was second only to that given the President of the United States a few weeks earlier!

Her face was rosier still next morning, when she came downstairs and saw at the breakfast table a handsome man, eating his favorite hoe cakes and honey.

"Papa!" she cried, and rushed to embrace him.

President Washington had left New York at dawn to come and escort his First Lady to the new capital.

Excitedly Martha and the children took their seats in the presidential barge, manned by thirteen men in white uniforms, to be rowed across the Hudson. For the first time she was hearing George called "Your Excellency."

"I can't call him Papa anymore," Martha thought. "It'll have to be something more dignified. Not the President, that's too cold . . . The General, that suited him. I mustn't forget."

As the boat came up the bay, cheering crowds—Governor George Clinton among them—gathered on the wharf to welcome the wife of the President to New York.

Acknowledging this warm greeting with bows and smiles, the tall President and his wife, who stood only as high as his heart, walked across the dock and entered a carriage to be driven to their new home on Cherry Street.

Her cheeks flushed, Mrs. Washington gazed out of the window. She felt George's hand tremble, as it held hers. Neither of them had wanted to leave Mount Vernon. But now that they were in New York, a sense of excitement filled them. What sorrows, what joys lay before them, as the first President of the United States and the first First Lady?

Chapter Twelve   Martha's "Lost Days"

AT SEVEN O'CLOCK ON THE FRIDAY EVENING FOLLOWING THE arrival of Martha Washington in New York, a line of carriages drew up at Number Ten Cherry Street, corner of Pearl, in the neighborhood now shadowed by Brooklyn Bridge. The President of the United States and his wife were holding their first reception.

Full dress was required, a fine excuse for ransacking trunks for imported silks and satins that had not seen candlelight since the Revolution. The cream of New York society, the wives and daughters of Congressmen, in their towering plumed headdresses and flower-garlanded skirts, not to mention the foreign ministers in their colorful uniforms, presented as elegant a list of guests as the city had seen for years.

The presidential mansion was called "the Palace." In reality it was far from palatial—a modest, three-story brick house, once occupied by the leader of Congress, and not even in the fashionable section of New York, then at Wall and Broad Streets. But it was cheap—Samuel Osgood, the Postmaster-General, being pleased to rent it to the President for nine hundred pounds a year.

"What are they like, these Washingtons?" people were asking.

There was nothing to be learned about them from the entrance hall of the Osgood house, which their guests had

seen many times and which was still furnished with the
Osgood belongings, rented along with the house. There was
a businesslike office, past which they moved slowly—was it
here that President Washington attended to affairs of state?
Then there was a drawing-room, where the President and
the First Lady were receiving. On the wall hung a large
portrait of Louis XVI in his state robes, a gift from the
French king to George Washington.

Under the portrait of the monarch stood President Washington, silver buttons on his brown suit, silver buckles on
his shoes, and his powdered hair gathered in a black silk bag.
Above his ruffled shirt of immaculate whiteness, his face was
so handsome that many a lady's heart fluttered as she curtsied
to him. Always distinguished-looking, George Washington,
nearing sixty, was even more striking in appearance than in
his youth.

At his side stood Martha, flourishing a fan and smiling.
She wore a full-skirted gown of white brocade trimmed with
silver. And on her powdered hair was a tiny white tulle hat,
its snowy ostrich feather curling down to touch her rosy
cheek.

Fifty-eight years old, but Martha was as straight-backed
as the day she made her bow to Governor William Gooch
in Williamsburg. And as bright of eye, too, as she received
the compliments of the crowd, pausing now and then to
lift her gaze to the noble face of the man beside her.

The first President of the United States—her husband.

As the New York ladies acknowledged Mrs. Washington's
bows with curtsies, a murmur of pleased surprise rose from
the crowd. She was such a little lady! And so dignified. And
younger than her husband, *years* younger. Who had spread
the rumor that the former Widow Custis was a plain, wealthy

woman who had captured the beau of the year—Virginia's hero, gallant Colonel Washington? Why, the wife of the new President was *charming!*

In the dining room the guests were impressed by the tea service engraved with the Washington coat-of-arms, as servants in the red and white livery of the family served them plum cake, tea and coffee. They were flattered when the President left his wife's side and chatted with them as familiarly as he would have done at Mount Vernon. Nor was his wife behind him in graciousness. She honored Mrs. Robert Morris, whose husband had raised the money for the Revolution, by drawing her down onto a sofa beside her. She was ready to engage other ladies in conversation, when an accident happened.

The ceilings of the house were so low that a young lady's headdress of ostrich feathers touched the candles in the chandelier and burst into flames. The lady shrieked. The President's aide, Colonel Humphreys, rushed to her rescue. Clapping the burning plumes between his hands, he put out the flames before their wearer was singed. Then Mrs. Washington went over to calm the frightened guest.

The reception continued. Indeed, it was just at its height when the clock struck nine. At that, Martha Washington rose and announced sweetly:

"The General retires at nine o'clock, and I usually precede him. Good night."

With a bow and smile, she moved gracefully up the stairs at the President's side, and disappeared.

Crestfallen, the guests accepted their dismissal. What could they do but ask for their wraps and leave? Behind them, servants quickly snuffed out candles and locked the doors. By ten o'clock the house was dark and quiet. Everyone was in bed.

Next morning the guests awoke to a furious discussion of Mrs. Washington's Friday levee—and their dismissal at the early hour of nine! There had been nothing very gay about the evening. In fact, it might be called dull, with its modest refreshments of plum cake, tea and coffee. No wine, no rich pastries and desserts. For people as rich as the Washingtons were *supposed* to be, wasn't it a disappointment?

Thus the talk went the rounds, with various offended New Yorkers agreeing stiffly that no one cared to be asked again to Number Ten Cherry Street.

But, as is usually the case when a party has a tang of novelty, things did not work out that way. Martha Washington's short and simple receptions proved to be an appetizer. Held each Friday evening, they were well attended by the old Knickerbocker families and the relatives of the government officials. And then and there a rule was set of early hours for the President and his family that has been gratefully observed by residents of the White House ever since.

When Martha reached New York, she had found George knitting his brows over social requirements. Should he give a reception each week for men only? Should he receive with Martha at her Friday levees? How many dinners for members of Congress were necessary? The First President and the first First Lady had no precedent to guide them. They had to make their own rules.

They knew they must ponder these matters and decide wisely. Whatever they did, other Presidents and First Ladies would be called upon to do likewise.

Colonel David Humphreys, Washington's aide, who had been Secretary of Legation in Paris and was used to the courts of Europe, wanted formal ceremony. George, ever the dignified statesman and fond of elegance, was inclined to agree with him. It was Martha who pleaded for simplicity. She wanted those courtesies to which her husband's high office was entitled, she told the men, but she begged that their entertainments be democratic enough not to be thought too royal.

Besides their levees, the Washingtons planned a series of dinners each Thursday during the session of Congress. With invitations issued for four o'clock, they waited five minutes after the time set for any latecomers. Then the President led the way into the dining room. "Gentlemen, we are too punctual for you," he told any stragglers-in. "I have a cook who never asks whether the company has come, but whether the hour of four has arrived."

The President sat halfway down the table, with the First Lady opposite him. Unless a minister was present, he said grace before sitting down, after which the guests were given a plain, but hearty family meal. On the table was the mirrored tray, which is today on the banquet table at Mount Vernon. Around it were placed the dishes of roast beef, turkey and chicken; the puddings and jellies at dessert time. From these, one of the President's young secretaries served the guests in the most informal fashion. The steward, ex-tavern keeper Samuel Fraunces, known as Black Sam because of his dark skin, dressed in a white apron and powdered wig, stood watching over six other servants in the Washington red and white livery.

What could be simpler than these Congressional dinners, without any excess of silver and wine and rich food, as displayed by the wealthy New Yorkers of the day? Nevertheless, dissatisfied people accused President and Mrs. Washington of "aping royalty."

Doctor David Stuart wrote them what was being said in

Virginia—that their receptions were "awkward imitations of royalty" with "more pomp than at St. James, and that your bows are more distant and stiff."

Reading David Stuart's letter, Martha's eyes filled with tears. Trying to please everyone, she and George had pleased no one. They must entertain lavishly enough to satisfy the aristocratic Knickerbocker families; yet not give offense to the strict Republicans.

They were living, the first President and his First Lady, the kind of life that is most distasteful to candid and honorable people; getting up in the morning after sleepless nights to talk over the gossip that had reached them, trying to console one another, to say that nothing mattered when they knew they were doing the right thing, yet knowing that before night came, some further malicious talk would hurt them.

The old influential New York families, the Livingstons, Beekmans, Van Rensselaers, and Jays, were disappointed in the Washingtons. The President did not attend another ball after the one given by the French minister in May, before Martha joined him. George's mother died in August, and the household went into mourning, even their servants wearing black cockades and arm bands.

When this period was over, New Yorkers saw that Mrs. Washington cared little for formal society. She never appeared at a public ball. And if she attended the Thursday Assemblies, a series of exclusive subscription dances, she did not dance and went home by ten o'clock.

Nor was Martha Washington's popularity increased by the fact that she refused to pay calls while in New York. She spent her days sewing beside a window that looked out on the East River, beyond which lay the small village of Brooklyn and the green forests of Long Island. And something akin to despair grew in her heart.

For the first time in her fifty-eight years, Martha was finding it impossible to adapt herself to circumstances. She was aware of what she was doing; she was making enemies for George and herself. But it was quiet and peaceful there in the bedroom on Cherry Street, and cruel criticism and lies could not reach her, so long as she was retired from her role of First Lady and was only Martha Washington. As for George—

Something ached inside of her at the thought of the man who had been her companion now for thirty years. This morning he had seemed old and tired. His rheumatism was bad. Burdened with cares of state, he had no time for medical treatment; yet he had found time to pat her hand, to ask when she had seen jolly Lucy Knox. Why not ask Mrs. Greene and Mrs. Montgomery, widows of his Generals, to tea? Martha was too much alone. She must see her friends . . .

"Oh, George, I can't—I can't see anyone," she had cried.

He had not pressed the point. "I know, I'm unhappy here, too," he murmured, kissing her gently. "My poor Patsy!"

Was she ill? Exhausted by the obligations of prescribed etiquette? Or desperately homesick for Mount Vernon? Martha did not know. She only knew that, even with George beside her, she was miserable. The Revolution had left her mentally and physically weary; the role of First Lady tired her to a degree that all the hardships of the war had failed to do. For the first time, she was finding it difficult to make new friends.

These were Martha Washington's "lost days" . . . the days which throughout her life, in letters and conversation, she was to refer to as those most barren of happiness.

To her niece, Fanny, whose husband, Major Washington, had been left in charge at Mount Vernon, Martha wrote a homesick, discouraged letter:

"I live a dull life here and know nothing that passes in the town . . . I never goe to any publick place . . . indeed I am more like a state prisoner than anything else, there is certain bounds set for me which I must not depart from . . . and as I cannot doe as I like I am obstinate and stay at home a great deal. . . ."

A few New Yorkers liked Martha Washington for her cordial manner, combined with well-bred dignity. William Johnston, in writing of a dinner at the President's, pays his "Lady" a nice compliment:

"I had the honor of drinking coffee with his Lady, a most amiable woman. I believe I shall become reconciled to the company of old women, for her sake. I have found them generally so censorious, and envious, that I could never bear their company. This made me marry a woman much younger than myself, lest I should hate her when she grew old; but I now really believe there are some good old women."

Martha's life in New York was made pleasanter when Tobias Lear, now the President's senior secretary, brought into the household as his bride a pretty twenty-three-year-old girl from his native Portsmouth.

"What would we do without the Lears?" Martha and George often asked one another.

Polly Lear took over many details of the receptions which Martha, with her dislike of the formality necessary to her position, was glad to be rid of. Tobias Lear handled the Washingtons' financial matters. He taught the children and managed the household. He wrote the President's letters and accompanied him each afternoon for a stroll on the Battery, the fashionable promenade of the day. And he took Martha shopping, usually to John Turner's dry-goods store.

Mistress Washington had never aspired to be a fashion leader, and after forty, she adopted middle-aged clothes. Her kerchiefs bordered with lace, a style she took from the Quakers, were usually worn over daytime dresses of stiff black silk or damask. Her cloaks were invariably of mulberry velvet, plain but of the best material.

Her one extravagance was gloves. She bought dozens of pairs to match each costume. And her one vanity now was her thick gray hair, once the color of a ripe chestnut. Each morning Lawrence Marey, a hairdresser, came to brush and curl and arrange her tresses. Then, when she had admired the creation, Martha hid it under a prim mob cap, of which she had a large collection.

Some of Martha Washington's caps were more becoming than others. Her New York caps of muslin and fluted lace, adorned with satin bows, were better suited to her round, pink face with its sweet mouth and hint of a double chin, than were the towering effects created for her later by the Philadelphia capmakers, which made the short, plump Mrs. Washington look top-heavy.

On the first of July, when Martha had only been in New York two months, she was made even more unhappy by a serious crisis in her life. George fell ill. A malignant carbuncle on his thigh forced him to lie on his side in bed for weeks, most of the time in great pain.

Frantic with worry, Martha nursed him herself, quick to soothe his pain and to relieve him from annoyance. Every noise disturbed the invalid. She ordered a chain stretched across the street to stop the passing of carriages. She had straw laid on the sidewalk. Nightly she prayed for cooler weather.

"Am I going to die, doctor?" George asked weakly. "Tell me, I'm not afraid to know."

Doctor Samuel Bard, his physician, admitted he was fearful.

Dropping to her knees beside her husband's bed, Martha took his hand and implored him to live.

George sighed. "Whether tonight or twenty years hence, it makes no difference. I am prepared—"

But he did not die. By the end of July he was better. Martha had had their new carriage remodeled so that George could lie on his side in it. And for several weeks he was carried out and put into it every day, driving around town for an hour with her, until gradually he recovered his strength.

Then, as now, Saturday was a school holiday; and nearly every Saturday, President Washington wrote in his diary: *"Exercised in the coach with the two children (Master and Miss Custis)—went the fourteen miles round."* The fourteen miles round was the circle of Manhattan Island, and Martha's favorite drive.

George and Martha were proud of their cream-colored English coach trimmed with scarlet, the Washington colors, which had arrived from London just before George's illness. On each of its four panels was a picture illustrating the four seasons, painted by the Italian artist, Cipriani. At the windows were hung Venetian blinds to keep out the sun, and black leather curtains for rainy weather.

There was always a crowd gathered across the street when the tall figure of the President, wearing a three-cornered hat and a blue military cape, came out of his house to enter the coach drawn by four high-stepping bay horses. Gallantly he

MARTHA WASHINGTON'S RECEPTION

handed in the First Lady, in her cloak of mulberry-colored velvet and plumed bonnet, and their two grandchildren. The postillions, in cocked hats, yellow gloves, and polished boots, jumped onto the lead horses. Fagan, the coachman, gave a crack of his whip. The Washington coach rolled off through the cobble-paved streets lined with narrow brick houses, each with its garden, and past the wharfs where the sailing ships were tied.

The Washingtons, being country people, were always glad when they reached the edge of the city, a short journey in those days, since New York was only a village on the tip of Manhattan. A drive of one mile up the Boston and Kingsbridge Road, over Murray Hill (now Lexington Avenue), brought them to the farms that covered the rest of the island. To McGowan's Pass (the northeast corner of Central Park) they went. Then the road grew rougher as they turned west and crossed the island by Harlem Lane (Saint Nicholas Avenue) to the west side (where General Grant's tomb stands). Today an automobile would cover this distance in an hour. Then it took the Washingtons all morning.

Presently the carriage turned south on the Bloomingdale Road (Broadway), the fashionable driving street of the city. Here was a parade of ladies in their carriages. Gay young blades sped by on horseback. Martha's neck ached from returning all their bows. And Nelly and young Washington, bright-eyed with excitement, thought they would never get enough of the crowds, the clop-clop of the horses' hoofs, and the roll of the coach beneath them.

But the children would not soon forget the day when they and Grandmama stepped into the carriage just as the bridle of one of the horses broke. The animal reared. He might have bolted if an Irish groom, James Hurley, had not jumped in front of the horse and held onto the broken rein.

The horses' harness was silver-plated, engraved with the Washington crest. The President's postillions wore their white liveries with scarlet waistcoats; the colors taken from the coat-of-arms of the Washington family. With the cream-colored coach and horses, the whole was indeed a royal equipage. Still there were New Yorkers who thought this turnout too modest for the President of the United States.

A Congressman, Colonel Thomas Rodney, describes in his diary the style, or rather what he considered the lack of it, displayed by the First Lady:

"After passing the ferry met Mrs. Washington in a coach, preceded by a Servant ½ mile ahead, and two Gentlemen on Horseback. This was her Suite. In old countries a Lady of her rank would not be seen without a retinue of twenty persons. The Motions of the President and His Lady is the public Talk of all Ranks at & near New York."

Such talk, when it reached Martha's ears, wounded her deeply. She had tried so hard to please. But her best apparently was never good enough. For a while she was so unhappy that she gave up her afternoon drives, until George Washington, distressed at finding his spirited wife pale and continually moping at home, gave her a gentle scolding.

"We might as well live as we please, Patsy; it's impossible to please everyone," he told her wisely. But his eyes were soft as he said it. He, too, was being hurt by adverse criticism, and well he understood her misery.

Dear George, how kind he was . . . how understanding! Almost shamefaced, Martha dried her eyes and straightened her cap. Her behavior, when viewed honestly, was cowardly and not worthy of her. She had a duty to fulfill—to stand by her husband's side in the high office by which the country had honored him. And George must not be ashamed of her.

Martha Washington would never learn to like living in the public eye. But gradually she forced herself to hide her distaste for its life of ceremony, and to acknowledge its many compensations and rewards. Hospitable and kindly by nature, she performed her duties as hostess at Number Ten Cherry Street with her usual courtesy and cheerfulness. Patiently she went through her "lost days."

But she expressed her feelings as to her "unwished-for situation," as she called it, to Mercy Warren, a Boston friend, in a letter so well spelled that it has obviously been edited:

"—I little thought when the war was finished that any circumstances would possibly happen which would call the General into public life again. I had anticipated that we should be suffered to grow old together, in solitude and tranquillity. . . . I sometimes think the arrangement is not as it ought to have been, that I, who had much rather be at home, should occupy a place with which a great many younger and gayer women would be extremely pleased.—When I was younger I should probably have enjoyed the gaieties of life as much as most persons of my age; but I have long since placed all the prospects of my worldly happiness in the enjoyments of the fireside at Mount Vernon—I have learned too much of the vanity of human affairs to expect felicity from public life. But I am determined to be cheerful and happy in whatever situation I may be. For I have also learned from experience that the greater part of our happiness, or misery depends on our dispositions and not on our circumstances. We carry the seeds of the one or the other about with us in our minds wherever we go."

The evenings that Martha Washington enjoyed the most in New York were those when she and George took friends to the theater, a tiny place on John Street, near Broadway, seating only three hundred people.

On the evening of November 24, 1789, George Washington had been asked to choose the play. He selected *The Poor Soldier*, in which Thomas Wignell, actor as well as manager of the troupe, took the part of Darby. And William Dunlap, a young dramatist, had written an interlude in honor of the President's visit.

The interlude, called *Darby's Return*, permitted Darby, an Irish lad, to tell of his adventures in the United States at the inauguration of President Washington.

"A man who fought to free the land from woe,
Like me, had left his farm a soldiering to go,
But having gained his point, he had, like me,
Returned his own potato ground to see,
But there he would not rest; with one accord
He's called to be a kind of—not a lord—
I don't know what; he's not a *great man*, sure,
For poor men love him just as he were poor,
They love him like a father or a brother—"

Seated in his box, his wife and friends around him, George Washington frowned. Nothing annoyed him like personal flattery.

Martha, knowing this, nervously fingered her fan, as the heroine of the play, Kathleen, asked Darby about the President.

"How look'd he, Darby? Was he short or tall?"

Martha felt George stiffen beside her. Coming, they both knew, was one of those distressing eulogies of his person, which the hero of the Revolution was obliged to listen to on so many public occasions.

But there was no cause for worry.

With an impish grin, Darby replied that he could not say what the President looked like, because at the inauguration *he had not seen him*. He had mistaken for George Washington a man "all lace and glitter, botherum and shine," until the show had passed.

At this saucy answer, there was a burst of laughter from the audience. And no one laughed harder than George and Martha Washington!

Wrapping her mulberry cloak around her at the end of the performance, Martha hummed the tune of a new piece of music, *The President's March*, composed by Feyles, the leader of the orchestra. It was played that night for the first time as the President and First Lady entered their box, intensifying the applause which greeted them. The audience, made up of many soldiers and sailors, veterans of the Revolution, recognized in the lively music the fife and drum beat, and began to cheer *The President's March*. Today it is known as *Hail Columbia*, from the first two words of its opening line, and is one of our great patriotic songs.

That Nelly and young Washington were as ardent theatergoers as their grandparents is shown by Tobias Lear's account book. Master and Miss Custis, aged eight and ten, were taken to such plays as *The Devil to Pay* or *The Wives Metamorphosed*, *The Drummer* or *The Haunted House*, and *The Duenna* or *The Double Elopement*, to which was added (they were all double features in those days) a pantomimical romance called *Robinson Crusoe* or *The Genius of Columbia*.

Part of the home attic was turned over to Nelly and Washington as a playroom, and there the youngsters held amateur theatricals, calling themselves the "Young American Company," after the Old American Company of Philadelphia.

But Martha saw to it that life was not all fun for Nelly and Washington Custis. The children continued their lessons under Tobias Lear. And Nelly, "a wild little creature who spends her time at the window looking at carriages & passing," as Martha wrote her niece, Fanny Washington, was being curbed to the extent of three music lessons each week and painting lessons under William Dunlap, who was a man of diversified talents, being also the author of *Darby's Return*.

That fall of 1789, George and Martha Washington decided that Tobias Lear was too occupied with his secretarial duties to serve as tutor to the young Custises. A Mrs. Graham's school was recommended for Nelly. Her announcement read:

Boarding and Education for Young Ladies

Mrs. Graham presents most respectful compliments to the Public. She proposes opening a School for Boarding and Educating young ladies, where will be taught on reasonable terms, Reading, English, Spelling and Grammar, Plainwork, Embroidery, Cloathwork, and various works of fancy Writing, Arithmetic, Geography, Drawing, Painting, Japanning, Philigree, Music, Dancing, and the French language. One of Mrs. Graham's assistants was for nine years in France, and has since assisted in some of the first Boarding Schools in London. For particulars apply at Mrs. Graham's, No. 5 Maiden Lane, New York.

Nelly started school as a day scholar in November. At the same time, young Custis began lessons under a Mr. Murdock. The boy had not done well under Tobias Lear, but then perhaps Tobias had been too fond of him, Martha thought.

The society of other boys might persuade her grandchild to take an interest in his studies.

It didn't, of course, for the good reason that Washington, like his father before him, was an indolent youngster with no love of study. Mr. Murdock could do no more with him than had Tobias Lear, who had honestly tried.

When Washington brought home a below-passing report card, his grandfather scolded him, just as he had scolded Jacky Custis. "I can govern men, but I cannot govern boys," he told Martha in discouragement.

With Nelly, it was different. She was sweet and docile— her grandparents' greatest joy. It was only necessary for Nelly to stand on tiptoe, holding to the button of her grandfather's coat as she whispered into his ear some request, to make his eyes soften. Whatever it was, he never refused her.

By winter, Nelly was old enough to attend her grandmother's teas, passing the silver sugar and cream bowls and catching the eye of all Mrs. Washington's callers.

Seeing the fuss everyone made of the child, Martha's heart sank. Nelly would be a vain little piece if ever there was one!

One day as a milliner waited on them in Mrs. Washington's bedroom, Nelly begged permission to try on two bonnets, one pink and one blue. Martha smiled as her granddaughter tried on the first one before the mirror, a plain blue silk affair; and then the pink, fluffy ruffles and one pink rose, all the while admiring her pretty round face with its dimpled chin and blue eyes.

Of course, Nelly decided on the pink bonnet as the most becoming, and indeed it was.

"May I have this one, Grandmama?" she asked sweetly.

Mrs. Washington removed her glasses, which she now wore

for sewing and reading. "No, my dear, not the pink," she said firmly. "The plain blue one, if you like."

And in spite of Nelly's tears, the pink bonnet went back to the shop.

But how could Martha Washington conceal from Nelly the truth about her dark good looks, for painters were constantly begging permission to paint the President's pretty granddaughter. It was enough to turn any ten-year-old's head.

The New Year of 1790 was warm enough for May. So unseasonable was it that the farmers of Manhattan began to plough their fields, and women appeared on the streets in summer dresses. And so many people crowded into Number Ten Cherry Street to wish the President and his family a "Happy New Year" that the air became hot and stuffy, and Martha, in her best black bombazine with tight sash and bodice, was faint with heat and fatigue.

Martha and George liked the old Dutch custom of paying New Year calls. But that crowded New Year reception made them realize that their Cherry Street house, in which they had lived for nine months, was entirely too small for their family. Looking around for larger quarters, they decided on the McComb house on Broadway, between Trinity Church and Bowling Green, where the French minister had lived.

The six-story house stood on a lawn sloping to the Hudson River. The drawing-room at the back of the house—Martha noted with pleasure its size—looked across the river to the forests of New Jersey. Their New Year reception of 1791 would be different; there would be ample room.

But there was to be no New Year's reception in the Mc-Comb house. The President's stay there was brief. By summer, Congress decided to move the federal government to Philadelphia while a permanent national capital was laid out on the Potomac, the site to be selected by President Washington. In August, Martha happily began to pack for the journey.

Liking to do things simply, the Washingtons had hoped to slip quietly away one morning. At daybreak, Martha had the children dressed, and after a hurried breakfast the carriage was called to the door. She was tying the strings of her bonnet, when out on Broadway they heard a band strike up *The President's March*. The children rushed to the window. There on the sidewalk stood Governor Clinton, his suite, and other New Yorkers, assembled to see the Washingtons off.

George laughed. "We're found out, Patsy. Come, we'll have to do our part . . ." Taking his grandson's hand, he led the way; Martha followed with Nelly.

Down Broadway the Washingtons' friends, led by a band, escorted them to the wharf and the presidential barge.

Standing in the stern of the boat, the President made a brief speech of farewell. He thanked the crowd that had assembled, as New Yorkers, for the manner in which he had been treated in their city, which he said he was leaving with regret.

As the boat moved away across the Hudson, Martha Washington stood beside her husband, smiling happily. Before going to Philadelphia to live, there was time for a brief visit back to Mount Vernon!

Leaving the presidential barge on the Jersey shore, the Washingtons entered their waiting coach for the journey home. In spite of the long hours in the lurching carriage over rutty roads, Martha's spirits rose with each mile as she neared her beloved Virginia.

Through the villages of New Jersey and Pennsylvania, their streets lined by crowds gathered to catch a glimpse of the President and his family, passed the Washington retinue. An outrider galloped ahead to warn of bad spots in the road. Then came the English coach, drawn by four horses, containing President Washington, his wife and grandchildren, with his secretaries riding on each side as escort. Behind them drove the open chariot with the maids. Last, the baggage wagon and mounted slaves leading extra horses.

There was a stop at Abingdon to permit Nelly and Washington to see their sisters, Eliza and Patsy, as well as another Stuart baby born during their absence. Then the Stuart coach joined the procession, Nelly and her sisters riding with the Washingtons and the three girls chattering all the way.

"How Eliza and Patsy have grown!" thought their grandmother, forgetting she had been away for fifteen months. "And isn't Eliza pretty! Prettier than dear Patsy . . ."

With a final lurch, the coach turned into the gate at Mount Vernon. George looked out eagerly on his side; Martha and Nelly on the other. "There's the bowling green!" said Martha. And there were the cabins. The spinning house. Her garden.

Mount Vernon had never looked so lovely to its homesick owners. Martha's eyes were like stars, as she groped for George's hand. Tomorrow they would walk together about the grounds; they would see how much each tree and bush had grown.

"Papa . . ." she breathed—he was no longer "The General," "The President"—"*we're home!*"

George nodded, too touched to answer.

From all sides the servants came running. The master and mistress of the plantation—not the President of the United States and the First Lady—had come home.

Chapter Thirteen   *Mistress President*

IN PHILADELPHIA, THE CITY FATHERS OFFERED PRESIDENT Washington the gift of a large house in the most fashionable neighborhood.

"If the Washingtons find a home they like, they'll want to stay in Philadelphia," people were saying. "Instead of the capital being moved south, it will remain in the City of Brotherly Love."

But the City Fathers did not know their independent President. George Washington wished to see the national capital situated on the banks of the Potomac. The most indiscreet thing he could do was to place himself under obligations to the Philadelphians. So declining the offer of the Ninth Street mansion, he rented a modest brick house owned by Robert Morris on High Street, now Market, between Fifth and Sixth Streets.

His choice was Martha's choice. Number 190 High Street, "too far out of town for fashion," boasted a stable large enough to hold twelve horses, which added to George's pleasure, as well as to that of his grandson, who already had a fine seat and his father's taste for blooded stock. To the east of the house was a walled garden, with peach and apple and cherry trees shading rows of flower beds. To the west was the home of Robert Morris. And Martha thought how pleasant it would be to live next door to the lively Mrs. Morris.

If the Washingtons could not have Mount Vernon, the Quaker atmosphere of this less stylish section of Philadelphia was second best. But the High Street house had to be enlarged to hold the President, his family, secretaries and servants. Deep bow windows extended the dining and drawing-rooms to a size suitable for entertaining. A kitchen ell helped to house Mrs. Washington's large stock of copper pots and pans. Yet even with these additions, the house was far from ideal. Whoever heard of an Executive Mansion with the President's office on the third floor, so that visitors on business had to climb two flights of stairs, walking past the family dining room and parlor?

"A totally unsuitable house for the President of the United States!" people were saying. "And next door to a hairdresser!"

Many government officials and Congressmen had not liked the transfer of the national capital from New York. Prices were higher in Philadelphia, houses difficult to rent and hard to remodel. The move had been urged on Congress by George Washington, they claimed, and the President had been influenced by his friend, Robert Morris, to promote Morris's real estate in Philadelphia.

"And haven't the Washingtons rented one of the Morris houses?" people added significantly.

The presidential family arrived in Philadelphia in November. But it was Christmas night before the High Street house was in condition for Martha to hold her first levee. She welcomed her guests in the "green room," which was behind the "yellow" or family sitting room, hung with curtains of green satin and furnished with mahogany furniture uphol-stered in green—a room made habitable only after a long struggle with fresh paint and Mrs. Washington's ingenuity with scissors and needle.

On a sofa before the fire sat the First Lady in a gown of blue velvet, over a white satin petticoat flounced with lace. Her gray hair was arranged moderately high, not half so high as the imposing structures of Lucy Knox and Mrs. Morris, who received with her. As in New York, liveried servants served the guests plum cake, tea and coffee. Martha's only concession to the gaiety of Philadelphia was to extend the closing hour of her receptions from nine to ten o'clock.

As that hour struck, there was a cordial good night, and lights out. The guests, not surprised, because whispers of the Washingtons' quiet habits had drifted down from New York, went on to merrier parties. George and Martha, rather worn out with their first taste of society after the peaceful months at Mount Vernon, retired to their bedroom on the third floor and were soon fast asleep.

As the days slipped by, Martha Washington was obliged to concede that it was possible to be the wife of the President of the United States and at the same time live a fairly uninterrupted private life.

Aside from the formal levees and Congressional dinners, which she had learned to accept as part of her position, there were quiet evenings in the yellow sitting room with the children, and Tobias and Polly Lear. Martha sewed or helped Nelly and Washington with their lessons. George read aloud; or if he was too tired, Tobias, who had a good, clear voice, took over the pleasant task. Polly sang a ballad. The parrot chuckled sleepily to itself in the cage, until yawns brought fresh candles and milk and biscuits for the children and a happy good night for all.

Martha had learned a great deal since that morning at Mount Vernon, when leaving private life behind, she mounted her coach to ride to New York. She had learned to take criticism not too seriously; to realize that it was made of the office, not of herself as a woman; and that it was often inspired by enemies of the administration. But when criticism was justified, she tried to profit by it.

Strengthened by her new philosophy, Martha Washington grew to like Philadelphia. She who had refused to pay calls in New York now surprised everyone by returning visits, and promptly, always on the third day. A footman would come to the door, knock and announce "Mrs. Washington," who then went in, escorted by Tobias Lear. And her carriage was often seen on the roads around Philadelphia, with the First Lady on her way to visit Mrs. Robert Morris at her country place, the Hills, or going to other estates on the Schuylkill and around Germantown, noted for a hospitality that reminded Martha of her own Virginia.

These were morning calls only. By three o'clock the carriage had returned to High Street, and George, who had perhaps come in from a walk with his secretary, Major Jackson, was ready to join Martha and the children for dinner. Thereafter only an Assembly or a new play at the theater on Chestnut Street could lure the Washingtons from their home.

The Philadelphia newspapers frequently announced: "The President and his Lady honored the performance by the Old American Company." The manager met them at the door, handed them in with much ceremony; and they were guided to their box by an usher who carried two candlesticks to light their way.

No occasion, from the opening of a circus to a balloon ascension, was considered complete without the attendance of the presidential family. They went to Richett's Circus, where George enjoyed the bareback and fancy riding. And

Martha took the children to see Bowen's Exhibition of Wax Works.

On Sundays the President and his family attended services at St. Peter's Church, the tall, impassive chief executive wearing his cocked hat and blue military cape with the red lining; his dignified little wife in a mulberry velvet cloak and bonnet, followed by pretty Nelly Custis and her red-cheeked brother.

We see them going down the aisle, preceded by a footman who opens the door of the square box pew, and, after ushering the family in, seats himself on a chair in the aisle, where he remains throughout the service. We see him handing them into the chariot at the conclusion of the service, Martha quiet and serene, as befits the day; the children a little restless, hungry, too, for the bountiful three-o'clock dinner that will grace the High Street table.

We can see them again, Martha and the children, as they drive out on another occasion, this time in a coach-of-state drawn by six horses. It is March 4th, 1793. George Washington is to be inaugurated for the second time as President of the United States.

Smiling and bowing, Martha acknowledged the cheers of the crowds, bidding Nelly and Washington to wave their hands at a group of children standing before Federal Hall, where the inauguration is to take place. Smiling and bowing, and yet finding time above the noise of the welcome to remind the children that the cheers were not for her or for them, personally, but for the wife and family of the President of the United States.

Martha entered the Senate chamber on the arm of her nephew, Bartholomew Dandridge; followed by the children, they took seats in the space reserved for the President's family.

ELEANOR ("NELLY") PARKE CUSTIS
*Granddaughter of Martha Washington, from
a painting by Gilbert Stuart*

Her heart swelled with pride as George entered; a white-haired, erect figure in black velvet, wearing a white satin vest, ruffled shirt, and silver-buckled shoes. In the four years since his first inauguration, she had learned something of the glory of the office of President. And something, too, of the responsibility that went with that office.

Facing the distinguished audience, President Washington made a short speech, expressing his gratitude at the honor of his reëlection. The oath was then administered by Judge Cushing of the Supreme Court. As the President left the Senate with his family, there was a burst of applause from the chamber filled with both Houses of Congress and the ministers of foreign countries.

In their coach-of-state, the Washingtons drove home through streets lined with people cheering the reëlected President. Another four years in Philadelphia had begun. What would they hold for Martha Washington? Reliving the events of the last year, she knew she had cause for anxiety. The previous August Philadelphia had suffered a yellow fever epidemic, resulting in the loss of many lives, including that of young Polly Lear, who had died in the Washingtons' own home.

Now, with summer ahead, would there be another epidemic? There was, and a serious one. By August the Philadelphians were leaving the city in droves. Martha, alarmed for the safety of the children, tried to persuade George to go to Mount Vernon. But he could not be induced to give up his duties until September, when they took a house in Germantown for a few months.

From there Martha Washington wrote to Fanny Washington, now a widow, and living at Mount Vernon:

"It would, my dear Fanny, be pleasing to me to come home this summer but the President thinks that the publick business will keep him in this place all summer—and it would not be agreeable to me to stay at Mount Vernon without him—if I could bear the journey I should like to make you a flying visit but you know I cannot as I am so much fatigued after I get home for several days—that I could not think of setting out again for some time—I do not know what keys you have—it is necessary that the beds and bed clothes should be aired I beg you will make Caroline put all the things out to air and Brush and clean the rooms that they were in. . . ."

Martha's thoughts were always at Mount Vernon. Whenever a Virginian came to see her, he was plied with questions. How were things going at home? Was the house kept as tidy as when she was there? Were the gardens thriving? The river—was it still as blue, as slow-moving?

Bryan Fairfax—Martha often thought of him. Five years earlier he had become rector at Christ Church, Alexandria. But after three years Bryan resigned from the ministry. Would he ever be happy at anything, Martha wondered? His wife, sweet Elizabeth, had died during the Revolution; two years later, Bryan had married Jane Donaldson.

And Sally Fairfax?

The Washingtons heard from Sally from time to time, but never very cheerful letters. She was still living in Bath, and very poor she must be, and bitter, too. Life had played Sally a mean trick. Robert, seventh Lord Fairfax of Cameron, had died a year earlier over in England. And because his heir, George William Fairfax, passed away first, the ambitious Sally would never become Lady Fairfax.

The Cameron title was left in abeyance. If it went to anyone, it would go to Bryan Fairfax.

Martha's heart was so big that she loved not only her grand-children but her nieces and nephews, as well. Her favorite had always been Fanny, Nancy Bassett's daughter. And now she was made very happy by the news that Fanny, left a widow with three small children two years earlier, was to marry Tobias Lear, also a widower, with one boy, Lincoln.

As a wedding present, the Washingtons gave the Lears three hundred acres of the Mount Vernon land, with a house on the property known as "Wellington." The marriage was a happy one for the eight months it lasted. In the spring of 1796 Fanny died, leaving Tobias Lear with four small children on his hands.

These little ones, without doubt, raced and played in the orchard behind the house on High Street, mothered by Martha Washington, who always seemed to have time to help her friends and comfort the troubled.

She worried a great deal at this time about her sister, Betty Henley. Martha had never been as close to this younger sister as she had been to Nancy. But now Betty, twice married and the mother of eight children, was ill. Remembering that she and Betty were the last of their family, Martha's heart ached for her.

Shortly before Fanny's own death, Martha Washington had written to her about Betty:

"I am much grieved to hear that my poor sister is in such a wretched situation. . . . Poor dear Betty has had a hard lot in this world. I hope her children will be a comfort to her as they grow up and not follow their unhappy Father's bad example. I often think of her with the greatest concern. I should be very glad if she would come up to see me when I go home."

"Bryan . . . Lord Fairfax!" George Washington exclaimed when they heard the news.

And Martha smiled, too. It was so absurd. Somehow it was impossible to imagine the pious Bryan Fairfax as an English nobleman.

"If Bryan gets the title, he'll have to give up his American citizenship," George explained, "go to England to live, and become an Englishman."

"And leave Virginia!" cried Martha. She could not imagine anyone trading that privilege for a title—anyone, that is, but Sally Fairfax.

Would not the homesick Mrs. Washington gladly have given up her title of First Lady to be back, that very moment, at Mount Vernon!

Two, perhaps three times, during the presidential years, Martha saw her home when the family slipped away for a rest after Congress recessed in March. A glimpse of the river —the tall green trees framing the comfortable white mansion. A little work in the garden. Then October. Another Philadelphia season, and Martha Washington was back in the house on High Street, acting her role of First Lady.

At the beginning of the President's second term, Martha decided that Nelly, fourteen, and Washington, twelve, were old enough to attend her receptions. Young Custis did not enjoy being made to dress up and bow like a little gentleman to his grandmother's guests. But Nelly loved it.

That year the young Custises were enrolled for dancing lessons at the Robardet's Classes. And Nelly's grandparents gave her the handsome mahogany harpsichord imported from London, "costing all of a thousand dollars," that is now in the music room at Mount Vernon. The gift must have inspired Nelly, for we hear no more of her being forced to practice her music.

How Nelly and Washington, and their young friends, lightened the old brick house with their laughter and fun! And what a comfort they were to George, worried and harassed by the unfriendly Republican newspapers, especially Nelly. It pleased Martha to see how her granddaughter's sunny disposition, sweetness and vivacity, never failed to draw her husband from his moods of depression.

Eliza Custis, Martha's oldest grandchild, whom the Vice-President, John Adams, describes as "a fine, blooming, rosy girl, who, I dare say, has had more liberty and exercise than Nelly," was also a favorite of the President—an affection which the seventeen-year-old miss heartily returned.

After a visit to her grandmother in Philadelphia, Eliza wrote to George Washington that the wish of her heart was to have his portrait.

He sent Eliza a miniature in a blue enamel case bordered with pearls, and with a lock of his hair in the back. "But I can't imagine the fondest desire of a young girl's heart is to have the portrait of an old man!" he told her.

Eliza, and her sixteen-year-old sister, Martha, who was quieter and not so pretty, were often at the Executive Mansion now. Their mother, Eleanor, who had been left a large fortune by Jack Custis, had lost most of it through unfortunate investments. The Stuarts had had to give up Abingdon and move to Hope Park, the Doctor's plantation twenty miles from Alexandria.

Nelly enjoyed nothing more than to have the "blooming, rosy" Eliza, and her other sister, Martha, with her. At their grandmother's receptions, the three girls, wearing their best frocks, helped to serve refreshments. And when the house was

full of young people, President Washington—believe[d] strangers to be cold and distant—would come out of his s[hell] and join the girls and their friends in dancing the Vir[ginia] reel.

That fall, lest she think herself grown up and ask for [too] many "liberties," Nelly Custis was packed off to schoo[l at] Annapolis. Her brother, Washington, was sent away, [too.] He was badly in need of discipline. His grandfather ho[ped] the time spent at his school, later to become part of the U[ni]versity of Pennsylvania, would rouse in the happy-go-luc[ky] lad some sense of responsibility.

Nelly's close friends at Annapolis were Elizabeth Bordl[ey] of Philadelphia and Martha Coffin from Portland, who spe[nt] many vacations with her at Mount Vernon. They wrote le[t]ters and scribbled verses, and had their portraits painted f[or] each other, just as school girls do today.

But no matter what young visitors were in the hous[e,] Nelly always accompanied her grandmother upstairs whe[n] she retired for the night. She read to her from the Bible an[d] sang a hymn. After that Nelly and Mrs. Washington, wit[h] Oney and Molly, Martha's maids, knelt in prayer.

That Nelly loved her Grandmama dearly is shown by a letter, written when she herself was a grandmother:

"I never loved anyone, not even my own children, as I loved Grandmama. Her equal I can never know. Love, admiration, respect, gratitude were all hers. Her judgment, her piety, her fortitude . . . I have never known in an equal degree in anyone. She never praised me in all her life. She feared more than anything to make me vain. When I was right, I looked into her eyes. It never required speech to tell me all I wished to know."

Kindness and common sense—those words described the middle-aged Martha Washington, and to these we may add a third, which she personified in public life: *discretion*. With old friends, where she felt secure, Martha Washington was the same impulsive, vivacious person. But with strangers, she had learned never to let a careless word escape her lips.

During the Revolution, Mrs. Washington had been more outspoken. It is believed she wrote an address published in a Philadelphia newspaper in 1780, entitled *The Sentiments of an American Woman*. Under the impression that she was the author, it was read from the pulpits of churches throughout Virginia. And she never denied the fact.

Now, as wife of the President, Martha Washington had learned to be cautious of what she said. Political discussions by her guests were not permitted at the Executive Mansion. She was herself careful not to express an opinion on public questions, except among her most intimate friends. Though diplomats and others often attempted to draw the First Lady into talking on topics of the day, she adroitly evaded doing so, until she earned for herself the reputation of being dull.

Yet Martha's convictions were as decided as those of George Washington, and in perfect harmony with his. Indeed, her sympathetic heart, sound sense, and good advice gave him much of his strength, and helped him to make wise decisions when he was overcome with doubts.

It is said that on the few occasions when they were separated, George's letters to his wife were filled with discussions of public affairs. And her answers, firmly stating her opinions, frequently told him what to do.

There came a crisis when Mistress Washington's sympathies were so deeply roused that she found it hard to hold her tongue. In Europe, the French Revolution had broken out.

George Washington watched with grave apprehension the trend of the times. He had been shocked at the beheading of the French king, whom he remembered as a friend of America. He was indignant at the news that his "boy," the Marquis de Lafayette, had been forced to flee Paris, and was a prisoner in Austria.

Alexander Hamilton and his party, the Federalists, agreed with the President in denouncing the lawlessness of the French Republicans. But opinion in Philadelphia was divided, just as the President's cabinet was divided. The downfall of the French monarchy was hailed with joy by Thomas Jefferson and his followers, who saw in the French struggle for liberty the triumph of their democratic ideas.

The misfortunes of the Marquis de Lafayette and his family gave the Washingtons the greatest anxiety. The Marquis's wife and daughters had hurried to Austria to share his prison with him. But his son, George Washington de Lafayette, had escaped to the United States with his tutor, Felix Frestal, and now begged the protection of the President.

George Washington's first impulse was to receive his French namesake into his home. But he realized that such a step would be dangerous to American policy at so critical a time in foreign affairs. Instead, he was forced to place the boy with Alexander Hamilton's family.

Martha was disappointed. Longing for a boy to mother, she would have liked to take young Lafayette into her home. "He could have Washington's room . . ." she thought.

Young Custis was at Princeton, moved there by his grandfather when the teachers at the Pennsylvania school confessed their inability to interest him in his studies. Once again George Washington was battling with the erratic Parke and Custis blood. Once again, he was writing to teachers and imploring them to overcome the boy's "indolence in every-thing that did not tend to his amusements."

Young Custis was as lazy as his sister was industrious. The only subject that held his interest was Roman history, and how, George Washington asked sternly, could he hope to grow to intelligent manhood with nothing more in his head than the adventures of Caesar?

The step-grandson, like Jacky, always promised to do better. "How just your letter! . . . That I have abused such goodness is shocking!" But he did not stay repentant long.

In Martha's opinion, however, it was never the fault of her grandson that he could not learn, and must be moved from school to school. It was always the fault of his teachers.

But she worried, of course. And when in January 1795 Martha Custis was married to Thomas Peter of Georgetown, the son of a friend of the President's, she was glad to have a wedding to occupy her attention.

"To think it's quiet little Patsy, not Eliza, who is marrying first!" Martha told George.

Vivacious Eliza Custis had long been unable to choose between a flock of beaux. Lately she had seemed interested in an Englishman, Thomas Law, but the match was totally unsuitable. Eliza was only nineteen. Thomas Law, the thirty-nine-year-old brother of Baron Ellenborough, Lord Chief Justice of England, had been married before and was the father of three sons. Martha, remembering with regret that she had introduced him to her granddaughter, prayed that nothing would come of it.

But something did. Fourteen months after Patsy's wedding, Eleanor Stuart wrote that Eliza and Thomas Law were to be married on March 20, 1796.

"This is terrible!" Martha wept, and George tried to comfort her. "We don't know a thing about this man, Papa. He may be an adventurer, accumulating that fortune in India! Isn't it to his advantage in America to marry into the President's family?"

George, too, was doubtful of the success of a marriage in which there was such a difference in ages. But Thomas Law was helping to build the new capital on the Potomac, now the President's absorbing interest. And that fact was enough to blind even George Washington to the Englishman's arrogance and egotism.

Martha knew better. She refused to attend the wedding at Hope Park. She demurred when Eliza asked that her young sister Nelly act as her bridesmaid. Nelly's own mother then added her plea. And the grandmother, of course, could not refuse.

The seventeen-year-old Nelly set off for the wedding, leaving Mrs. Washington to wonder how her innocent darling could fit into the sophisticated celebration that would make Eliza the bride of Thomas Law.

Nelly's first letter brought the news of a dance at Georgetown, given in Eliza's honor. "This ball was different from the ones you gave in Philadelphia," Nelly wrote Grandmama. "I had a lovely time. But all the young people were friends." The boys and girls seemed to her to show their liking for each other too openly. She would "never give herself a moment's uneasiness on account of any of the young men of the present day" she assured her grandparents, and went on to give a lively description of the party.

Martha read between the lines of Nelly's letter and her hand trembled. Her darling was growing up!

But George was highly entertained.

"We should be glad Nelly can write us so frankly," he

told his wife, and answered his granddaughter's letter at once —an answer which is known as his "love and duty letter."

In it he shows his affectionate amusement at Nelly's determination to remain fancy-free, and warns her not to be too sure of herself. "Do not boast too soon or too strongly," he says, and goes on to write Nelly as to the proper way for a young lady to handle herself in love affairs.

He also wrote to Washington Custis at Princeton, enclosing a ten-dollar bill "to purchase a gown &c. . . . if proper." But he cautioned him to consult his teachers as to the style of the gown, lest he be "distinguished more by folly than by the dress." He rejoiced at the assurance the boy gave that he was studying hard, and added, "It is you yourself who is to derive immediate benefit from this. Your country may do it hereafter. . . ."

That Martha should have burdened George Washington with young Custis's affairs at a time when he carried a vast weight of public business is the part of her character least easy to analyze. She saw her husband's stern, sad face, and understood the conditions which oppressed him. The new treaty with England was unpopular. There was trouble with France. . . .

President Washington had issued a Proclamation of Neutrality to keep America out of France's quarrel with England. This had deeply hurt the French people, who remembered their help to America in the Revolution. From a friend, France had turned into an enemy. And from being a man above party bickering, George Washington was being forced to take sides in quarrels. It followed, inevitably, that he should be attacked in the basest, most personal manner. No one dared openly to accuse the President of dishonest conduct, yet by innuendos and falsehoods his political enemies were doing everything they could to destroy his popularity.

This was the moment of George Washington's greatest humiliation, and his devoted wife knew it. There were days when every public appearance was torture to him, and when each move he made meant a flock of new enemies. Days in which Martha, frantic with worry, knew that her husband was not eating, not sleeping, not even answering the questions she put to him.

Some women would have wept and wrung their hands. But not Martha Washington. She was sixty-five now, and more weary than ever with public life. But she had work to do, and she did it. She gave receptions and dinners. She wrote cordial little notes to people she disliked (and what unhappy hours that effort cost her!). She drew her husband, tired, discouraged and unhappy, into the warmth of her companionship, until even the tired statesman was forced to lift his head and carry on.

Martha Washington had grown in worldly wisdom and poise since those days of bitter revolt in New York. The violence of political controversy blew over her snowy head like a summer breeze. At home, in the green parlor, all was serenity and graciousness.

Callers found her there, plump and rosy-cheeked, seated under a portrait of President Washington.

"I've never seen a *good* likeness of the General," she would say, hoping perhaps that her listener would not agree. "The only merit in his many portraits is their resemblance to each other."

True enough, as any schoolchild of today will tell you when asked to describe the Father of His Country. But certainly not true of the portraits of Martha Washington. The artists for whom she sat, Gilbert Stuart, Robertson, Pine,

"Bryan . . . Lord Fairfax!" George Washington exclaimed when they heard the news.

And Martha smiled, too. It was so absurd. Somehow it was impossible to imagine the pious Bryan Fairfax as an English nobleman.

"If Bryan gets the title, he'll have to give up his American citizenship," George explained, "go to England to live, and become an Englishman."

"And leave Virginia!" cried Martha. She could not imagine anyone trading that privilege for a title—anyone, that is, but Sally Fairfax.

Would not the homesick Mrs. Washington gladly have given up her title of First Lady to be back, that very moment, at Mount Vernon!

Two, perhaps three times, during the presidential years, Martha saw her home when the family slipped away for a rest after Congress recessed in March. A glimpse of the river —the tall green trees framing the comfortable white mansion. A little work in the garden. Then October. Another Philadelphia season, and Martha Washington was back in the house on High Street, acting her role of First Lady.

At the beginning of the President's second term, Martha decided that Nelly, fourteen, and Washington, twelve, were old enough to attend her receptions. Young Custis did not enjoy being made to dress up and bow like a little gentleman to his grandmother's guests. But Nelly loved it.

That year the young Custises were enrolled for dancing lessons at the Robardet's Classes. And Nelly's grandparents gave her the handsome mahogany harpsichord imported from London, "costing all of a thousand dollars," that is now in the music room at Mount Vernon. The gift must have inspired Nelly, for we hear no more of her being forced to practice her music.

How Nelly and Washington, and their young friends, lightened the old brick house with their laughter and fun! And what a comfort they were to George, worried and harassed by the unfriendly Republican newspapers, especially Nelly. It pleased Martha to see how her granddaughter's sunny disposition, sweetness and vivacity, never failed to draw her husband from his moods of depression.

Eliza Custis, Martha's oldest grandchild, whom the Vice-President, John Adams, describes as "a fine, blooming, rosy girl, who, I dare say, has had more liberty and exercise than Nelly," was also a favorite of the President—an affection which the seventeen-year-old miss heartily returned.

After a visit to her grandmother in Philadelphia, Eliza wrote to George Washington that the wish of her heart was to have his portrait.

He sent Eliza a miniature in a blue enamel case bordered with pearls, and with a lock of his hair in the back. "But I can't imagine the fondest desire of a young girl's heart is to have the portrait of an old man!" he told her.

Eliza, and her sixteen-year-old sister, Martha, who was quieter and not so pretty, were often at the Executive Mansion now. Their mother, Eleanor, who had been left a large fortune by Jack Custis, had lost most of it through unfortunate investments. The Stuarts had had to give up Abingdon and move to Hope Park, the Doctor's plantation twenty miles from Alexandria.

Nelly enjoyed nothing more than to have the "blooming, rosy" Eliza, and her other sister, Martha, with her. At their grandmother's receptions, the three girls, wearing their best frocks, helped to serve refreshments. And when the house was full of young people, President Washington—believed by strangers to be cold and distant—would come out of his study and join the girls and their friends in dancing the Virginia reel.

That fall, lest she think herself grown up and ask for too many "liberties," Nelly Custis was packed off to school at Annapolis. Her brother, Washington, was sent away, too. He was badly in need of discipline. His grandfather hoped the time spent at his school, later to become part of the University of Pennsylvania, would rouse in the happy-go-lucky lad some sense of responsibility.

Nelly's close friends at Annapolis were Elizabeth Bordley of Philadelphia and Martha Coffin from Portland, who spent many vacations with her at Mount Vernon. They wrote letters and scribbled verses, and had their portraits painted for each other, just as school girls do today.

But no matter what young visitors were in the house, Nelly always accompanied her grandmother upstairs when she retired for the night. She read to her from the Bible and sang a hymn. After that Nelly and Mrs. Washington, with Oney and Molly, Martha's maids, knelt in prayer.

That Nelly loved her Grandmama dearly is shown by a letter, written when she herself was a grandmother:

"I never loved anyone, not even my own children, as I loved Grandmama. Her equal I can never know. Love, admiration, respect, gratitude were all hers. Her judgment, her piety, her fortitude . . . I have never known in an equal degree in anyone. She never praised me in all her life. She feared more than anything to make me vain. When I was right, I looked into her eyes. It never required speech to tell me all I wished to know."

Martha's heart was so big that she loved not only her grand-children but her nieces and nephews, as well. Her favorite had always been Fanny, Nancy Bassett's daughter. And now she was made very happy by the news that Fanny, left a widow with three small children two years earlier, was to marry Tobias Lear, also a widower, with one boy, Lincoln.

As a wedding present, the Washingtons gave the Lears three hundred acres of the Mount Vernon land, with a house on the property known as "Wellington." The marriage was a happy one for the eight months it lasted. In the spring of 1796 Fanny died, leaving Tobias Lear with four small children on his hands.

These little ones, without doubt, raced and played in the orchard behind the house on High Street, mothered by Martha Washington, who always seemed to have time to help her friends and comfort the troubled.

She worried a great deal at this time about her sister, Betty Henley. Martha had never been as close to this younger sister as she had been to Nancy. But now Betty, twice married and the mother of eight children, was ill. Remembering that she and Betty were the last of their family, Martha's heart ached for her.

Shortly before Fanny's own death, Martha Washington had written to her about Betty:

"I am much grieved to hear that my poor sister is in such a wretched situation. . . . Poor dear Betty has had a hard lot in this world. I hope her children will be a comfort to her as they grow up and not follow their unhappy Father's bad example. I often think of her with the greatest concern. I should be very glad if she would come up to see me when I go home."

Kindness and common sense—those words described the middle-aged Martha Washington, and to these we may add a third, which she personified in public life: *discretion*. With old friends, where she felt secure, Martha Washington was the same impulsive, vivacious person. But with strangers, she had learned never to let a careless word escape her lips.

During the Revolution, Mrs. Washington had been more outspoken. It is believed she wrote an address published in a Philadelphia newspaper in 1780, entitled *The Sentiments of an American Woman*. Under the impression that she was the author, it was read from the pulpits of churches throughout Virginia. And she never denied the fact.

Now, as wife of the President, Martha Washington had learned to be cautious of what she said. Political discussions by her guests were not permitted at the Executive Mansion. She was herself careful not to express an opinion on public questions, except among her most intimate friends. Though diplomats and others often attempted to draw the First Lady into talking on topics of the day, she adroitly evaded doing so, until she earned for herself the reputation of being dull.

Yet Martha's convictions were as decided as those of George Washington, and in perfect harmony with his. Indeed, her sympathetic heart, sound sense, and good advice gave him much of his strength, and helped him to make wise decisions when he was overcome with doubts.

It is said that on the few occasions when they were separated, George's letters to his wife were filled with discussions of public affairs. And her answers, firmly stating her opinions, frequently told him what to do.

There came a crisis when Mistress Washington's sympathies were so deeply roused that she found it hard to hold her tongue. In Europe, the French Revolution had broken out.

George Washington watched with grave apprehension the trend of the times. He had been shocked at the beheading of the French king, whom he remembered as a friend of America. He was indignant at the news that his "boy," the Marquis de Lafayette, had been forced to flee Paris, and was a prisoner in Austria.

Alexander Hamilton and his party, the Federalists, agreed with the President in denouncing the lawlessness of the French Republicans. But opinion in Philadelphia was divided, just as the President's cabinet was divided. The downfall of the French monarchy was hailed with joy by Thomas Jefferson and his followers, who saw in the French struggle for liberty the triumph of their democratic ideas.

The misfortunes of the Marquis de Lafayette and his family gave the Washingtons the greatest anxiety. The Marquis's wife and daughters had hurried to Austria to share his prison with him. But his son, George Washington de Lafayette, had escaped to the United States with his tutor, Felix Frestal, and now begged the protection of the President.

George Washington's first impulse was to receive his French namesake into his home. But he realized that such a step would be dangerous to American policy at so critical a time in foreign affairs. Instead, he was forced to place the boy with Alexander Hamilton's family.

Martha was disappointed. Longing for a boy to mother, she would have liked to take young Lafayette into her home. "He could have Washington's room . . ." she thought.

Young Custis was at Princeton, moved there by his grandfather when the teachers at the Pennsylvania school confessed their inability to interest him in his studies. Once again George Washington was battling with the erratic Parke and Custis blood. Once again, he was writing to teachers and imploring them to overcome the boy's "indolence in every-thing that did not tend to his amusements."

Young Custis was as lazy as his sister was industrious. The only subject that held his interest was Roman history, and how, George Washington asked sternly, could he hope to grow to intelligent manhood with nothing more in his head than the adventures of Caesar?

The step-grandson, like Jacky, always promised to do better. "How just your letter! . . . That I have abused such goodness is shocking!" But he did not stay repentant long.

In Martha's opinion, however, it was never the fault of her grandson that he could not learn, and must be moved from school to school. It was always the fault of his teachers.

But she worried, of course. And when in January 1795 Martha Custis was married to Thomas Peter of Georgetown, the son of a friend of the President's, she was glad to have a wedding to occupy her attention.

"To think it's quiet little Patsy, not Eliza, who is marrying first!" Martha told George.

Vivacious Eliza Custis had long been unable to choose between a flock of beaux. Lately she had seemed interested in an Englishman, Thomas Law, but the match was totally unsuitable. Eliza was only nineteen. Thomas Law, the thirty-nine-year-old brother of Baron Ellenborough, Lord Chief Justice of England, had been married before and was the father of three sons. Martha, remembering with regret that she had introduced him to her granddaughter, prayed that nothing would come of it.

But something did. Fourteen months after Patsy's wedding, Eleanor Stuart wrote that Eliza and Thomas Law were to be married on March 20, 1796.

"This is terrible!" Martha wept, and George tried to comfort her. "We don't know a thing about this man, Papa. He may be an adventurer, accumulating that fortune in India! Isn't it to his advantage in America to marry into the President's family?"

George, too, was doubtful of the success of a marriage in which there was such a difference in ages. But Thomas Law was helping to build the new capital on the Potomac, now the President's absorbing interest. And that fact was enough to blind even George Washington to the Englishman's arrogance and egotism.

Martha knew better. She refused to attend the wedding at Hope Park. She demurred when Eliza asked that her young sister Nelly act as her bridesmaid. Nelly's own mother then added her plea. And the grandmother, of course, could not refuse.

The seventeen-year-old Nelly set off for the wedding, leaving Mrs. Washington to wonder how her innocent darling could fit into the sophisticated celebration that would make Eliza the bride of Thomas Law.

Nelly's first letter brought the news of a dance at Georgetown, given in Eliza's honor. "This ball was different from the ones you gave in Philadelphia," Nelly wrote Grandmama. "I had a lovely time. But all the young people were friends." The boys and girls seemed to her to show their liking for each other too openly. She would "never give herself a moment's uneasiness on account of any of the young men of the present day" she assured her grandparents, and went on to give a lively description of the party.

Martha read between the lines of Nelly's letter and her hand trembled. Her darling was growing up!

But George was highly entertained.

"We should be glad Nelly can write us so frankly," he

told his wife, and answered his granddaughter's letter at once
—an answer which is known as his "love and duty letter."

In it he shows his affectionate amusement at Nelly's determination to remain fancy-free, and warns her not to be too
sure of herself. "Do not boast too soon or too strongly," he
says, and goes on to write Nelly as to the proper way for a
young lady to handle herself in love affairs.

He also wrote to Washington Custis at Princeton, enclosing
a ten-dollar bill "to purchase a gown &c. . . . if proper."
But he cautioned him to consult his teachers as to the style
of the gown, lest he be "distinguished more by folly than by
the dress." He rejoiced at the assurance the boy gave that he
was studying hard, and added, "It is you yourself who is to
derive immediate benefit from this. Your country may do it
hereafter. . . ."

That Martha should have burdened George Washington
with young Custis's affairs at a time when he carried a vast
weight of public business is the part of her character least
easy to analyze. She saw her husband's stern, sad face, and
understood the conditions which oppressed him. The new
treaty with England was unpopular. There was trouble with
France. . . .

President Washington had issued a Proclamation of Neutrality to keep America out of France's quarrel with England.
This had deeply hurt the French people, who remembered
their help to America in the Revolution. From a friend,
France had turned into an enemy. And from being a man
above party bickering, George Washington was being forced
to take sides in quarrels. It followed, inevitably, that he should
be attacked in the basest, most personal manner. No one dared
openly to accuse the President of dishonest conduct, yet by
innuendos and falsehoods his political enemies were doing

everything they could to destroy his popularity.

√ This was the moment of George Washington's greatest humiliation, and his devoted wife knew it. There were days when every public appearance was torture to him, and when each move he made meant a flock of new enemies. Days in which Martha, frantic with worry, knew that her husband was not eating, not sleeping, not even answering the questions she put to him.

Some women would have wept and wrung their hands. But not Martha Washington. She was sixty-five now, and more weary than ever with public life. But she had work to do, and she did it. She gave receptions and dinners. She wrote cordial little notes to people she disliked (and what unhappy hours that effort cost her!). She drew her husband, tired, discouraged and unhappy, into the warmth of her companionship, until even the tired statesman was forced to lift his head and carry on.

Martha Washington had grown in worldly wisdom and poise since those days of bitter revolt in New York. The violence of political controversy blew over her snowy head like a summer breeze. At home, in the green parlor, all was serenity and graciousness.

Callers found her there, plump and rosy-cheeked, seated under a portrait of President Washington.

"I've never seen a *good* likeness of the General," she would say, hoping perhaps that her listener would not agree. "The only merit in his many portraits is their resemblance to each other."

True enough, as any schoolchild of today will tell you when asked to describe the Father of His Country. But certainly not true of the portraits of Martha Washington. The artists for whom she sat, Gilbert Stuart, Robertson, Pine, and the three Peales, reveal in each picture a different woman.

James Peale, commissioned to paint her miniature, was told to appear for the first sitting at seven o'clock in the morning. The artist took a walk down the street before he could make up his mind to sound the brass knocker at the Executive Mansion at so early an hour.

When he did so, he was greeted by a brisk little woman in a starched white cap, who said tartly, "You're late, Mr. Peale."

Blushing, the artist explained that he had hesitated to disturb her at an hour when most ladies were still asleep.

Mrs. Washington laughed. "I've already attended family prayers, given Nelly a music lesson, and read the newspaper while I waited for you. Come, let's get on with the picture."

Martha Washington's "lost days" were drawing to an end. President Washington had refused a third term. And by spring the family would be off, bag and baggage, for Mount Vernon.

When Washington's sixty-fifth birthday came on February 22, 1797, two weeks before their departure, Philadelphia celebrated the occasion with a birthday ball that was also a farewell. When the President entered Rickett's Amphitheater with the First Lady on his arm, they were greeted with "tumultuous applause."

Martha Washington was a stately figure that gala night in orange satin trimmed with flowers. Her petticoat was lemon silk, with wreaths of roses caught with silver braid. Orange plumes nodded in her puffed white hair. Black lace mittens covered her hands.

Styles in hair were changing; lofty headdresses had toppled. Nelly wore hers in the latest fashion, in curls over her bare shoulders. Her gown of green brocade was looped over a white satin petticoat. "How pretty she is!" thought many a young man as Martha's demure granddaughter passed to the platform, where the presidential family were to be seated on a sofa under a canopy.

Nelly did not remain there long. She danced, and how she loved it! Danced with Colonel Hartley, Lawrence Washington, and the other "genteel beaux" of the day, in tight breeches, coats of striped silk with high collars, and hair powdered and perfumed.

George Washington, who had not danced since the Fredericksburg ball after Yorktown, was so warmed by the hearty reception that he *walked* sedately, not danced, through the steps of the minuet.

This left Martha Washington alone on the sofa, a small dignified figure, far more distinguished looking, although she wore no jewels, than the wives of the foreign ministers seated around her, who glittered with diamonds to the summit of their headdresses.

Twelve thousand people had come to the birthday ball. There was such a rush to go to supper that, according to John Adams, "there was danger of being squeezed to death." The Vice-President had the honor of handing-in Mrs. Washington, and the President followed. "The applause the Washingtons received is indescribable," he wrote. "The President and Mrs. Washington were in good spirits, and, I am persuaded, have not spent so agreeable an evening for a long time. Every countenance bespoke approbation; even political enemies forgot their enmity, and joined heartily in the festivity."

The band played, and everyone sang the popular song written for the President's sixty-fifth birthday:

"Come, boys, close the windows and make a good fire,
    Wife, children, sit snug all around;
'Tis the day that gave birth to our country's Bless'd sire,
    Then let it with pleasure be crowned.
Dear wife, bring your wine, and, in spite of hard times,
    On this day at least we'll be merry;
Come, fill every glass till it pours o'er the brim,
    If not with Madeira—then Sherry."

The enthusiasm was sincere. Everyone wanted to show affection for the retiring President. Catching her husband's eye, Martha Washington smiled. It was easy enough to be gay tonight when within a few weeks all this pomp and ceremony would be over.

On the 4th of March, 1797, George Washington attended the inauguration of his successor, John Adams. In a firm, clear voice, he read a brief valedictory which brought tears to the eyes of the hushed assembly.

That night the Washingtons gave a dinner for President Adams and his wife, at which the foreign ministers and their wives, Thomas Jefferson, and others were present. The meal was festive enough. But at the end, George Washington rose, glass in hand, and said:

"Ladies and Gentlemen, this is the last time I shall drink your health as a public man. I do it with sincerity, wishing you all possible happiness."

The simplicity of these words and the quiet tired voice that spoke them put an end to all merriment. A hush fell over the table. Even those who had most often criticized George Washington and had said of the First Lady that her unassuming manners were more suitable to the wife of a Virginia planter than that of the President of the United States were sorry to see them go.

The dinner for the Adamses was the last to be cooked by Hercules, Martha's famous chef. Next day, as the kitchen pots and pans were being packed, "Uncle Harkness," as he was called, disappeared. A Negro dandy, captivated by the delights of Philadelphia, he had run away rather than return to Mount Vernon. Although the Washingtons hunted for him a long time, he was never found.

Martha had recently lost another slave; Oney, who had been with her since White House days, also escaped. Oney's work had been mostly fine sewing and hand laundry. No one could prepare Martha's caps with the same skill in clear-starching, frilling and quilling. Her other maid, Molly, was so clumsy that Martha begged George to advertise for Oney's return.

But President Washington, who had never approved of slavery, refused to do so. To Martha's chagrin, he actually seemed to welcome Oney's rash step, and when later the woman turned up in Boston, giving as her reason for running off a wish for freedom and a desire to learn to read and write, he frankly stated that she showed good sense.

With only Molly to help her, packing for the journey to Mount Vernon was an arduous task. But so light of heart was the home-going Mistress Washington that she turned her hand with right good will.

At last came the morning of their departure, a March day, clear and fresh. With services to their country over, the Washingtons stepped into a coach. The horses' heads were turned homeward. In the carriage with them were Nelly and her brother, together with another boy—a French lad about Nelly's age—George Washington de Lafayette and his tutor, Felix Frestal. Now that George Washington had retired from

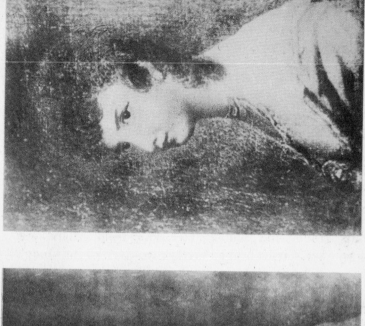

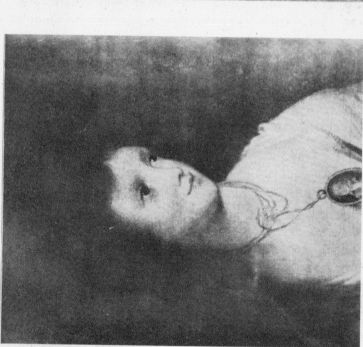

Left. ELIZA PARKE CUSTIS, GRANDDAUGHTER OF MARTHA WASHINGTON

Showing the miniature of President Washington painted for her in Philadelphia

Right. MARTHA PARKE CUSTIS, GRANDDAUGHTER OF MARTHA WASHINGTON

public life, there was no reason why his French namesake should not make his home at Mount Vernon.

The household furniture had been sent to Virginia by boat. But the baggage wagon that followed the coach was piled high with trunks. Nelly's pet dog barked on the top of the load, frightening Martha's parrot in its cage. Along the way, George Washington wrote to Tobias Lear, who had remained in Philadelphia:

"On one side, I am called upon to remember the parrot, and on the other, to remember the dog. For my own part, I should not pine much if both were forgot."

The Washingtons, private citizens intent on their own simple pleasures, wanted to avoid parades. But how could they? At every town bells rang and cannons boomed, and guards of honor rode out to meet and escort the retiring President and his party.

It was on the evening of March fifteenth that the coach passed through the west gate at Mount Vernon, up the long drive, and stopped before the door of the white mansion, now shadowy in the twilight.

The Washingtons were at home, for good, this time.

Martha was suffering from a cold she had caught in Philadelphia. But she soon recovered in the sunshine and quiet of her cozy sitting room. George forgot his rheumatism in the pleasant farming tasks that again occupied his days. And Nelly, writing to a friend, expressed the joy of the entire family:

"We arrived here on Wednesday without any accident after a tedious journey of seven days. Grandpa is very well and much pleased with being once more Farmer Washington."

Chapter Fourteen

BUT TWO SHORT YEARS WERE LEFT TO MARTHA AND GEORGE Washington to be together at Mount Vernon. Martha must have sensed the quick passing of those precious days, for in a letter to Lucy Knox, she says: "The twilight is gathering around our lives." Then she adds more cheerily:

"The General and I feel like children released from school, and nothing can tempt us to leave our roof tree again. I am settled down to the pleasant duties of an old-fashioned Virginia housekeeper; steady as a clock, busy as a bee, and cheerful as a cricket. I cannot tell you how much I enjoy home after having been deprived of one for so long, for our dwelling in New York and Philadelphia was not home, only a sojourning."

There was the pleasant task of getting settled at Mount Vernon once more. Nelly's harpsichord was put in the music room. But where should they hang the Trumbull portrait of General Washington standing by his horse? The shaving stand given the President by the French minister, and other pieces, must also be uncrated and set in place, to go down through the years as part of the historic furnishings of the mansion.

For the first time in twenty-five years, Martha and George could regard themselves as permanent residents of their plan-

262

tation. Life in the big white house beside the Potomac was never sweeter. The halls rang with the voices of sixteen-year-old Washington Custis and his friend, young Lafayette, who was one year older. Nelly, at eighteen, considered herself too dignified to romp with the boys, yet often she forgot herself long enough to dash to the harpsichord and pound out gay tunes which the three young people sang until they were weak with laughter. And watching them were Martha and George Washington, serene in the last and best years of their lives.

There were no more gallops for them across the green fields of the plantation; no more gay hunt balls and dinners for the neighboring gentry. Martha's wide-hooped ball gowns and scarlet riding habit were packed away in cedar-lined closets not far from George's uniforms and swords. Now she was content to be the white-haired, rosy-faced old lady of the pictures best known to us, wearing dresses of dove-gray and mauve, and frilled mob caps of crisp linen and fluted muslin, tied with neat black ribbons; content to sit quietly by the side of the man who had been her husband for thirty-eight years.

That summer Mount Vernon was once more the center of the youthful gaiety of the neighborhood, with Nelly's friends and admirers constantly coming and going. Afternoons, the girls and their beaux played bowls on the green. And when evening came, candlelight shone softly on dancing figures in the wide hall of the mansion.

Out on the dim piazza, Martha and George and their guests sat on the famous Windsor chairs, watching the young folk and nodding their heads in time to the music. Then Nelly, pink-cheeked and breathless, would emerge, twirling her flounces, and beg Grandpapa to be her partner in the

minuet. The attention flattered him. Almost he was persuaded, but eventually he shook his head. George Washington's dancing days were over.

In the fall of 1797, the Washingtons took a trip they had
long promised themselves. They went to visit the Federal
Capital, rising on the Maryland banks of the Potomac.

It had not taken much coaxing to set Martha packing for
this journey. Her two granddaughters, Eliza Law and Martha
Peter, were living in Washington City, as the national center
was to be called. And there were new babies in both house-
holds.

The Washingtons went first to stay with Eliza in the
house which Thomas Law had built on Capitol Hill, a home
torn down to make room for the House of Representatives'
Office Building. Speculating in Washington City real estate,
the wily Englishman had lost no time in selecting a good lot
for himself.

Thomas Law had not changed much, as Martha was quick
to see. A conceited braggart, she told herself as she kissed her
granddaughter Eliza, and hastened to the nursery to see her
first great-grandchild, a baby girl named for her mother. Eliza
had everything—a handsome home, a prosperous husband, a
beautiful child. And yet, searching her granddaughter's face,
Martha knew that hers was not a happy marriage.

Very different was the Thomas Peter home on K Street.
Here was the thing Martha liked best in a house—comfort
without ostentation. Tom Peter, under the guidance of his
father, the first mayor of Georgetown, was fast becoming one
of the important young men of the new capital. Patsy was
the same sedate girl of her unmarried days, proud of her
husband, absorbed in the care of her little Martha-Eliza, and
expecting a second baby in December. As Mrs. Washington

clasped Patsy in her motherly arms, tears of relief dimmed
her eyes. Here, unquestionably, was a happy home.

She would have liked nothing better than to remain in
the house on K Street, fondling her great-grandchild and
gossiping with capable Patsy Peter. But each morning, Pierre
L'Enfant, the young French engineer who had laid out the
city, came to act as guide to the illustrious visitors.

At the time of Martha's first visit, work on the national
capital, which was to become one of the most beautiful in
the world, was progressing slowly. The ten-mile square tract
between Rock Creek and the Anacostia River, selected by
George Washington, was mostly wilderness. The walls of
the President's house, the unfinished capitol, and a few scat-
tered houses along unpaved streets constituted the town. Yet
the four people who looked at it on an autumn morning in
1797 were so familiar with the plans that they could visualize
the Washington of the future.

Proudly, Major L'Enfant explained to Martha the two
points from which the boulevards were to radiate—the House
of Congress and the home of the President. Connecting the
capitol and the executive mansion would be a landscaped mall,
or park.

"Why, the town's laid out like Williamsburg!" she exclaimed with approval.

An interesting moment for Mrs. Washington was their visit
to a tract of land called Square 21, west of the present Naval
Hospital. George had bought this lot to build on it a small
house for his own use.

There is a story relating to his purchase of this land, which
he told that day to L'Enfant, while Martha listened, highly
amused.

It had been necessary to buy a farm owned by a Scotsman,

David Burns. The man refused to sell, although President Washington pointed out to him the advantages he would derive from the sale. The peppery owner listened for a while, then exclaimed, "I suppose you think people are going to take every grist that comes from you as pure grain. *What would you have been, if you hadn't married the Widow Custis!*"

"You see, gentlemen, that illustrates the sentiment of the country in regard to our marriage," George concluded. And Martha's laughter, which joined his, was as clear and spontaneous as Nelly Custis's own.

She smiled happily all the way back to Mount Vernon, seated beside her husband in the family chariot. The visit to the Federal City had been a success. She was tired, after eight days of it; she would be glad of the peace of Mount Vernon. But she rode along planning in her mind the house they would some day build in the national capital.

"There must be a garden on that southern slope," Martha murmured sleepily.

George smiled, and his fingers closed over hers.

"Yes, Patsy," he said softly. "Wherever you are, there must always be a garden."

In the fall of 1797, good news reached Mount Vernon from France. The Marquis de Lafayette had been released from prison. Now his son could safely return home.

Motherly Martha Washington kissed George's French name-sake good-bye with regret. Nelly, too, was sorry to see young Lafayette go. She had hoped to dance the minuet with him at the next Washington's Birthday Ball. But there were always partners galore for pretty Nelly, and one graceful Frenchman less was a loss quite easily borne.

The winter of 1797-8 was a cold one. The Washingtons drove in their sleigh into Alexandria on February eleventh, not the twenty-second. Elsewhere the new calendar had been accepted, and the President's birthday was celebrated on the twenty-second. But Virginia knew her native son had been born on the eleventh and clung to that date until after his death. So while he lived, George Washington was a man with two birthdays a year.

The ball was held at a tavern, "The Sign of the Grapevine." When the musicians struck up *The President's March*, and the General entered with Martha on his arm, the dancing began.

Of all the girls, no one was prettier that night than Nelly Custis, in her short-waisted white dress with puffed sleeves, as she returned with sweeping curtsies the courtly bows of her partner in the minuet.

Martha Washington, a white-haired lady in dove-colored satin, took her seat sedately with a row of old friends along the wall of the tavern. There was no sofa on a raised platform for the ex-President and his wife to sit on—their neighbors in Alexandria would have scoffed at the idea. The arrangement suited Martha, who was delighted to be again the wife of a Virginia squire. George stood talking with the men about crops and horses, serene in the thought that no one would berate him about the Jay Treaty or ask if he thought there would be a war with France.

That night at Alexandria was the last birthday ball that the Washingtons would attend. Twilight was gathering around their lives, as Martha had told Lucy Knox. But it was a twilight that fell softly and was lightened by memories of two full and well-spent lives.

Even Washington Custis seemed to be settling down. In

Princeton, Martha was sure her grandson had at last found the college that suited him. He wrote his grandparents such nice letters. He promised to study so hard.

Her complacency was shattered by a note from President Smith of Princeton; a note that gave George Washington "extreme disquietude," and caused him to write his grandson a sharp rebuke. The records reveal a most ingratiating reply from the charming young scamp:

"Dearest Sir, did you but know the effect your letter has produced it would give you consummate pleasure. My very soul, tortured with the stings of conscience, at length called reason to its aid, and happily for me triumphed. That I shall ever recompense you for the trouble I have occasioned is beyond my hopes. However, I will now make a grand exertion and show you that your grandson shall once more deserve your favor."

Tears came to Martha's eyes as she read these repentant words. She persuaded George to write the boy, assuring him that they would "bury in oblivion all that has passed."

To prove that he had reformed, young Custis produced a delicious bit of renunciation. He wrote: "The fourth of July will be celebrated with all possible magnificence; the college illuminated and cannon fired; a ball will be held at the tavern in the evening." And he adds nobly, "but I shall not attend, as I do not consider it consistent with *propriety*."

To this George Washington, shocked by the apparent lack of patriotism on Custis' part, replied: "If it has been usual for the students of Nassau College to go to balls on the anniversary of the Declaration of Independence, I see no reason why you should avoid it, as no innocent amusement or reasonable expenditure will ever be withheld from you."

Again the spoiled boy scored. Not only did he get credit for self-sacrifice, but he also attended the party!

So the pleading, repentant letters traveled between Mount Vernon and Princeton, with the usually realistic Martha assuring herself and her husband that her grandson's conduct would improve.

Meanwhile, the Washingtons' greatest comfort was the dutiful Nelly, who only once, so history relates, caused them a moment of anxiety.

The romantic young girl was fond of wandering alone in the woods of Mount Vernon in the dark. Martha, who regarded these strolls as unsafe, asked her grandchild to promise not to go out alone after sunset.

But on the next moonlight evening, Nelly was missing. Servants were sent to bring her from the secluded woodland paths, back to the candle-lit drawing-room. The General was walking up and down with his hands behind him. Martha, seated in her wing chair by the hearth, lost no time in scolding her granddaughter.

"Don't you remember your promise, Nelly," she asked in a hurt voice, "not to go out after dark alone?"

The moon-struck miss knew she was at fault; she could offer no excuse. Blushing, she asked Grandmama's pardon and started to leave the room. As she was shutting the door, she heard her grandfather say, "My dear, I would say no more—perhaps Nelly was *not* alone."

Turning abruptly, Nelly went back into the room. "Grandpapa, you brought me up to speak the truth," she told him, "and when I told Grandmama I was alone, please believe *I was alone*."

To hide the twinkle in his eyes, the General made Nelly one of his most courtly bows. "My child, I beg your pardon."

He must have smiled broadly at another romantic adventure of Miss Custis's, which occurred about that time.

It was a strict rule in the family that everyone must dress for three-o'clock dinner. The General himself changed from his riding clothes, whether they had company or were alone. And he expected his household to do likewise.

At ten minutes of three one afternoon, Martha, in black moire and a lace cap, joined her husband at the foot of the stairs. But where was Nelly?

As the meal was announced, the girl rushed in with Martha Dandridge, a young niece of Mrs. Washington's, just in time to sit down at the table. Martha stared at the girls in shocked surprise. They still wore their calico morning dresses, and what was worse, *curl-papers*. If the General noticed their unusual attire, he made no comment. Nor did Mrs. Washington speak to them as dinner progressed.

The family was still at table when a coach was seen rounding the serpentine drive.

"Who can that be?" cried Nelly.

Forgetting their favorite dessert of almond trifle, the girls jumped up and ran to the window in a flutter of excitement. What distinguished guests could be arriving?

They knew soon enough when the carriage drew up at the door. Out of it stepped two handsome French officers and Charles Carroll of Carrollton, only son of the signer of the Declaration of Independence, who came frequently to Mount Vernon to court Nelly.

That young lady remembered her plain calico gown; she clutched her curl-papers in despair. "May I be excused from table, Grandmama?" she gasped. "I must change my dress and fix my hair."

"You'll remain as you are," was Martha's reply. "What is

good enough for General Washington is good enough for his guests!"

It would seem that she believed young Carroll's love would even survive the sight of Nelly in curl-papers, for of all her granddaughter's beaux, Martha liked him best. Charles Carroll had been educated in Europe. He was heir to a large fortune. Martha was in favor of Nelly's encouraging him.

But George had other plans for his grandchild. He wanted Nelly to marry his nephew, Lawrence Lewis.

Lawrence, one of the six children of Betty and Fielding Lewis, had become a member of the Mount Vernon household in the spring of 1798. A tall handsome young man of twenty-one, who resembled his Uncle George, he had come to help the Washingtons to entertain the crowds of people again flocking to Mount Vernon.

America was once more on the verge of war—this time against France—and the nation had turned to George Washington for guidance. His days were filled with conferences and the writing of anxious letters to his friends. An army was being raised. And who must lead it but the victorious general of the late war, George Washington! Martha, at sixty-seven, saw their peaceful life again shattered by another threat of war.

Urged to do so by President Adams, George Washington accepted the army command, with the understanding that Alexander Hamilton be made acting commander, so that he need only take the field in an emergency. Overnight, it seemed to Martha, the household at Mount Vernon went on a war-time footing. Tobias Lear became George's military secretary, with the rank of Colonel. Washington Custis, home from Princeton, was assigned to the staff of General Pinckney. Lawrence Lewis's commission gave him the title of Major,

which he used all his life. Even Nelly became the godmother
of a regiment of young men raised in the neighborhood and
began making a silk flag for her troop, spending hours on
the tiny stitches in bursts of patriotic zeal.

But war was not all silken flags, handsome soldiers in uniform, and farewell balls when the troops marched away.
Watching Nelly, who had played with her dolls through the
fierce battles of the Revolution, Martha Washington sighed
deeply. War was a long and ghastly affair of illness and suffering, dirt and vermin, poverty and incredible deprivation.
Could it happen to a woman three times·in her life?

It seemed that it could, and for the General's wife there
was the usual acceptance of responsibility. When the call to
arms came, Martha Washington responded as naturally as
did her soldier-husband. If their country needed them, well
on in their sixties and worn by years of service, they were
ready. General Washington went off to review troops. And
Martha began to oil the spinning wheels, plant a war garden,
and make plans for hospital care of the soldiers.

But in the end, war did not come. The French government
was overthrown by Napoleon Bonaparte, who, for reasons
of his own, was friendly toward America.

Even this grim summer of 1798 had its pleasant interludes.
Whenever they could do so, the Washingtons slipped away
to be alone in the little house they had built in Alexandria,
at the corner of Pitt and Cameron Streets. And one day they
went to Mount Eagle on Great Hunting Creek, to say good-
bye to their old friend, Bryan Fairfax.

Bryan was going to England to test the worth of his claim
to the Cameron title.

"Not that I want to be Lord Fairfax myself," he hastened
to assure the Washingtons. But he wished the title for his son,

Thomas, and he must be sure that the claim was sound.

Returning home that day, Martha could not keep her mind off Sally Fairfax. The years rolled back; she was a bride again, newly arrived at Mount Vernon, shy and embarrassed before the sharp-tongued queen-like Mistress Fairfax, who reigned next door at Belvoir. But Martha had grown in the intervening years, grown in mentality and in understanding. Now when she thought of Sally it was without a pang of envy. She saw Mrs. Fairfax as poor and elderly, perhaps ill, and living a lonely life.

"Why, I'm actually sorry for her!" thought Martha in surprise.

When they reached Mount Vernon, Martha followed George into his library. He was seated at his tall tambour desk.

"George, I want you to write a letter to Sally Fairfax for me," she told him. Martha had always hated letter-writing. These days her husband took care of all her correspondence. "Bryan can take the letter to England."

Washington turned, a surprised look on his face. He had written to the Fairfaxes ever since they had gone to England, but Martha had never so much as sent them a message.

"Yes, it's the kind thing to do," continued Martha, arguing with herself. "Sally is old and poor, bitterly disappointed, no doubt, that the title passed her by. I have so much. I'd like to show her some act of kindness."

Looking down at George Washington's handsome face, his wife knew why she had always envied Sally Fairfax—why she had been relieved when her neighbor went away. Sally was so much cleverer . . . so much more fascinating. How could George help but compare such a lovely creature with his plump little wife?

But even as Martha faced squarely the reason for her envy, it seemed to vanish into thin air. George and she—forty years of marriage had been theirs, years spent at Mount Vernon, in camp and in presidential mansions, in complete serenity and sympathy, and with ever increasing affection and devotion. Not even Sally Fairfax could come between them now.

So with her hand on her husband's shoulder, Martha Washington dictated a letter to her old neighbor which included the following friendly words:

"—I shall proceed having so good an opportunity as is afforded by Mr. Fairfax's voyage to England, to assure you that although many years have elapsed that my affectionate regard for you has undergone no diminution, and that it is among my greatest regrets, now I am again fixed (I hope for life) at this place, at not having you as neighbor . . ."

When the letter was finished, Martha read it over.

"That's good!" she said briskly. "Now sign my name to it, dear, and let's go to dinner."

Martha turned away with a light heart. A drop of sealing wax on the letter, and the ghost of Sally Fairfax was laid forever.

On the sixth of January, 1799, Martha and George Washington celebrated their fortieth wedding anniversary. The house was still hung with Christmas evergreen brought in from the woods. Songs were sung, with Nelly playing her harpsichord and Lawrence Lewis his violin. And the chintz guest rooms overflowed with all the relatives who had assembled to congratulate the famous pair.

Stuarts, Laws, Peters, Dandridges, and Washingtons filled

the long table in the banquet room at dinner. And like a queen at the head of her table, sat Martha Washington—a round, bespectacled little woman of sixty-eight, with a sweet unlined face, and abundant snow-white hair.

When it was time for toasts, George Washington rose and held his glass high. "To my bride—" he said.

The eyes of Martha and George met above his wine glass as he drank to her health. And hers sparkled as brightly as on their wedding day forty years before.

Martha did not feel old; she could not think of George as old, although she heard the neighbors refer to him as "the old General." It pleased her when guests at Mount Vernon exclaimed at General Washington's erect figure; when young people told her how his stride was so long and manly that going to see the deer in the park, they had not been able to keep up with him.

It had been a shock to Martha when first she heard Washington Custis call his grandfather "an old gentleman." A visitor to Mount Vernon had asked where the General might be found.

"If you see an *old gentleman*," Washington replied, "in a white hat, with an umbrella attached to his saddle, that person, sir, is General Washington."

"An old gentleman"—her George! Martha flushed. He was not old, not really, although nowadays he talked continually about the past, and the changes in Mount Vernon since he had come there to live with his brother Lawrence, bringing his new surveying instruments and his copybook.

The eight years of the Revolution had placed a heavy strain on George Washington, his wife knew. His service as President had brought him discouragements that were in themselves aging. Then there was Washington Custis, a constant trial. The boy was a failure at Princeton, a failure at Saint John's College, Annapolis, to which he had been transferred.

Finally, even his indulgent grandmother was forced to admit the uselessness of sending the boy to *any* college. And he had come home for good, to see signs of a romance which was to brighten George Washington's last years by adding a third link to the chain that connected his family with Martha's.

Propinquity had helped Lawrence Lewis's suit. He had become Nelly's favored admirer, much to his uncle's satisfaction.

The story of Lawrence's proposal is one of the pretty legends of Mount Vernon.

One evening Nelly and Lawrence strolled together in Martha's garden. The girl showed her suitor the "Wishing Rose," where she and her brother had come as children to make a wish. If they bowed three times before the white rosebush and asked for something, that wish, they believed, would come true.

"Lawrence, it always did!" Nelly laughed. "You see, Grandmama and Grandpapa were often in the garden, out of sight but within hearing. And they gave us everything we asked for."

"Can you still ask the rosebush for what you want?" Lawrence asked softly.

At the look of love in his eyes, Nelly's heart beat faster. "Yes, Lawrence. . . . But first you must bow."

Solemnly he bowed three times before the "Wishing Rose." Solemnly he asked the rosebush to give him the girl he loved.

THE MUSIC ROOM AT MOUNT VERNON

*In the foreground is the harpsichord which General Washington
imported from London for Martha Washington's
granddaughter, Nelly Custis*

MARTHA WASHINGTON'S SITTING ROOM AT MOUNT VERNON

*Across the hall from the Music Room. Beyond the open door is
the stairway leading to General and Mrs. Washington's bedroom*

Nelly did not answer in words. Breaking off a white rose, she handed it to her future husband.

The culmination of George Washington's fondest desire is recorded simply in his diary:

"The Rev^d Mr. Davis & Mr. George Calvert came to dinner & Miss Custis was married about Candlelight to Mr. Law^r Lewis."

It was a sunny Washington's Birthday of 1799, the air as balmy as May, when the gay crowd assembled at Mount Vernon for Nelly Custis's wedding.

The slim, starry-eyed bride was never more beautiful than in her gown of white satin. Her veil was held on her dark hair by a white ostrich plume, the badge of the Federalist Party, for Nelly, intensely partisan, could not forget politics even at her wedding. She was given in marriage by her grandfather, who at the bride's wish wore his Continental uniform. The Reverend Thomas Davis, rector of Christ Church, Alexandria, performed the ceremony.

After the benediction, the bride first embraced her darling Grandmama. When she kissed her grandfather, there were tears in his eyes. George Washington was deeply touched that Nelly had chosen his birthday for her wedding.

A banquet, followed by dancing and singing, marked the beginning of the wedding festivities. Next day General and Mrs. Washington gave a second dinner party "in honor of Major and Mrs. Lewis." Later the young couple went to the Federal City to visit the Peters, to Hope Park to stay with Nelly's mother, and on a round of visits to Lawrence's family.

On their return to Mount Vernon, the Lewises were given a real surprise. From his nine thousand acres General Washington had selected two thousand in the western part of his estate as a gift to them. On this land, Martha and George hoped that eventually Nelly and Lawrence would build a house of their own. But for the present they must live at Mount Vernon.

They were precious days, these last days of the old Mount Vernon life, and Nelly did much to make them so for her grandparents. Evenings the family gathered in the music room, where young Mrs. Lewis played her grandmother's favorite tunes on the harpsichord, accompanied by Lawrence on his violin.

One of the favorites, *The Boston Boys*, she had to sing over and over.

> "The Boston Boys in their old games, Sir,
> Called old things by their right name, Sir.
> But spryness now they call elastic
> And every Jim is now gymnastic.
> Heigh, ho, I grieve, I grieve,
> For the good old days of Adam and Eve."

If anything could have added to Martha's joy that year, it was the coming on the first of December of a daughter, Frances, to Nelly and Lawrence. How pleased Martha was to hold another great-grandchild in her arms! Especially Nelly's child. And how fortunate that Frances came when she did, so that her great-grandfather could know the happiness of her arrival!

Afterwards Martha was to wonder if George knew that his end was near. He kept saying, "This is probably the last time I'll do this!" over anything so simple as a trip to Alexandria or a boating party on the river. It disturbed Martha, who firmly expected many more years of robust living.

George had been depressed by the death of his brother Charles. "I'm the last one of my family left," he had said. And he was alarmed by a dream that he could not shake off for days.

He had dreamed that he and Martha were seated in their summerhouse beside the Potomac, talking over the happy life they had spent. Suddenly there was a blinding light. An angel stood by Martha's side, whispered in her ear, and she vanished.

"I never felt better!" his wife tried to reassure him.

But she could not draw George from his thoughts of death. In November he refused to go to the dancing assemblies in Alexandria, although Martha was willing to attend, on the chance that a bit of frivolity might bring him cheer. And George began to plan for a new family burial vault to replace the old one which was in bad repair.

"This change," he told Lawrence Lewis one day, "I must make first. I may need it soon. I'm of a short-lived family and can't live much longer."

But General Washington had just come in from his usual ride. There was healthy color on his cheeks and his manner was lively. Lawrence thought he had never looked so well or so handsome.

On Saturday, the seventh of December, 1799, Martha and George drove up to Mount Eagle to dine with Bryan Fairfax and his family.

Martha had seized on the news that Bryan was back from England. "Come on, Papa, let's go and see if he has the title!" she cried gayly. Surely, the visit to Mount Eagle would take George out of himself!

Bryan greeted the Washingtons in the purple costume,

from hat to shoes, he had worn to England, causing the English to imagine that all the American clergy dressed in this eccentric fashion. At the dinner table he told them about his trip. He had addressed a petition to George III. Now it rested with the House of Lords as to whether they would recognize his right to assume the title of Baron of Cameron.

"And did you see Sally?" Martha asked.

Yes, Bryan had gone to Bath to see his sister-in-law. He had found her living "in gentile poverty," in a house smaller than the lodge-house on her lost Yorkshire estate, Towlston Manor.

"Sally does not even have a carriage," Bryan told the shocked Washingtons. "George William was forced to lay down his carriages when he sold Towlston."

But Sally had greeted Bryan coldly. She did not want sympathy. At seventy, still beautiful, she held her head high.

"No, I've no thought of returning to America, that barbarous country," she said. "I'm an Englishwoman, and proud of the fact. I'll stay where I am."

Thus Bryan had left her—an aging, unhappy woman, who would live on for twelve more bitter years.

On the Wednesday following, the Washingtons invited old friends to dinner: Bryan Fairfax, his son Thomas and daughter Elizabeth, John Herbert, George William Fairfax's sister, Mrs. Warner Washington, and her son Whiting.

Around the candlelit table they talked of the old days. It was late when the guests left. George and Martha went out on the front steps to bid them good night. "There's a ring around the moon, Bryan," said George, gazing at the sky.

"It means rain," Bryan answered.

It meant sleet and snow. But next morning George Washington rode out in the storm to make the rounds of his farms, as usual.

The following day, it was still snowing. George complained of a sore throat, and did not go for his daily horseback ride. But in the afternoon he tramped through three inches of snow to mark trees for cutting. His hoarseness increased, but he made light of it.

He appeared almost his usual self that evening, as he sat with Martha and Tobias Lear reading the newspapers. Lawrence Lewis and Washington Custis were at New Kent on business. Nelly was upstairs in bed, recuperating from the birth of her child.

When Martha joined her husband in their bedroom over the library, she reminded him that he had been sitting up too late for a man with a cold. But he said he felt better. Covering the fire, George undressed and lay down on the large square bed with the white canopy, which stands today in the Washington bedroom at Mount Vernon.

During the night of December 14, 1799, George Washington's cold developed into acute laryngitis. About three-thirty in the morning Martha was wakened by his hand on her shoulder. "I'm very sick . . ." he gasped. Although he spoke and breathed with difficulty, he would not let her get up and call a servant for fear she might catch cold. At daybreak the maid, Caroline, appeared to make the fire, and was asked to call Tobias Lear. Doctor Craik of Alexandria was sent for by messenger.

The stout Scotch doctor, James Craik, Washington's comrade through two wars and his physician for forty years, arrived at nine and applied the usual remedies. But as the day wore on, the sick man's breathing became more labored. To Martha's affectionate inquiries as she smoothed down his pillow, he answered, "I'm very ill. . . ."

About four o'clock George turned to his wife, who was seated near his bed. There she had been all day, reading to him from time to time from the Bible. "When will Lawrence and Washington return from New Kent?" he wanted to know. "About the twentieth of the month," Martha answered, clearly. But he did not seem to hear her voice.

The day dragged itself into darkness. George was now in great pain, breathing hard, restlessly changing his position in bed. At five o'clock he spoke to Doctor Craik. "Jim, I die hard, but I'm not afraid to go."

His life-long friend pressed Washington's hand in silence, too moved to speak. Leaving the bedside, the doctor went over to the fire to hide his grief.

That left Martha alone near the foot of the bed, awaiting the end with great self-control. The last look George should have of his "dear Patsy" would not reveal her helpless grief. He should see her as he had always wanted her, brave and smiling.

At ten o'clock, the General turned to Tobias Lear, whispering: "I'm going. Don't let my body be put into the vault until three days after I'm dead."

Lear bowed his head.

"Do you understand?" Washington asked.

Lear replied, "Yes, sir."

" 'Tis well."

At a little after ten, he lay dead on the big mahogany bed, famous as the deathbed of George Washington. At the head stood Tobias Lear and Doctor Craik. At the foot, where she had remained constantly, was Martha.

"Is he gone?" she asked in a calm voice.

Tobias Lear could not speak. He held up his hand as a signal that he was.

" 'Tis well," Martha repeated George's last words in the same quiet tone. "All is over now. I've no more trials to pass through. I'll soon follow him."

Chapter Fifteen   *Widow Washington*

O<small>N</small> A CHILLY DECEMBER AFTERNOON, AS THE SUN HUNG low, Martha Washington followed her husband's body down the slope from the house to the family tomb beside the river.

There were others in the solemn procession—the militia of Alexandria leading to the sound of muffled drums; the clergy; military and Masonic officers; the General's horse led by black-clad grooms; relatives, intimate friends, and servants— all gathered to say farewell to America's great soldier and statesman.

But to the little woman in black mourning garments, there was none other present than her husband in the six-foot casket. For the last time, Martha was going with George down the path grown familiar through years of strolls together.

Staunchly she walked, head up, refusing the aid of those dearest—Eleanor Stuart, who had loved George Washington as a father; the Laws and Thomas Peter, Doctor Craik, Bryan Fairfax, and red-eyed Tobias Lear.

Arriving at the tomb on the bank of the Potomac, the soldiers halted. Mrs. Washington took her place beside the casket. The Reverend Davis, who had married Nelly, began the words of the Service of the Dead:

"*Lord, thou has been our refuge from one generation to another . . .*"

As overhead the wind stirred the leafless branches of the

trees, the love and courage of Martha Washington went with George on his long journey.

"So teach us to number our days, that we may apply our hearts unto wisdom . . ."

Soon the simple funeral service was over. The body of America's first President, with the miniature of "dear Patsy" around his neck, was laid to rest in the soil of his beloved Mount Vernon.

Still erect, Mrs. Washington turned back to the house, and graciously offered food and drink to the mourners. She had not slept two hours a night since her husband's death, yet she flung fatigue aside and with calm dignity accepted condolences and murmured farewells.

But by nightfall the carriages had all driven away, leaving the house suddenly too large and too empty. Mount Vernon had lost its master. George Washington, who had walked for over forty years through its rooms, was gone. Martha was left to carry on a lonely life without him.

Looking at her white face, Doctor Craik dismissed his chaise and announced that he would spend the night. He did not like the strained expression in her eyes, the steady pace she had set herself since George's death, fearing to relax lest she break down.

When Martha said she must hurry to the Negro cabins to give the slaves the food the guests had left, good old Doctor Craik put his arm around her.

"Patsy, you're going to lie down." The burr in his Scotch voice grew soft. "And, dear, don't you want to cry?"

The next moment Martha Washington was sobbing her heart out on the stout shoulder of the understanding old Scotchman who had seen her son and husband die.

George Washington's illness had been so short that his

nearest relatives could not reach his bedside before he died. Lawrence Lewis and Washington Custis, the two men of the household on whom Martha could have leaned, were at the White House, down in New Kent. Eleanor Stuart, the Laws and Thomas Peter came with all speed, but did not reach Mount Vernon until the day of the funeral. As for Nelly, ill and crushed with sorrow, she could be of little aid to dear Grandmama other than to sob out her heart in sympathy.

So Martha Washington, although overwhelmed with grief, mustered her courage and planned each detail of her husband's burial. A plain mahogany casket was brought from Alexandria. She ordered his body carried down from their bedroom and laid out in front of the Italian mantelpiece.

With Tobias Lear she inspected the family vault on the river bank, built by the youth, George Washington, after the death of his brother, Lawrence. And she asked that a wooden door be made for the bricked-up entrance of the tomb.

"For it will soon be necessary to open it again," she told Tobias.

Did Martha really believe that her days on earth were few? Or was it only the anguished cry of a woman bereft of her husband? *"I shall soon follow him"*—she often repeated her prediction made at George's bedside. And it had the sound of a prayer.

Martha was by temperament loyal and intense. At twenty-six, the widowed Mrs. Daniel Parke Custis had declared that her life was over. She was sixty-eight now, and her second loss was the more poignant, yet her healthy body and spirit would sustain her beyond her seventieth birthday. For the Widow Washington, there were full years ahead.

The news of George Washington's death had not reached

Congress, in session in Philadelphia, until the day of his funeral. Plans were made for a memorial service, for which Lighthorse Harry Lee, father of the Civil War general, Robert E. Lee, would write an oration: "First in war, first in peace, and first in the hearts of his countrymen."

Congress also decided to erect a marble tomb for the first President, and possibly for his wife, in the crypt of the still unfinished Capitol.

When Martha learned that the government wished to take George's body from the grave on the lawn at Mount Vernon, she broke down completely. After a quick, stunned glance at the announcement, she hurried to her room and flung herself on her bed in tears.

Was George never to be left to her alone! Because it was her duty, she had given him to the Continental Army. In the same spirit, she had given him to the Presidency. Even in private life, they had had little time together. There were always guests at Mount Vernon, and official duties to take George from her side. And now, in death, was he to be taken from her again? To be taken from their beloved Mount Vernon?

For a long time she wept bitterly. And then her sobs subsided. Rising from her bed, she wiped her eyes and straightened her cap.

Life-long habits of doing one's duty are hard to break. When Martha Washington sat down at her desk to answer the letter from the Congressional committee, she was resigned. In a handwriting that shook only a little, she penned the words which (so she thought) would separate her in death from the husband whose life she had shared with the world, in camp and public office and home:

"Taught by the great example which I have so long before me never to oppose my private wishes to the public will—I must consent to the request made by Congress—which you have had the goodness to transmit to me—and in doing this I need not—I cannot say what a sacrifice of individual feeling I make of a sense of public duty."

Never in her life had Martha Washington made a more painful decision. But, fortunately, she was not called upon to make this sacrifice. Congress did not carry out its proposed plan. George Washington's body lies beside his wife's in the new vault at Mount Vernon, built according to his directions, at the foot of what is known as the Vineyard Enclosure.

In the attic of the Mount Vernon mansion we visit today is a bedchamber so tiny that only a bed, a chair or two, and a dressing table can be put in the cramped space under the sloping roof.

To this small third-floor room, with its dormer window overlooking the Potomac, Martha Washington moved after her husband's death. The apartment on the floor below which she had shared with him was locked. Custom had it in those days that a room must be abandoned for two years after a death occurred within its walls. But Martha could not have brought herself to occupy alone the quarters she had shared with George. Instead, she chose this nook over her old room, because from its window she could look out at his tomb.

For many days during that lonely winter she sat by the window, hands idle for the first time in her life.

"Is there anything I can do for you?" urged Nelly Lewis, now well again and willing to run up the steep flights of stairs a dozen times a day to comfort her grandmother. "Would you like to hold the baby?"

The shawled figure turned from the window. The hazel eyes behind the spectacles were sad, but resigned. Frances was a rosy girl, with her mother's dark curls and natural vivacity. Any great-grandmother would be proud of her.

"The child needs a new blanket," Martha reproved her granddaughter, as she took Frances in her arms. "This one is a disgrace."

A few hours later, Nelly's heart rejoiced to hear Grandmama's knitting needles clicking through the pink wool of a new baby blanket. And before the week was out, so bravely did Martha try to pick up her life, that she was directing the cutting of the summer clothing for the slaves.

Callers came—old friends to express their sympathy, and public figures to do honor to the memory of George Washington. Martha greeted them all, a tiny motherly figure in frilled mob cap and plain black gown. But her manner was that of a great lady.

The national capitol had been moved to Washington City. The fourteen miles to Mount Vernon was a long distance in those days. Yet many of the Congressmen made the trip to pay their respects to the Widow Washington. Gentlemen in knee breeches and silver-buckled shoes were these Congressmen. Many of them still wore wigs, although that custom was passing. And they sat in the halls of Congress with their hats on.

They were sure to be invited to have a meal with Mrs. Washington at Mount Vernon. As of old, the table was bountifully spread with platters of cold meats, garnished with parsley and vegetables from her garden. And behind the handsome silver service, their hostess would be seated to pour tea and coffee for her guests.

"We were all Federalists, which gave her pleasure," a Massachusetts Congressman describes his visit. "Her remarks were pointed, and sometimes very sarcastic, on the new order of things and the present administration. . . . She appeared in good health, but like one who has sustained a loss that will always remain fresh in her mind. She spoke of the General with affection, and observed that, though she had many mercies, she felt as if she was a stranger among her friends, and could welcome the time when she should be called to follow her husband."

This was a time when party feeling ran high between the Federalists, George Washington's party, and the Democrats, for Thomas Jefferson, Democratic leader, had been elected President to succeed John Adams. Martha Washington, who had lost none of her lively interest in politics, took an active part in the conversation. As a private citizen, she could again say what she thought. There was no need to curb her tongue lest she injure George Washington's career. And her comments on "the present administration," were "pointed and sometimes very sarcastic."

Widow Washington enjoyed these glimpses into the political world. Her seclusion was no longer precious to her, since George was no longer there to share it.

It was at one of these Congressional dinners that she originated the famous Washington Pie. Wishing a dessert to take the place of mince pie, one quickly prepared, for possibly the Congressmen had arrived unexpectedly, she gave orders to her kitchen staff to make a pie-like layer cake with a filling of custard and jam.

Tradition says that when it was first served President Jefferson was a guest, and that some of the Congressmen had brought their wives. These ladies asked Mrs. Washington for the recipe for Washington Pie, which boomed into popularity on the tables of social Washington, and from there was introduced all over the country.

The Mount Vernon family group was now composed of Nelly Lewis, her husband and child, and Martha's darling grandson—jolly young Washington Custis.

Washington was still a bachelor. "But one of the wealthiest young men in Virginia!" his grandmother thought proudly. She rejoiced in her grandson's bachelorhood, even as she approved his interest in Mary Lee Fitzhugh. The girl's mother had been a Randolph; her father, the wealthy William Fitzhugh of Ravensworth, a member of the Continental Congress and friend of George Washington.

There had always been pretty ladies to distract the Custis heir. From Annapolis, during his stay there, had come disquieting rumors that the sixteen-year-old boy was "paying much attention to a certain young lady." General Washington cautioned him: "Recollect the saying of the wise men, 'There is a time for all things,' and this is not a time for a boy of your age to enter into engagements which might end in sorrow and repentance."

To which young Custis answered: "The report of my being *engaged* to the young lady in question is strictly erroneous. That I gave her reason to believe in my attachment to her I candidly allow, but that I would *enter into engagements* inconsistent with my situation, I hope your good opinion of me will make you disbelieve."

Eventually Washington Custis was to take Mary Fitzhugh for his bride, and settle down. He would develop land opposite the Federal City, left him by his father, into an estate named "Arlington," from the ancestral Custis home on the eastern shore of Virginia. And there he was to build a house modeled after the temple of Paestum, out of deference to his life-long interest in Roman history. But that would be following his grandmother's death.

Her grandson was Martha's joy; but it was to Nelly and Lawrence Lewis that she looked for help in running the Mount Vernon plantation. And the Lewises, who would have liked a home of their own on the land General Washington had given them as a wedding present, never seriously considered moving from Mount Vernon as long as Mrs. Washington lived.

Leaving the running of the house to Nelly, Martha Washington was content now to spend her time with little Frances. She liked nothing better than to listen to the child's innocent prattle, to teach her to play with the toys that had delighted her own children and grandchildren. Frances seemed to be her dear Nelly, a baby again.

She found pleasure in making her great-granddaughter an intricate patchwork quilt, its pieces cut with six sides in the shape of hexagons. Another source of pleasure for her was wrapping up locks of George Washington's hair and sending them as remembrances to people who had loved him.

One day Martha enjoyed a visit from her old friend, Bryan Fairfax. Bryan had heard from England that the House of Lords had recognized his right to assume the title of Baron of Cameron.

Bryan, Lord Fairfax, eighth Baron of Cameron.

Over a cup of tea, Martha gazed at her clerical neighbor and tried to imagine him as an English Lord. She wished that George could know of it, and smile with her at the incongruity. She wondered how Sally Fairfax had taken the news. Bryan now had Sally's coveted title—pious, simple Bryan who

MARTHA WASHINGTON
From a painting by Gilbert Stuart

did not want it at all!

"The committee wrote me that in order to assume the title of Lord Fairfax, and a seat in the House of Lords, I must become a British citizen, and that I'll never do," Bryan said emphatically. "I'm an American, Patsy, and proud of it. My son can do as he wants, when his turn comes. I'll continue to call myself plain Bryan Fairfax."

Martha Washington beamed her approval. She had always liked Bryan the best of the Fairfax family. How different he was from Sally, who had preferred a title to being an American!

"This country needs men such as you, Bryan," said Mrs. Washington, as she poured him a second cup of tea. "If only George could hear you speak!"

So they sat before the fire, talking and laughing gently, the strange new nobleman and the winsome old lady—almost the last of the friends of Colonial Virginia.

The Lewises went several times that winter to visit Nelly's sisters, Patsy and Eliza, in the Federal City. And Nelly wore her white plume, badge of the Federalists, at parties given for President Jefferson and his cabinet. Mrs. Lewis wrote that she was "very vain of the plume, and whenever I wish to look particularly smart, I become a Major General!" But Nelly's bravery in flaunting her party principles was greater than her tact. Times had changed. And the Federalists, the party of George Washington, were now in the minority.

The marriage of Patsy Peter had turned out happily, as her grandmother predicted. Already Patsy's prosperous young husband was planning to leave their K Street house and build a larger home on the heights of Georgetown—Tudor Place, designed by William Thornton, the architect of the Capitol, and still standing today.

The Lewises had driven out to the site selected; a tree-clad hill stretching from the present Q Street to R Street, and overlooking the busy wharfs of Georgetown. As they gazed down the Potomac toward Mount Vernon, Patsy told Sister Nelly how on the north of the house she would plant a garden like her grandmother's, and elsewhere a maze of fragrant box.

Life was gayer in the Law household, with a hectic round of parties for all foreigners who came to Washington. Eliza's ego-ridden Englishman fancied himself a dramatist. That winter of 1801, he was writing a play and promoting the first theater to be built in Washington City, at the corner of C and Eleventh Streets. In fact, he was full of promotion schemes, all of which took money; and money was something that Thomas Law, once a rich man, was beginning to find very scarce, due to his speculations in real estate.

Meanwhile, his handsome young wife was left very much to her own devices. Neglected, restless, dissatisfied, Eliza spent her time on visits to her mother at Hope Park and to her grandmother at Mount Vernon, where she frequently brought her little girl.

This same year, 1801, had brought a new baby to Mount Vernon; another little girl whom Nelly Lewis called Martha. But "precious Frances" was still her great-grandmother's favorite and constant shadow, just as Nelly had been at her age.

Writing to a friend, Mrs. Lewis says:

". . . little Frances is the darling of her Grandmama and seems to afford her comfort and amusement. My Beloved Parent is delighted when my child is fond of her, calls her

Grandmama and gives her sweet kisses. My only fear is that my daughter will be spoilt. She is indulged in every thing, stays with Grandmama the most part of every day and is never denied anything she takes a fancy to."

Nelly gives a pretty picture of little Frances "running about, singing, and much delighted with the doll" purchased by her mother in Alexandria. "As soon as Lawrence returns from the farms, he plays on the violin for her to dance," she adds.

Martha Washington smiled, watching the little sprite dance, thinking of Nelly as a child, and, though the picture was dimmer, of her own Pat, "the Dark Lady." She often caught herself daydreaming these days. The knitting needles would fall from her hands, the yarn in a tangle of pinks or blues, while her eyes rested on the river or the blazing fire and her thoughts traveled back through the years. Not to New York. Not to Philadelphia. Nor even to the stirring days of the Revolution. But to Williamsburg, and the White House, and her own childhood on the Pamunkey.

Martha was not very well that summer. "I have always one complaint or another—I never expect to be well as long as I live in this world—" she wrote Tobias Lear's mother. But she was not really ill; she was old and tired, and the zest for running things had left her. The vivid, active little woman, who had done a man's job in the management of two plantations, was through with her work.

Gradually Martha relinquished all responsibilities, spending her days knitting and playing with Nelly's babies. Always too busy to indulge in much reading, she now devoured in quick succession the popular novels of the day: *Ouabi*, an Indian tale, by Philena, "a lady of Boston"; *The Prince of Abyssinia*, by Samuel Johnson; *Jilts* or *The Female Fortune Hunter*.

George Washington, who had expressed himself forcibly against the evil of popular novels, would have frowned on Martha's pastime; yet, after his death, she bought a collection of these books. Bearing her name neatly written on the fly-leaves, they were later sold at the auction of the Washington library of military and agricultural books.

The Lewises' own home was rising on their property overlooking the Potomac, its plans drawn by William Thornton, architect of Tudor Place for the Peters. Some day Nelly and Lawrence would have to move there. For George Washington had left Mount Vernon, after Martha's death, to his nephew, Bushrod Washington, the son of his brother John Augustine.

Nelly played with the idea of housekeeping in letters to friends. She wrote Mrs. Pinckney:

"Our little dwelling will be finished this summer, so that by next season, I hope to be well fixed—then shall I expect my good friends will have some curiosity to see me a housekeeper, and allow me the delight of entertaining them."

But by the time "the little dwelling," a large, rose-brick Georgian Colonial house, called "Woodlawn," was finished, Martha Washington was too feeble to be left alone.

The running of the Mount Vernon mansion and the deeds of charity were turned over to Nelly; Major Lewis ran the farms and, with the help of Tobias Lear, handled all legal matters, until the estate was settled in accordance with George Washington's will.

That will, labored over with the General's habitual precision, had brought to his "dear Patsy," whom he would not have hurt for the world, the greatest unhappiness of her widowhood—*he had given their freedom to his own slaves after her death.*

Along with other enlightened men of his time, George Washington never approved of slavery. He had wanted to free his own slaves during his lifetime, but could not, because many of them had intermarried with the dower slaves of Martha's first marriage, who belonged to her heirs.

It was inevitable that George Washington's slaves should learn of the clause in his will which gave them their freedom at Martha's death, and that their delight should give everyone on the plantation the gravest concern.

It was also inevitable that Martha should develop a sensitivity that may have been based on fact, and may have been based on imagination. In any event, she conceived the idea that these slaves, eager to be free, were trying to hurry her death.

Nothing specific, of course; just little things which annoyed her. That fire in the attic room permitted to go out, with no firewood handy to warm the room at her early rising hour . . . That trifle served with soured cream, a dish that caused Mrs. Washington a bad digestive upset . . . The afternoon the horses almost ran away as Martha took her drive. Had the coachman, one of George's slaves, touched them too sharply with his whip?

Before long, Martha Washington began to believe her life was in danger. Brooding deeply, she worked herself into a fit of fever which left her weak and ill. She refused to eat . . . perhaps the cook was poisoning her! She refused to drive out . . . She sat in her attic room, the door bolted, and asked the family to come to her alone, unattended by servants.

Finally one day, when the Lewises and Washington Custis were at Hope Park, Martha became badly frightened over the behavior of an awkward slave who served her noonday meal. As darkness fell, her hysteria increased. She thought she smelled smoke . . . realized she was alone on the third floor of the big house, and imagined the slaves were trying to burn it down . . .

Old, alone and helpless, she sent a frantic plea for help to her husband's nephew, Bushrod Washington.

Judge Washington was attending the Supreme Court when the note reached him, but with Chief Justice Marshall he hurried at once to Mount Vernon. After listening to the trembling old lady's complaints, he shook his head and promised to remain until the Lewises and her grandson returned. Later he took them aside, and repeated the story. Sorrow and loneliness were preying on Martha Washington's mind, he suggested. But her grandson scoffed at the notion—Mrs. Washington's mind was as strong and reliable as it had been at fifty. Nelly, worried, was not so sure . . . Her grandmother was failing, that was apparent. She had not been herself for weeks.

The situation went from bad to worse. Finally, the family found it necessary, "for prudential reasons," as Washington Custis was to write in his memoirs, to free the slaves while the mistress of Mount Vernon still lived.

But it was too late. Serious damage had been done to Martha's health, leaving her too weak to combat the attack of bilious fever which came early in May, 1802. Doctor Craik, at her side from the start, was baffled by her apathy.

"Come, come, Patsy," he scolded her. "You must help me. You're only seventy—you have ten good years before you. Fight, woman, fight!"

When Nelly came to her bedside, Martha was cheerful enough, interested in what the children were doing, and asking after the health of Eleanor Stuart, who was ailing. But when she was alone, she lay in the little attic room (she had refused to be moved down stairs), her large brown eyes on the window, thinking, thinking.

So they remained beside her, Nelly and Lawrence, and sometimes Doctor Craik. Tender and considerate, they talked when she wished it, or sat in silence when her eyes were closed.

They could not watch her every moment, it was not humanly possible. One night, as her faithful servant, Molly, slept outside the door, Martha Washington slipped from the bed and moved, a small frail figure, across the room to her desk.

From a secret drawer she took a bundle of George's letters, tied together with mulberry-colored ribbon. By the flickering candle-light, she read them over, one by one. Letters from camp, from New York and Philadelphia, written during his Presidency, when she was at home at Mount Vernon. Letters for her eyes alone. Letters, she decided, which should never be shared with a curious world.

And knowing that she was soon to die, Martha Washington held each piece of paper to the flame of the candle and burned it.

One letter Martha could not bring herself to destroy. *"My dearest . . ."* it began, and it told her that her husband had assumed command of the Continental Army. No other letter could equal it for tenderness. Smiling, she kissed the paper and replaced it in the secret drawer, where Patsy Peter, who inherited the desk, was to find and treasure it.

Destroying George Washington's letters from the sight of prying eyes had occupied many hours. It was dawn when Martha blew out the candle and crept back to her bed.

Determination had lent strength to her weary body. As she laid her head on the pillow and felt the comforting warmth of the patchwork quilt, she looked rested somehow, and almost young again. Exertion had brought the color to her cheeks. Her eyes were bright with fever.

When the drowsy Molly roused herself to answer her mistress's call, she found her lying quietly in the dim light, her eyes resting, as always, on the dormer window facing the river.

"Get Mistress Lewis," she whispered. "I am failing."

Suddenly the room was full of people: Nelly and her husband, Doctor Craik, Washington Custis, the weeping servants. Was Mrs. Washington worse? It was the seventeenth day of the fever. Had the crisis come? Doctor Craik felt her pulse, frowned, and motioned to the others to leave the room. But Martha, lifting her head, called Nelly's name.

She must see the Reverend Davis of Christ Church, Alexandria, she said distinctly. He had buried her husband. Now he must come to give her, George's widow, the last sacrament.

Red-eyed but calm, Nelly promised to do Grandmama's bidding. "But you'll be well soon," she assured her. Martha shook her head, and lay back on her pillow.

"Fetch my best white gown," she told Nelly, "and see that I'm buried with my miniature of your grandfather on my breast, even as he wore mine to his grave."

At that her mind clouded a bit and mistily she slept. Finger to her lips, Nelly led her husband and brother from the room. The doctor took his station by the bed, watching.

All morning Martha Washington lay there, loved and honored, and encircled by every hope that kindly hearts could feel. And yet, she was alone. Little and old and tired, and

ready for a long journey, at the end of which she would see
the face of the man in the miniature she always wore.

But before that meeting could be, her mind wandered back
to the farthest past; she was a girl of fifteen, tearing across
the tobacco fields on her pony, Fatima. Her first ball . . .
young Mountjoy who had laughed at her . . . the meeting
with Daniel Parke Custis who had made her the happiest
young wife in Virginia. Their four children—Daniel, Frances,
Pat, Jacky—how long ago it had been since she had guided
their first steps.

Memories flowed over her now . . . her first widowhood
. . . it had been hard to go on without Daniel's kindly presence—those intricate business affairs which had so baffled her;
her ignorance, her grief.

And then the glory of a new love . . . the little room in
which she lay spread into a series of rooms, each larger than
the last. A soldier's bride in white satin and pearls . . . Mistress Washington, seated in the House of Burgesses, listening
to her husband's faltering speech . . . a young hostess at
Mount Vernon, eager to appear well before Colonel Washington's boyhood friends . . .

Friends. James Craik, bending over to lay his hand on her
brow, was one of them. She stared at him with her big hazel
eyes, and then the sight of his honest Scotch face was gone.
Her friends were the Fairfaxes, the old Lord, George William
and Sally. She must be worthy of George in their sight. She
must . . .

"Quiet, Patsy," cautioned Doctor Craik. "Here, try to
sleep . . . this will help."

The potion calmed her, and for hours she slept. It was late
afternoon when her mind drifted back to the scenes of the
Revolution . . . the wounded soldiers needed her; she was

ready with food and medicine and bandages . . . "Lady Washington" they called her. She could hear their cheers . . . she could see their faces; but no, it was the face of one tall soldier who wore a general's uniform.

"Who is it?" she whispered. "*George?*"

After that the attic room was quiet throughout the cool May evening. Nelly and Washington Custis, standing beside their grandmother's bed, could hardly restrain themselves from speaking to her. She looked so happy, so at peace. But something stopped them . . . was it the touch of another presence—that of George Washington, come to welcome his "dear Patsy"?

A mocking bird sang beneath the window. Martha's eyes opened. This time, she *saw—*

"George," she repeated, and sighed contentedly.

The clock struck midnight. And Martha Washington, her hand in Nelly's, her grandson Washington beside her, breathed her last.

On the next day there was published this notice in the *Washington Federalist*, written in the florid language of the times:

"Died, at Mount Vernon, on Saturday evening, the 22nd ultimo, Mrs. Martha Washington, widow of the late illustrious General George Washington. To those amiable and Christian virtues, which adorn the female character, she added dignity of manners, superiority of understanding, a mind intelligent and elevated. The silence of respectful grief is our best eulogy."

Newspapers all over the country proclaimed Martha Washington's passing. Yet most of the American people, watching the rise of Napoleon Bonaparte, hoping for the acquisition of West Florida and of the rich valley of the Mississippi, which would result in the Louisiana Purchase the following year, regarded the news as an echo of a past generation.

General Washington . . . the Revolution. How long ago that seemed, although it was but nineteen years! But in Mrs. Washington's death, the older citizens of the nation realized that the link which bound America to its first President was broken; and they sincerely mourned the loss of their first First Lady.

They dressed Martha Washington in her favorite white dress, and laid the miniature of George Washington on her breast. Then relatives and loving friends went with her, on a sunny May day, down the same path that she had walked with George two and a half years earlier. The oaken door of the family tomb swung open. And Martha's body was laid beside the man whose wife she had been for forty years. But her intrepid spirit was winging its way back to God Who had made it strong, and whom it had served.

In the ivy-covered mausoleum to which the bodies were later moved, Martha Washington sleeps, rightfully honored, for an eternity of deep contentment. She lies in the beloved soil of Mount Vernon, by the side of the man whom she loved. For her there is no more parting. Her dream of everlasting life with George Washington, beside the blue Potomac, has at last come true.

BIBLIOGRAPHY

BIBLIOGRAPHY

Conkling, Margaret Cockburn. Memoirs of the mother and wife of Washington. Auburn (New York), Derby, Miller and Company, 1853 (c1850)

Hervey, Nathaniel. The memory of Washington; with biographical sketches of his mother and wife. Boston and Cambridge, J. Munroe and Company, 1852

Lossing, Benson John. Martha Washington. New York, J. C. Buttre, 1865 (c1863)

Lossing, Benson John. Mary and Martha, the mother and the wife of George Washington. New York, Harper and Brothers, 1886

Minnigerode, Meade. Some American ladies; seven informal biographies. New York and London, G. P. Putnam's Sons, 1926. Contents: Martha Washington; etc.

Walter, James. Memorials of Washington and of Mary, his mother, and Martha, his wife, from letters and papers of Robert Cary and James Sharples. New York, C. Scribner's Sons, 1887

Wharton, Anne Hollingsworth. Martha Washington. New York, C. Scribner's Sons, 1907 (c1897)

Custis, G. W. Parke. Recollections and Private Memoirs of Washington by his adopted son. Philadelphia, William Flint, 1859

Hughes, Rupert. George Washington. 3 vols. William Morrow, 1926

Fitzpatrick, John C., edited by. The Diaries of George Washington. 4 vols. Houghton Mifflin Co., 1925

Foster, Genevieve. George Washington's World. Charles Scribner's Sons, 1941.

Prindiville, Kathleen. First Ladies. The Macmillan Company, 1940

Earle, Alice Morse. Home Life in Colonial Days. The Macmillan Co., 1941

Earle, Alice Morse. Child Life in Colonial Days. The Macmillan Co., 1940

Decatur, Stephen, Jr. Private Affairs of George Washington, from the Records and Accounts of Tobias Lear, Esquire, His Secretary. Houghton Mifflin Co., 1933

Lossing, Benson John. Mount Vernon. New York, Townsend & Company, 1859

Rosé, Grace Norton. Williamsburg—Today and Yesterday. New York, G. P. Putnam's Sons, 1940

Harland, Marion. Some Colonial Homesteads and Their Stories. G. P. Putnam's Sons, 1897

Wilstach, Paul. Mount Vernon. Doubleday, Page & Company, 1916

Moore, Charles. The Family Life of George Washington. Houghton Mifflin Company, 1926